Talking Books

Children's authors talk about the craft, creativity and process of writing

James Carter

London and New York

First published 1999
by Routledge
11 New Fetter Lane, London EC4P 4EE

Simultaneously published in the USA and Canada
by Routledge
29 West 35th Street, New York, NY 10001

Routledge is an imprint of the Taylor and Francis Group

Transferred to Digital Printing 2003

Typeset in Palatino by Keystroke, Jacaranda Lodge, Wolverhampton

British Library Cataloguing in Publication Data
A catalogue record for this book is available from the British Library

Library of Congress Cataloging in Publication Data
Talking books : children's authors talk about the craft, creativity
  and process of writing / [edited by] James Carter.
      p.   cm.
      Contents: Brian Moses – Benjamin Zephaniah – Ian Beck – Neil
Ardley – Terry Deary – Helen Cresswell – Gillian Cross – Berlie
Doherty – Alan Durant – Philip Pullman – Celia Rees – Norman
Silver – Jacqueline Wilson.
      Includes bibliographical references (p.   ) and index.
      1. Children's literature, English—History and criticism—Theory,
etc. 2. Authors, English—20th century—Biography. 3. Children's
literature—Authorship. I. Carter, James, 1959– .
    PR990.T35 1999
    809'.89282—dc21
                                                    98–32051
                                                    CIP

ISBN 0–415–19416–4 (hbk)
ISBN 0–415–19417–2 (pbk)

With all my love I dedicate this book to Sarah – my wife and very best friend.

Contents

Introduction
Talking about *this* book

Where do your characters come from?

How long does it take to write a book?

What did you read when you were a child?

How did you become a writer?

These are just a few of the questions that are commonly asked of children's authors, and clearly there are no singular or definitive responses. Essentially, what *Talking Books* sets out to do is to show how some of our children's authors respond to these and many other similar questions. By doing so, the authors help to demystify and demythologise something of the writing process. They reveal that creativity needs to be nurtured, that writing is a craft skill that requires much time and dedication – and most of all, that a readership comprised of children and young adults is as discerning and discriminating as its adult counterpart.

Some of the writers featured here you will be familiar with already. You will have their books in your classroom or you will have shared their work with young readers. All of these writers have been chosen because they each have something unique and invaluable to contribute to this book about the craft, creativity and process of writing for children – not because they are deemed to be the very best in their field (of which there are a great many more). Collectively, their work represents the panoply that is contemporary children's literature – including poetry, information books, picture books, short stories, novels and graphic novels, fairy tales, educational texts, stageplays as well as television dramas – and encompasses a variety of voices, styles, genres and subject matters.

At the outset of this project, an eclectic list of children's writers was drawn up, one that sought to achieve breadth and balance in terms of gender, race and genre. And whilst the first two of these categories may not have been realised, the latter certainly has. And because the implied audience for *Talking Books* was to be Primary and Secondary teachers, it was deemed important to choose authors that are or have been regular visitors to schools. As a result, a number of the authors here discuss how contact with their readers informs their writing.

Here's another question to add to those above: *How much do we really know about the people who write for children?* And the answer has to be: *Very little.* For, in the main, and to adapt the old adage, children's writers are read but rarely heard. Unlike luminaries such as film and television icons, sports personalities and politicians, writers for children are not high profile individuals that receive regular media attention. So, in response to this situation, this text serves as a forum in which each of these authors can provide a sustained insight into their writing lives.

Talking Books is, in effect, a collection of monologues – reworked transcripts from in-depth interviews recorded onto cassette tape. To achieve uniformity, focus and coherency, the monologues are divided into individual sub-sections:

An introduction to . . . : in which the authors introduce themselves by responding to a series of questions about their books, their lives and their interests.

1 *How the reader became a writer*: the authors reflect upon their biography – in terms of the books that inspired them as young readers and also how they came to be published writers.

2 *Writing: routines and reflections*: the authors highlight various issues related to their work – such as their writing methodologies and how they perceive the writing process.

3 *Growing a book / poem*: the authors talk in detail about the evolution of one or two of their titles.

4 *Visits to schools*: the authors reflect upon their work in schools and how contact with their readership informs their writing.

5 *Specialist subject*: the authors explore an issue of interest related to their work.

Selected current titles: a list of most of the authors' current books.

(Please note that the sub-sections of the monologues vary slightly from author to author, according to the topics covered during the original interviews.)

The final part of *Talking Books* is a useful miscellany that brings together contacts, organisations and addresses for those that wish to find out more about children's books and their authors.

Although initially intended for an educational market, *Talking Books* does have a potential range of audiences and purposes. Self-evidently, it is up to each reader to decide how they wish to utilise the material. Some teachers may choose to use this text to discover more about the writers whose books they read with their pupils, whereas others may wish to extract certain passages, either to create author profiles or to share the authors' words with young readers. Perhaps other teachers may decide to adopt some of the writers' activities and methodologies into their regular classroom practice. Librarians and academics may find the text helpful for providing biographical or bibliographical details. Would-be and aspiring writers of any age could find much here of use to them. And alternatively, a more general reader may simply find it interesting to discover how children's writers approach and perceive their work.

As assembler of this book, I was conscious of the fact that the market does not have anything quite like *Talking Books* at the present time, and it was often the enthusiasm and support of the writers involved that enabled me to see the project through with confidence. To all of these writers I am most grateful for their warmth and generosity – for inviting me into their homes, for giving up their time and for talking candidly and at length about their work. In addition, I must thank them not only for rummaging through their attics, offices, garden sheds and filing cabinets for old manuscripts and artwork, but also for helping me with the revision of the transcripts.

Special words of thanks must go to a number of illustrators. First, to Ian Beck for his brilliant artwork for the cover. Thanks too to Nick Sharratt for producing the wonderful illustration of himself and Jacqueline Wilson, which he generously donated to this book. Thanks also to Peter Bailey for providing the splendid illustration for Philip Pullman's *Clockwork* that was not included in the published version of the book. Further thanks to Jilly Wilkinson for the fascinating work-in-progress artwork for Norman Silver's *The Blue Horse*.

From meeting these authors and researching this text it became only too evident that there are numerous unsung heroes and heroines in the publishing world – such as agents, editors, editorial assistants, designers, marketing staff and publicity assistants – people whose names are forever absent from the pages of children's books, people who have a great influence over the books that we read. I wish to extend my thanks to those people – and in particular, Alice McLaren at Puffin, Naomi Cooper at Transworld and Suzy Harvey (formerly of Scholastic) – for their assistance and help and dedication to this book that was above and beyond the call of duty. I thank you Suzy for suggesting I interview Celia Rees, Ian Beck and Terry Deary. I wish you the very best with your degree. Jude Bowen and Ian Critchley of Routledge also deserve much credit for all their enthusiasm and positivity.

Further gratitude must be extended to various members of staff at Reading University – to Tony Watkins for coming up with the concept of a collection of interviews, to Catriona Nicholson and Dudley Jones for their ongoing support and advice, and especially to Michael Lockwood for his encouragement, his invaluable input and his never-ending supply of excellent ideas.

Others I must mention are: Prue Goodwin at the Reading and Language Information Centre (at Reading University), Jan Powling of the author visit agency 'Speaking of Books', Ed Zaghini at Young Book Trust in London, Kim Reynolds at Roehampton Institute, Bethan Roberts at Faber & Faber, David Fickling at Scholastic, Sue Unstead at Dorling Kindersley, Linda Banner at Orchard Books, Angela Redfern (previously of Reading University), Betty and Peter Barker, Pete Stevenson, as well as Nigel Gough, Margaret Wing and Leslie Westwood at the finest bookshop in the cosmos – Bookcentre in Woodley, Reading.

Most of all, I wish to thank my editor, Helen Fairlie, for her limitless creativity, her acute insight, her unfailing patience and her sensitive guidance – as well as being the only person with the imagination and foresight to take on a project such as this.

James Carter

Acknowledgements

We are most grateful for permission given to reproduce extracts/illustrations/ materials from the following:

Neil Ardley

Eyewitness No. 12: Music
101 Great Science Experiments
The Way Things Work – with text and illustrations by David Macaulay
(all Dorling Kindersley)

Ian Beck

Tom and the Island of Dinosaurs
Text and illustrations © 1993 by Ian Beck. Extracted from TOM AND THE ISLAND OF DINOSAURS published by Doubleday, a division of Transworld Publishers Ltd. All rights reserved.

Peter and the Wolf
Text and illustrations © 1994 by Ian Beck. Extracted from PETER AND THE WOLF published by Doubleday, a division of Transworld Publishers Ltd. All rights reserved.

Emily and the Golden Acorn
Illustrations © Ian Beck
By arrangement with Transworld Publishers Ltd.

Ian Beck's Picture Book (Scholastic Ltd, 1994)

Tim and Charlotte – Edward Ardizzone
© Edward Ardizzone Estate 1951, published by Scholastic Ltd 1999

Helen Cresswell

The Bongleweed (by permission of Oxford University Press)
The Piemakers (by permission of Oxford University Press, 1967)
Illustration from *The Piemakers* copyright © V.H. Drummond
Moondial (Faber & Faber)

Gillian Cross

Cover illustration by George Smith for WOLF by Gillian Cross (Puffin, 1992) Copyright © George Smith, 1992

Cover illustration by Mark Longworth for THE DEMON HEADMASTER by Gillian Cross (Puffin, 1997) Copyright © Mark Longworth, 1997

Terry Deary

Bloody Scotland (Scholastic Ltd, 1998)
Illustrations – Martin Brown
Shakespeare Stories (Scholastic Ltd, 1998)
Illustration – Michael Tickner

Berlie Doherty

Cover illustration by Sophy Williams for DEAR NOBODY (Hamish Hamilton, 1991) Copyright © Sophy Williams, 1991

Alan Durant

Extract from MOUSE PARTY Text © 1995 Alan Durant. Illustrations © 1995 Sue Heap. Reproduced by permission of the publisher Walker Books Ltd, London

Brian Moses

Don't Look at Me in that Tone of Voice: 'The Lost Angels' (Macmillan)
Knock Down Ginger: 'Readathon Sleepathon' (Cambridge University Press, 1994)
Other poems by Nicola Burridge, Sarah Jackson and James Rogers

Philip Pullman

His Dark Materials 1: Northern Lights and *The Subtle Knife* (Scholastic Ltd)
Rough Illustration for *Clockwork* by Peter Bailey

Celia Rees

Blood Sinister (Scholastic Ltd)

Norman Silver

Artwork for *The Blue Horse* by Jilly Wilkinson

Jacqueline Wilson

Double Act – © Jacqueline Wilson 1995. Extracted from DOUBLE ACT published by Doubleday, a division of Transworld Publishers Ltd. All rights reserved.

Illustrations (Ruby) © Nick Sharratt
          (Garnet) © Sue Heap
By arrangement with Transworld Publishers Ltd.

The Suitcase Kid –
Illustration © Nick Sharratt
By arrangement with Transworld Publishers Ltd.

Illustration of Nick Sharratt and Jacqueline Wilson – by Nick Sharratt

Benjamin Zephaniah

'Who's Who' (p. 48, 7 lines) from TALKING TURKEYS by Benjamin Zephaniah (Viking 1994) Copyright © Benjamin Zephaniah, 1994

Text and graphics of 'Civil Lies' (pp. 58–59) from TALKING TURKEYS by Benjamin Zephaniah (Viking 1994) Copyright © Benjamin Zephaniah, 1994. Illustrations Copyright © The Point, 1994

'Part Wan' (p. 42, 9 lines) from TALKING TURKEYS by Benjamin Zephaniah (Viking 1994) Copyright © Benjamin Zephaniah, 1994

8 lines from 'Going Lotto' (p. 69) from FUNKY CHICKENS by Benjamin Zephaniah (Viking, 1996) Copyright © Benjamin Zephaniah, 1996

All above materials – Reproduced by kind permission of Penguin Books Ltd.

Individual poems:

'I Love Me Mother and Me Mother Loves Me'
'Benny's Wheels'
'Wot a Pair'

Extract from *Oxford Book of Poetry* (Oxford University Press)

Other poems by Mahmood Jamal and Bina Sudra.

Every effort has been made to trace all copyright holders. In the event of any queries please contact Routledge, London.

An introduction to . . . Brian Moses

WHAT SORT OF BOOKS DO YOU WRITE? Poetry for children (my main area of interest), picture book texts, some books for teachers and a few information books.

WHAT ARE YOUR BOOKS ABOUT? Difficult to say with regard to my poetry as I write about anything and everything. Lots of ideas come from travelling around. The picture books are often in verse. Information books have tended to be historical as that's another area of interest.

BORN: 18 June 1950.

EDUCATION: Holy Trinity Primary School and Chatham House Grammar School in Ramsgate, Kent. I went on to teacher training college in Eastbourne and then I did a B.Ed. degree at Sussex University.

LIVES: St Leonards-on-Sea in East Sussex.

PREVIOUS OCCUPATION: I was a teacher for 12 years.

FAMILY: I have a wife, Anne, and two daughters – Karen (13) and Linette (6).

HOBBIES: I'd love to say something interesting like hang-gliding over active volcanoes in Ecuador, but really I like reading and collecting books, travelling and racing my mountain bike around the woods!

MOST TREASURED POSSESSION: A rather battered copy of Palgrave's *Golden Treasury* – inscribed Pte. H. Moses 7389233, R.A.M.C. This book accompanied my father during the North Africa and Italian campaigns of World War Two and owes its appearance to a dip in the Mediterranean when my father's kitbag fell from the quayside.

AWARDS: 1979 Eric Gregory Award from the Society of Authors for folio of poems by poet under 30. A South East Arts bursary, awarded for writers working in one genre who want to write in another. As a poet I've always been interested in writing a novel. I've now finished it, but so far it's unpublished.

LANGUAGE TRANSLATED INTO: Welsh.

FAVOURITE CHILDREN'S BOOKS: Most books by Robert Westall, *The Midnight Fox* by Betsy Byars and *Walk Two Moons* by Sharon Creech.

FAVOURITE POEM: 'When You Are Old' by W.B. Yeats.

FAVOURITE MUSIC: Bob Dylan, Mary Chapin Carpenter.

FAVOURITE FILMS: *One Flew Over the Cuckoo's Nest* and Zeffirelli's *Romeo and Juliet*.

FAVOURITE PLACES: Vancouver, especially the huge downtown area of Stanley

Park with its trails and lagoons. The west coast of Guernsey, particularly at sunset. The old part of Whitby. The bookshops of Bath. The Troodos Mountains in Cyprus.

WHAT WERE YOU LIKE AT THE AGE OF 11? Shy, nervous and bookish.

ENJOYS VISITING SCHOOLS BECAUSE: I love working with children.

WHY DO YOU WRITE? It's something that's in me, I just need to write.

IF YOU WEREN'T A WRITER: I'd still be a teacher.

AMBITIONS: To keep on writing and paying the bills!

WHICH FOUR WORDS DESCRIBE YOU BEST? Untidy, enthusiastic, idealistic, impulsive.

WHAT WOULD YOU LIKE TO HAPPEN IN THE TWENTY-FIRST CENTURY? For my children to grow up in a more harmonious world.

WHICH OF YOUR POEMS WOULD YOU LIKE TO BE REMEMBERED FOR? 'The Lost Angels' or 'The Cowpat-Throwing Contest'. In fact, 'The Cowpat-Throwing Contest' was banned by BBC Radio 5 for fear of offending teachers!

WEBSITE: www.poetryzone@ndirect.co.uk

I HOW THE READER BECAME A WRITER

The first books I can remember being absolutely hooked on were Enid Blyton's. Though after I'd read about fifteen *Famous Fives* I got to the stage where I realised that they were all exactly the same! So then I got into things like *Jennings* and *Billy Bunter* and *Just William* and *Biggles*. I loved series books – knowing that when you'd finished one you could go on to another. I used to belong to Boots' Library and I got all those books out from there.

The books I still revisit from my childhood are the *William* books. It's a mark of a great book if you can enjoy it as both a child and an adult. And it's the same with the *Asterix* books. These books work on different levels – appealing to both a child and an adult reader. I try and do this with my poetry now. I know that when I do a performance there'll be adults there, so I want things that they can tune into as well.

I can remember writing poetry at primary school. We were occasionally asked to write a poem, and I would struggle with the spelling, punctuation, the neatness and the form of it. What I actually wrote about was the last thing that the teachers were interested in. As long as it looked nice and was technically good. At secondary school, it was very much a question of analysing and criticising and chopping up a poem and seldom being left with any image of the poem as a complete entity at the end of all this. And that really turned me off poetry for a while.

By fourteen, I was reading Ian Fleming's novels, despite my father's disapproval! And I got into music – Bob Dylan and the Rolling Stones, and later on Jimi Hendrix.

All those guys were doing wonderful things with words in the context of song. It was the 60s lyrics that made me appreciate words for the first time. I began learning the guitar, but I didn't succeed. I didn't get beyond the usual three chords. And I tried to write songs, and it wasn't until one day that somebody told me what a dreadful noise I was making that I put the guitar on one side and just concentrated on lyrics and songs. I was about sixteen, seventeen when I was doing this. I was a rebel at that age. I loved the rebelliousness of the 60s, and I was heavily into Flower Power in 1967. But I think the teenage Brian Moses would have been quite impressed with the middle-aged Brian Moses – to be working with words, because I was into song lyrics.

When I left school I got a summer job driving a van for a photography company. I had a lot of spare time with that job and I read a lot in the van. One afternoon, I went into a bookshop and I picked up a book with Roger McGough's name on the cover. The only reason I knew McGough was that he was in a group called The Scaffold. It was a poetry book. Normally I would have put it down straight away, but I didn't. I started reading McGough's poems. And that was *Penguin Modern Poets 10 – The Mersey Sound* with Roger McGough, Adrian Henri and Brian Patten.

That book changed my life. I read and I read and I read that book all summer because the poems were accessible. They were written colloquially. They were about things I was interested in. They were about falling in love. They were about rebellion. They were about daft ideas, crazy things. And that book was an absolute 'Road to Damascus' experience for me. I started writing poetry from that moment on. The poems were terrible pastiches of the Mersey Poets. And I don't think I was beyond nicking the odd line or two from various writers at that point just to get something that sounded good! I did that for many years. I wrote terribly bad versions of those poets in the hope that one day the first spark of an original voice would shine through.

I went to college and I had my first poem published in the college magazine. I went around on a high. Wow, I thought, I'm published! And then I saw an advert in the paper – it was a new poetry magazine starting up that was asking for poems and they accepted another of my poems. This was a surrealist poem about a seaside resort in winter. When I graduated I was still writing obscure stuff that was getting published in the huge network of small magazines that existed in the early 70s. I don't think these magazines were ever read by anybody other than the poets who were writing stuff for them! It was a very cliquey kind of thing. But it was valuable in that I was getting published, and it meant a lot to me at that time. With a friend, Jeff Bleakly, I even started a magazine called *Malenka*. The title's a corruption of the French – *mal encre* – bad ink. And we were publishing all this stuff and we didn't even understand a lot of it!

And then I became a teacher. I did a lot of poetry with the children. I used to read all my favourite stuff by Michael Rosen, Roger McGough and, later on, Kit Wright. Much of the time I found that the sort of poems I was looking for – for our class topics – I couldn't find. And so I started writing them myself and using them with the children. The children's responses were quite favourable, probably because I was their teacher and they were being kind to me. And that encouraged me to keep writing more and more.

I was still writing stuff for adults because I was in a group at the time called The Pork Show. It was a group of poets and musicians. There was myself, Pie Corbett and four musicians. We went out on the road – and did no end of performances, at schools, festivals, pubs and wine bars. This was essential for me – as I was finding my voice and learning how to handle an audience, which was important for what I did later on.

Pie Corbett and I were working at the same school at this time. We started up an after-school writers' club. It was a tough school, and the kids were pretty streetwise – but we had about twenty-five kids come along to our club. Their writing was so honest. They were so keen to be little surrealists and have fun with words that we all had a fantastic time. Pie and I saved all the poems from these kids and we put them in a book that we wrote for the other teachers in our school. The headteacher, Graham Bond, said we should get it published. So we sent it to Oxford University Press as we liked the anthologies that John Foster had done for them. After three months, an editor from OUP rang me up and said they wanted to publish it. Two and half years later, and after a lot of tinkering around with it, *Catapults and Kingfishers* was published. We were just in the right place at the right time, and they happened to be looking for a book like that. It was the first unsolicited manuscript they'd published in fifteen years! And that book launched my career.

Then I did a term as Teacher Fellow at what is now the University of Sussex, in Brighton. I was going into other schools, where I was working with children and performing poetry. And over the next couple of years East Sussex Council kept taking me out of my own classroom to go to other schools to perform. I began to think, why not try and do this full-time? As soon as I had a full diary – having sent mail-shots around to all the schools in the area – I left and became a full-time writer and performer.

Roger McGough is still someone whose poetry and wordplay I admire immensely. I had the great pleasure of doing both a radio programme and a live performance with Gareth Owen whose work on the page and delivery on stage I find totally engaging. I also enjoy Charles Causley, Kit Wright, Shel Silverstein. Two recent books that have particularly impressed me are *The Last of The Wallendas* by Russell Hoban and *Plum*, the first collection by Tony Mitton. I'm pleased to say that I was one of the first anthologists to pick up on Tony's work!

2 WRITING: ROUTINES AND REFLECTIONS

I work in my office, which is a purpose-built extension at the back of our house. It's a very pleasant, light, airy room that has a nice view of lots of trees and it's where I like to write. But I can write in all sorts of places, such as hotel rooms and even trains.

My first draft is done either by hand or by dictaphone. I take a dictaphone around with me everywhere I go. If I'm in the car and I get an idea, I'll speak it into the machine. I always do a lot of work with a poem on paper first. Then there arrives a time that it just needs to go onto the computer. Then I jigsaw the lines around until it's finished. One quality that I try to achieve with my poems is that they work both on and off the page, in that they can be read silently or performed.

I store all my ideas in notebooks and on disc. I keep all my poetry notebooks, and all of the ideas are dated. I'll remember a poem by the place I wrote it in. And I can usually remember quite accurately the year and time I would have written it. Sometimes I'll go through the notebooks, taking out ideas I want to use. Here's something I jotted down a few years ago that I've recently developed. I saw a sign saying 'Carpet Showroom' and I looked at the word 'carpet' and I thought it could be 'car pet'. So I wrote a poem called the 'Car Pet Showroom'.

Ideas come from anywhere and everywhere. An idea is like a knock on the door. Ignore the knocking and whoever it is goes away. When an idea comes knocking, I can't afford to ignore it. I grab it quickly before it can escape. Ideas often come from what I read. Once I read a report on the front of *The Times* – and the headline was 'No Kissing'. It was about a private school where the headteacher had introduced the six-inch rule, which meant that children of the opposite sex were not allowed to get closer than six inches of each other because there had been reports of these children kissing in town on a Saturday afternoon. So I wrote a poem called 'No Kissing' in the voice of the children at the school. Also, my poem 'Croc City' was inspired by an article in an American paper about the problem with alligators in the sewers of New York. I couldn't make it work with alligators, so I used poetic licence and changed it to crocodiles.

Other ideas come from what I hear. I was at a school about four years ago, sitting in the staff room. I suddenly realised that the staff were all telling each other what they wore in bed at night! And that's how my poem 'What Teachers Wear in Bed' started. And then that poem eventually kicked off the collections *The Secret Lives of Teachers* and its sequel.

I write for children because I experienced initial success with the stuff I wrote for that age group. When you feel that children are enjoying what you write it encourages you to pursue it. And I loved children's literature, and I really wanted to be a part of it. It was Auden who said that although there are good poems that are only for adults, there are no good poems that are only for children. I do readings for adults sometimes, and I still read a lot of the stuff I write for children. But I will read a lot of my unpublished teenage poetry, which is also suitable for adults.

You should never write down to children or assume that they know less than you do. I see so much writing for children where people are writing in such a bland way, because they feel this is all children can take. I believe in taking a few risks – at whatever level I'm writing for. I try to write what I think children want to hear rather than what I think they ought to hear – with things like my teachers' poems. And fortunately, teachers have come along with me, and they've enjoyed the poems too.

What I enjoy about poetry is that you can create a poem quickly and it's there and you feel good that you've done something that day. I like to see my poems building up in a folder, moving towards a new collection. And I suppose because I'm attracted so much to music and the rhythms of music, I'm attracted to the rhythms of poetry and language. I love words and how poetry allows you to string words together in a variety of ways. For me, a poem is a snapshot giving you a brief glimpse, but a glimpse that is often so powerful that it can stay with you forever. It enables you to look at the world in a different way. Writing poetry is something I'll always do.

In total, I must have written about 1,500 poems in about thirty years. My weekly output varies so much because I divide my time up between visiting schools and writing. I find that I collect lots of ideas on my travels and my notebook gets full while I'm away. When I come back, I might spend the first day writing three or four poems because I've gone through the notebook and found various things I want to work on. There are times when I'll write nothing at all for six weeks and then I'll write several.

A poem takes anything from five minutes to a year to write. An average poem will initially take an hour or two – but I'm always tinkering away at it afterwards. Then I'll perform it and modify it. And then maybe perform it to a different audience and modify it again. Performances can help me to see if there are any flat points. And sometimes I'll start to write a poem, put it away for a couple of months, and then go back to it, and do a bit more to it – and it might take a year to get written. I don't think I ever quite know when a poem is finished. The only time I'll finally leave it alone is when it's published in a book.

Some poems will need a lot of work before they're right. When I did my *Hippopotamus Dancing* and *Knock Down Ginger* collections, for instance, I had a very good editor who told me that twenty of the poems were fine, but that another ten needed a lot of work. At first I hit the roof! But later I compromised – three of those ten I knew worked well in performance, but the other seven I worked on, and they became much stronger poems. I'll always show Anne, my wife, my work and she'll tell me what's working and what's not. As with my editors, Anne is able to see things in my poems that I can't, because I'm too close to them. I can't be objective. And I'll say to children during my school visits that it's good if they can work with friends on a regular basis – and start by saying what they like in each other's poems and then go on to say what needs a bit more work. It can really help if you can build up that level of trust in a response-partner situation.

Lucy Maddison illustrates most of my work at the moment. I'm very happy with what she does with my poems. We seem to have developed a sympathetic relationship. In my mind, a good illustration should complement a poem, it shouldn't overtake or overstate it. Ideally, it should lead the reader into the poem and I think Lucy does that really well.

I think there are a lot of people who feel they can write children's poems because they feel it's easier to write for children than it is for adults. That's a total misconception. A child audience is the hardest audience you'll ever meet. Children will soon vote with their feet if what you're giving them isn't what they want to hear. A lot of material that's being sent in to publishers is just people thinking 'Oh, I can do this, you know.' And they'll send off any old rhyming rubbish. We've got to keep the standard up. We can keep the humour, but it's got to be clever humour and not just lavatorial stuff. I may have written a poem like 'The Cowpat-Throwing Contest', but I'll stand by it. It is based on historical fact. I think it's a good poem – it's well structured and I think it works! The theme may be distasteful, but I've seen teachers and children creased up with laughing at that poem!

3 GROWING A POEM

'The Lost Angels'
(from the collection *Don't Look at Me in that Tone of Voice!*)

The poem began when I was on holiday in France with my family. We were staying on the Normandy coast and we went along to an aquarium. We thought it was going to be like a British sea life centre, but it wasn't, it was run down and tatty. The first room we went into was about the size of a classroom, and there was a round tank, rather like a back garden swimming pool. The water in the tank was green and slimy and there were three enormous turtles inside, trying desperately to swim around in the water. I love turtles, and my daughter Karen does too. We were very, very sad to see the turtles kept in captivity when they should be in the ocean. I just couldn't imagine what it must have been like for these poor creatures in this tank, desperately trying to live in a natural way. They must have been totally confused by the environment they found themselves in.

Karen and I stayed with the turtles a long time, just looking at them. We tried to get as close as we could to them, without getting bitten. We watched people's reactions as they came into the room and listened to what was being said. We didn't really look round much more of the aquarium after that, we just left. In the evening, we found ourselves sitting down and writing poems about the turtles. And I was struck by the resemblance between the front flippers of a turtle and an angel's wings. And that's why I called the poem 'The Lost Angels'. Initially, it started in a different way. It began:

Fish show no emotion
or nothing that I can detect
Though perhaps to another fish
who knows what signals they send

The only line from that that I kept eventually was 'who knows what signals they send'. And it went on:

But today I saw creatures with angels' wings
Floating and falling in a fish tank in France

And in this, the final version, I changed the beginning as I wanted it to be a performance poem, and I needed the first four lines to be quite direct and to explain what it was all about:

In a fish tank in France
we discovered the lost angels
fallen from heaven and floating now
on imaginary tides.
And all along the sides of the tank,
faces peered, leered at them,
laughing, pouting,
pointing, shouting,
while hung above their heads, a sign
'Ne pas plonger les mains dans le bassin.'
Don't put your hands in the tank
– the turtles bite seriously.
And who can blame them,
these creatures with angel's wings,
drifting past like alien craft.
Who knows what signals they send
through an imitation ocean,
out of sight of sky,
out of touch with stars?

Dream on, lost angels,
then one day, one glorious day,
you'll flap your wings
and fly again.

After the first four lines I wanted to say something about what was happening in that room with these turtles, and it became 'And all along the sides of the tank, / faces peered, leered at them'. I do tend to put quite a lot of internal rhyme into a non-rhyming poem – and also with 'laughing, pouting, pointing, shouting'. When we were at the aquarium I copied down the sign 'Ne pas plonger les mains dans le bassin', which I incorporated to give it an authentic French ring, as it were!

Now, I'm not quite sure whether I should have brought the alien craft image into the piece or not. But people say it works. The whole idea of 'Who knows what signals they send' was influenced by a couple of novels I've read – Russell Hoban's *Turtle Diary* and *Changes in Latitudes* by Will Hobbs. Both of these books talk about turtle migration and homing instincts.

I don't know why there are two stanzas – one long and one short. Perhaps the short one is simply a coda. I wanted a bit of hope at the end, although in reality there isn't : 'Dream on, lost angels, / then one day, one glorious day, / you'll flap your wings / and fly again.'

When I perform this piece, I always pause after the word 'fly' – 'You'll flap your wings and fly –' and the children in the audience will often say '–away!' and I say '-again!'

This is something of a spiritual poem for me, and something I'd like to do more of. I'll always write the humorous poems, but in a way I'd like to concentrate on the more serious ones at some point in the future. However, I have always written serious ones, and you'll find them in all my books. I've had a lot of reaction to this poem, initially from Macmillan who said they really liked it. I sometimes ask the children during a school visit which their favourite poem was, and occasionally someone will say 'The Turtles Poem' – and I'll know I've reached through to another turtle fan!

'Readathon Sleepathon'
(from the collection *Knock Down Ginger*)

Some years ago I had a phone call from one of the teachers at Rainham High School for Girls asking if I wanted to get involved with their 'readathon–sleepathon'. She explained that this is an event in which their Year 7 girls come to school with their sleeping bags and extra food and home clothes and they camp out in the school hall overnight. And throughout the night they read books. It's a sponsored event in which all the proceeds go to a charity for children with cancer.

The teacher asked if I would like to come along in the evening – so I did! And I read all these spooky poems and nobody could sleep much after that! As I was driving home after the event, my eyes kept closing all the time. I had to do something to stop myself falling asleep – so I got out my dictaphone and started recording my impressions of the event I had just taken part in. That recording eventually became this poem.

It started out as a picture of the school hall, a bit like a refugee feeding station with all these sleeping bags everywhere:

> Mary is sleeping by Janice, and Janice is next to Louise,
> and Louise is squeezed beside Tracy who's pressed
> against Alice's knees.

Again, there's a lot of internal rhyme and assonance in there.

> And Sally is pally with Gemma, and Gemma is talking
> with Claire,
> and Claire is thinking that maybe she should have stayed
> home and washed her hair –

I like this phrase 'readathon–sleepathon'. I suppose it's a little bit like the kind of thing that Shel Silverstein, the American poet, does. He makes up words to rhyme, which is what I was doing here:

> but it's the readathon–sleepathon
> a ghosts-at-midnight screamathon
> and anyone who's anyone
> is reading at the readathon.

Then there's a few more details about the girls taking part:

> But Ann-Marie would dearly love to be at home in bed,
> Lying safely in her room while silence fills her head,
> and Nicola is tired and would like to go to sleep
> but all that talk of ghosts has given her the creeps.

And the next part is actually true, because one girl was petrified of going to the toilet after I'd read the ghostly poems:

> And 'I need to go to the toilet, Miss, I'm not going on my own,
> someone had better come with me, it's not like being at home.'
> 'Hey, come and give me a kiss, Miss, my Mum always does,
> and tuck me up really tight, Miss, go on, make a fuss – '
>
> at the dramathon, the pyjamathon,
> I'd rather run a marathon,
> but anyone who's anyone
> Is reading at the readathon.

I was constantly trying to find different rhyming words to go with 'readathon':

> It's been going on for 19 hours and it's been lots of fun,
> but now it's early morning and someone wants her Mum.
> In just a few more hours we can all creep home to bed,
> dream of money raised and the number of books we've read –
>
> at the readathon, the pleadathon,
> the money-for-people-in-needathon,

> and anyone who's anyone
> Is reading at the readathon.
>
> And then when it's finally over and everything's cleared from the floor,
> when everyone's saying goodbye and heading for the door
> it's a readathon, a stampedathon,
> a mega-brill stampedathon,
> a guaranteed repeatathon –
> will you be here next year?

And they invited me back the following year, and I went and read the poem to them!

This poem didn't take very long to write. Once I got going with the rhythm and the pattern of it, it came fairly immediately. And I sent a copy of the poem to the school a week after the event. As I said, most of it was written on the dictaphone, and it was just a matter of transferring that to the page. It was pretty much a single draft. And I chose rhyme for this one as it adds to the humour and it gives it more of an uplifting feel. And I wanted it to be a kind of jaunty, lively read – and I think rhyme does that with this piece.

4 VISITS TO SCHOOLS

I've always loved performing poetry, right from the days I was in the group The Pork Show. Poetry, for me, is written to be performed. I love being in front of an audience. I get a real buzz from a performance in school that's going really well. My biggest audience ever was 625 children. And it's great if the teachers are prepared to come and enjoy themselves in a school session. Occasionally, I'll go to a school and get a real po-faced bunch of teachers sitting down the side and the kids are enjoying themselves but the teachers just won't let themselves go. Though it's great when the teachers do, because then everyone is joined together in the sheer enjoyment of poetry!

I think children enjoy my sessions because I show them a side to poetry that they don't necessarily realise exists – that it's not just something that sits on the page, it's something that can be brought to life, using different voices, instruments and movements.

During a performance I'm constantly modifying what I'm doing as I go along. I'll look at the audience and decide which poems I'll do next. Even if I've prepared a performance list, it's not set in stone; I'll see how it's going, and I'll gauge the responses and act accordingly. For the writing workshops I have something like thirty different sessions I could do, and I'll draw on one of those, often depending on how the class react to my initial talk. I'll try and find out what sort of class they are, what their imaginations are like, and whether they can think quickly and then I'll fit one of my activities to that group of children.

One workshop that I've done over the years begins with me telling the class that writers are liars and thieves and that we steal and use the stories that people tell us. Then I'll tell them about a story I was told by a girl I met in a school on Guernsey. This girl had a budgie that her dad accidentally sucked up into the vacuum cleaner when he was cleaning out the cage. So they got the budgie out of the dust bag, and the budgie was a bit dusty and he was coughing a lot. So they washed him and put him back on his perch, and the next day he was fine. Then I'll tell the children that there's a new breed of super budgies on Guernsey! And I'll say to the children that I want them to take an ordinary creature – and by means of lying, boasting and exaggerating, I want them to turn it into a super creature. And they seem to have great fun doing this. Occasionally, I'll write a poem on the board with them to begin with, and at other times I'll put a list of things up that they may want to think about – such as size, shape, colour and the food the creature eats.

Another workshop I've been doing for a few weeks now is called 'Dreams'. I'll get the children to imagine that anything can dream – any object, any animal, anything. And I'll make a few suggestions, such as 'What does a goal post dream of?' or 'What does a tree dream of?' I did this yesterday in a local school and we had some amazing ideas – from a flea dreaming that it can jump as high as the Eiffel Tower to a crisp dreaming of being sweet – all kinds of things!

In the workshops I'll say that I'd rather their poems didn't rhyme, but some children still want to. And if they do, I'll say that I'm tough on rhymes, and I won't accept a word that is just there for the sake of it. A rhyme must be there because it adds to the poem. The other thing I'm tough on is that a poem must look like a poem on the page from the start. A poem is not chopped-up prose. So if anyone thinks they can get away with writing a story or description, they must think again! I'll actually go quickly round the class to see what the children are doing. And if they're struggling, I'll suggest various things they can do.

When I respond to children's work I'll give a positive comment first. I always respond initially with encouragement. It makes it easier for the child then to accept that one or two bits of their poem could benefit from re-jigging. And I'll pinpoint certain lines and suggest ways to change or develop the poem. I do emphasise the need to find a poem's rhythm, especially if there's no rhyme, they must find the rhythm. Sometimes you can do that with words or lines that repeat themselves – or with assonance, internal rhyme or alliteration. So, it's using all the tricks a poet has to get an interesting rhythm into the poem. I'll rarely talk about metre, but with an older or more able group we might count the syllables. With syllable counting we'll take a possible first line to a poem, count the syllables and then try to make the other lines of the poem the same number of syllables. Or, we'll adopt a pattern – 10–8–10–8 or something similar. This tightens up a poem and strengthens its rhythm. And I'm always saying to children that there are no wrong ways to write, it's just that some ways are better than others.

Another piece of advice I give children is that if they want to write seriously, then they should keep a writer's notebook. But they mustn't think that they're going to write a story or poem every time they open it. I'll suggest that they go back over their day, to find interesting or funny things that they've heard or seen. Then a notebook becomes a treasure chest of ideas. And when they've got time to write something they can open it up and see what jumps out as inspiration.

What's the nicest compliment a child has ever paid my work? In response I'll read a couple of poems written by pupils from some of the schools I've visited over the last ten years. This one's by James Rogers, of Cuxton Primary School in Kent, who was 10:

When Brian Moses came to school
we wrote poetry all day
When Brian Moses came to school
two policeman arrested
the Head for making children
bored with discipline
When Brian Moses came to school
he took us to the woods
and I trod in dog's dirt
When Brian Moses came to school
he said nice was not a nice word to use
When Brian Moses came to school
I felt like a real poet.

And this one's by Sarah Jackson from Sandham Middle School on the Isle of Wight:

At Sandham Middle School one Monday morning
a poet came who wasn't boring
Brian Moses was his name
he made poetry a game
Out to break nice and early just for today
poetry's over and Brian's on his way
To another school to teach more children like me
how great poetry can be

I offer a whole variety of activities to schools. I do presentations of my poetry to the whole school, or for juniors and infants separately. I run writing workshops with individual classes of children. And, because of the books I have done for Heinemann and Longman recently, I get asked to do INSET training days for teachers on the new Literacy Hour. I also give talks on the work of the writer and how books are produced.

I do family writing evenings too – where we invite children and parents as families to school. During the evening I'll read some poetry, talk about writing and get everybody – whole families – sitting around a table with a big sheet of paper sharing ideas and memories for writing. One of the exercises I use is called 'If my whole life flashed before me, I wouldn't want to remember . . .' And the families will go through all their embarrassing moments! The conversation and the laughter that goes on during that half an hour in which they share their memories is wonderful. And I think it shows that writing poetry is tough, and that children in school achieve so much every day. But overall it's a fun evening, having fun with words.

And there's an 'Establishing the Reading Habit' evening where I'll take along a couple of boxes of recently published books and my favourite books for children. I make a display and talk to parents about what makes a good book for children. I'll start the evening off by reading them a story. And I'll talk about the books I like and how to choose a good book, how to tell what's worth buying, and what's suitable for different age ranges. We finish with the families looking at the books I've brought in. If there's time, parents will take a book with their children into a corner and read together. But overall, I do more visits for children in schools – I probably do a couple of family evenings a term.

Just recently I've begun doing 'writers' trails' in schools. Schools invite me in to develop a trail around their school grounds. The idea is that the children will go to various points along the trail where they'll find an activity which will inspire them to write in a creative and imaginative way. Occasionally I'm asked to go on school trips and to get the children to write on location. I do a regular trip with a small group of schools where we walk along the South Downs. We spend a couple of days writing about what we see, how we feel about the landscape, like the white horse on the hillside and other geographical features that we come across.

About five or six times a year I'll do a residency in a school, and stay there for a week or so. Popular places have been the Isle of Wight, the Channel Islands, Yorkshire and Cyprus. I've just come back from a residency at Castle Cornet on Guernsey. I was employed by the museum service over there to set up a 'writers' trail' around the castle. Children from the local schools were brought along, and the idea was that I would try to give them a more imaginative response to the castle as opposed to the usual scenario of the children being given a worksheet and being asked to fill in gaps and tick various boxes. We wrote about all kinds of things – from the spooky aspects of the castle – such as Prisoner's Walk – to the views and the things the castle has seen and heard over the centuries. We tried to empathise with the German soldiers that were stationed there in World War Two. Some children wrote poems and diary entries in the voices of the German soldiers – about their experiences in the war and being away from home. The quality of the writing was brilliant. By writing on location you get a more direct experience, and this informs the children's writing in a wonderful way. This visit was one of the highlights of my writing career so far. It was great fun. I was there for a week, actually living in the castle. This poem was written by one of the children during the residency:

Ways of entering a castle

You can enter the castle crestfallen like a cheerless ant,
You can enter quietly like a speechless mum.
You can enter noisily like a roaring bear,
You can enter a castle as if you were a wonderful magician.
You can enter a castle by flying down from high above like George of the Jungle
You can enter bad tempered like a boiled beetroot
OR you can enter a castle normally just like my mum and me
(Nicola Burridge, aged 10, Amherst Junior School, Guernsey)

Teachers can prepare for my visits by familiarising the children with my poems, by showing them my books – so they know who this author who's coming along is. It's always more enjoyable for me if the children are coming up and saying 'Why did you write such-and-such?' or 'What do you mean in this poem?' My aim is to give 101 per cent when I go into a school and I want that commitment back from a school, because I know then that we can have a really good day. Sadly, I don't always get that – sometimes children won't be in the classroom on time or won't have anything to write with, and this happens too often. I need the children to be there and to be ready to write with me. And no teacher marks books during my workshops or performances! If they come into the hall with a pile of books expecting to mark, I will not begin my performance! It gives the wrong message to the kids and it's very bad manners.

School visits are so important to my writing as well. Visits can generate ideas, they give me an insight into what children are interested in – the latest crazes and what they're reading. Overall, they help me to keep in touch.

5 COMPILING ANTHOLOGIES

I have to thank my friend Anthony Masters for getting me involved with anthologies. He knew that I was quite keen to do books and he introduced me to Caroline Walsh, who used to be the poetry editor at Blackie. At that time Blackie had got quite a nice series of poetry anthologies on their list, and Caroline asked what ideas I had. I told her that I'd like to do a family anthology and that turned into *You Just Can't Win*, which is now out of print. After that, we did a collection of shape and puzzle poems entitled *My First Has Gone Bonkers*.

Then I got involved with Macmillan, who at that point were wanting to develop a poetry list, and so I was there from the start. The first thing we put together was *The Sandwich Poets* series – and the first collection from this series was *Rice, Pie and Moses*, now reissued as *An Odd Kettle of Fish* – which included poems by John Rice, Pie Corbett and myself. Pie Corbett and I are actually the editors of the series. The main criterion of *The Sandwich Poets* series is that the poets are actively performing in schools.

The anthologies that I really enjoyed myself were the ones that John Foster compiled for Oxford University Press – *A First Poetry Book*, *A Second Poetry Book*, and so on. They were just wonderful. They made us all look at how to present poetry in a different way. They were benchmarks that we all tried to reach up to.

Anthologies originate with me or with my editor, Gaby Morgan. We'll talk on the phone and I'll send in proposals. Gaby then takes these to a publisher's meeting and if the ideas are adopted then we're off on our next title.

Sometimes, a single poem can spark off an anthology – that's what happened with both *The Secret Lives of Teachers* and *Aliens Stole My Underpants*. With *The Secret Lives*, I originally took the idea for the collection to another publisher, but they turned it down. I told them I was sure it was going to be a bestseller! But they said it wouldn't sell. So then Macmillan took it on, and, 50,000 copies later, I was proved right!

School Trips – which has only just come out – was another that originated with me. I've been on so many school trips myself, and we were looking for another school-based collection. And I thought that teachers themselves would be fascinated by school trip poems as they've all got horrendous tales of school trips to tell! Other collections I'm currently doing are *We Three Kings* (a Christmas anthology) and

Minibeasts. There's also going to be a brothers and sisters collection called *I'm Telling On You*, as well as *My Gang* – a friendship collection.

When I'm compiling the Macmillan anthologies I look for lively and humorous poems which children are going to relate to. Though sometimes – as with *Parent-Free Zone* – I'll put a couple of more serious poems in. For example, there's one in that anthology by Jackie Kay on divorce. Again, with *We Three Kings*, I think people will be quite surprised in that there's some quite thoughtful pieces in there, alongside the more humorous poems. The majority of poems I choose will be new poems, mainly because you're not tied up with any problems of copyright, you only have to pay the poet, and you don't have to request permissions from rights departments. Probably 75 per cent of the poems in these Macmillan anthologies are published for the first time.

The various stages each book will go through are as follows. First, Gaby Morgan will send me a commission letter, and I'll write back accepting the commission. Then I'll get my contract and I'll send letters out to about seventy or eighty poets that I keep on my database. The letters will give details of the theme, nature and intended age group of the anthology and will request any suitable material that the poets may have. There's usually a deadline of 2–3 months on that. When all the poems are in, I'll have a huge pile to go through. I do an initial sorting-through for those poems that aren't right, and then I'll whittle it down to a pile of fifty poems that I'll send on to Gaby. In the end, we'll choose about thirty poems. I'll write to each of these poets saying that we've accepted their work, and asking if they'll accept the conditions of the contract. At the same time we'll also send them a typeset version of their pieces to ensure that we've copied the poems correctly. If the poets agree the terms, I'll then return the typeset versions to Gaby at Macmillan. Meanwhile, the cover will be designed, and the illustrations will be drawn – usually by Lucy Maddison. Also, the blurb for the back of the book will be written. A couple of proofs are made, and then the books are printed, bound and distributed to bookshops.

SELECTED CURRENT TITLES

Poetry

Hippopotamus Dancing and Other Poems (Cambridge University Press)
Knock Down Ginger and Other Poems (Cambridge University Press)
Croc City (Victoria Press)
An Odd Kettle of Fish – with John Rice and Pie Corbett (Macmillan)
Don't Look at Me in that Tone of Voice! (Macmillan)

Poetry anthologies

Aliens Stole My Underpants and Other Intergalactic Poems (Macmillan)
I'm Telling On You! – poems about brothers and sisters (Macmillan)
More Secret Lives of Teachers (Macmillan)
My First Has Gone Bonkers (Puffin)

Poems About Me (Wayland)
Poems About Me and You (Wayland)
School Trips (Macmillan)
The Secret Lives of Teachers (Macmillan)
We Three Kings – Christmas poems (Macmillan)

Literacy hour anthologies

Storyworlds – four anthologies in support of the National Literacy Strategy
  (Heinemann)

Picture books

Play With Me (Ginn)
Ten Tall Giraffes (Ladybird)
The Dragons Are Coming (Ginn)
Shoo Fly Shoo (Ladybird)

Picture books – non-fiction

The War Years: The Home Front (Wayland)
The Wartime Cookbook : Food and Recipes from the Second World War – with Anne
  Moses (Wayland)
I Feel Angry / I Feel Sad / I Feel Frightened (Wayland)

Books for teachers

Catapults and Kingfishers – Teaching Poetry in Primary Schools (OUP)
My Grandmother's Motorbike – Story Writing in Primary Schools (OUP) – both titles
  with Pie Corbett
Stories from the Past (Scholastic)

An introduction to . . . Benjamin Zephaniah

WHAT TYPE OF BOOKS DO YOU WRITE? Poetry for children and adults, and also plays for stage, radio and television. I've just finished a novel – *Face*, for teenagers – which is a new territory for me.

WHAT ARE YOUR BOOKS ABOUT? In my children's poetry I write about issues that I'm concerned about – such as animals, the environment, bullying and racism. I think back to when I was at school and to the things that people weren't writing about then, and I think that I'll write about them now.

BORN: I was born in Coleshill just outside Birmingham. Strangely enough, I really don't know the exact date of my birth. It was 1958, but I don't know whether it was 15 March or 15 April – there was a genuine mix-up. The hospital has records for both dates. So I feel like the Queen, in that I've got an official birthday, which is 15 April, and an unofficial one!

EDUCATION: I went to St Matthis Infant School in Handsworth and then Deykin Avenue School in Witton, which was a school I really liked. I went to various secondary schools.

LIVES: East Ham, London.

PREVIOUS OCCUPATIONS: I've never really done anything else – but I was a painter and decorator for a couple of weeks and I once made policemen's whistles for two and a half days!

FAMILY/PETS: I'm married to Amina. Since Danny the cat died we don't have any pets. I may seem a bit of an extremist on the issue of pets – I don't think we can own animals. I never used to say Danny was my cat – Danny lived with me. We were companions.

HOBBIES: I restore classic cars. I'm doing one at the moment. The shell of it is a TR7. My other hobby – which I tell people about when I'm on stage and the audience thinks I'm joking – is collecting money! I collect bank notes from all over the world. And I love keeping fit and doing Kung Fu.

MOST TREASURED POSSESSION: I don't think that I have a soul, I think that I am a soul. And it's not part of me, it *is* me. So my most treasured possession is my body. That's why I look after it and keep it healthy.

AWARDS: *City Limits* Poet of the Year Award – which I won three years running. I'm an Honorary Citizen of Memphis. And I've just accepted an Honorary Doctorate from the University of North London.

LANGUAGES TRANSLATED INTO: Various poems have been translated into Arabic, Spanish, French, Danish, German, Italian, Zulu and Xhosa. I've had a play translated into French.

FAVOURITE PLACE: It doesn't matter where it is, but it's a forest. It's where I can get exercise, be with animals and have fresh air.

FAVOURITE BOOKS: *A Book of Nonsense* by Mervyn Peake; *Red Shelley* by Paul Foot; and I have an 1853 first edition of *The Political Works of Shelley* – somebody gave it to me as a present.

FAVOURITE LINES OF POETRY: It's not a poem, but it's a great line. It's by Adrian Mitchell:

Most people ignore most poetry because most poetry ignores most people.

And this is by Mahmood Jamal. It's one of my faves:

There is punk poetry and junk poetry
There is monk poetry and drunk poetry
There is sad poetry and mad poetry
But above all there is good poetry
And there is bad poetry.

FAVOURITE MUSIC: I was on *Desert Island Discs* a little while ago, and these were the records I chose – 'Fire in Babylon' by Sinead O'Connor; 'Chura Liya' by Bally Sagoo; 'Last Year's Men' by Leonard Cohen; 'Marcus Garvey' by Burning Spear; 'Me Can't Believe It' by Michael Smith; 'Ku Klux Klan' by Steel Pulse; 'Little Ukelele' by George Formby; 'Take Five' by Dave Brubeck – if I'm auditioning saxophone players I'll always get them to play this because it's quite a difficult piece to play; and the one that didn't get on to the show was 'Around Midnight' by Miles Davis.

FAVOURITE FILMS: *The Jerk* with Steve Martin.

WHAT WERE YOU LIKE AT THE AGE OF 11? I had an enquiring mind and I was forever asking questions. I always wanted to know 'Why?' And I was also fascinated with girls!

ENJOYS VISITING SCHOOLS BECAUSE: I never had a poet visiting me – we just had a fireman and a policeman. I just wish that a poet had come into my school when I was young – it would have just fired me up so much. But I know what schools are like – they can be hard work, so I like to go in and blow the kids away!

WHY DO YOU WRITE? There was a poet survey conducted in Britain, America and Canada. This question was in that survey too. Something like 80 per cent of the poets responded with 'depression'. I was the only one to say 'oppression'!

IF YOU WEREN'T A WRITER: If I couldn't make a living from poetry I'd still do it. I'm a qualified Kung Fu teacher, so maybe I'd do that. I still do teach kids today, but usually kids who have suffered from bullying or discrimination or some kind of abuse. And it's not so much about self defence as building confidence.

AMBITIONS: I want to be good at what I do.

WHAT FOUR WORDS DESCRIBE YOU BEST? Passionate, loud, serious and immature!

WHAT WOULD YOU LIKE TO HAPPEN IN THE TWENTY-FIRST CENTURY? I know we're never going to have a Utopian society, but I'd like to see a world without armies.

WHICH OF YOUR POEMS WOULD YOU LIKE TO BE REMEMBERED FOR? I don't think I've written it yet. To date it would be this one from *Talking Turkeys*:

Who's who

I used to think nurses
were women,
I used to think police
were men,
I used to think poets
were boring,
Until I became one of them.

WEBSITE: http://www.oneworld.org/zephaniah/

I HOW THE READER BECAME A WRITER/PERFORMER

If I was caught reading a book in our house, my parents would come up to me and say, 'Haven't you got anything to do?' I can't remember there being many books in our house, but we did have the Bible and a copy of *Pilgrim's Progress*. One thing we did have a lot of was oral poetry – tapes from Jamaica, of people like Louise Bennett. Also, my mum would tell me poems from her childhood. We read the Bible a lot, as my family were real preachers. I always recognised the Psalms as poetry, it's like praise poetry, praising God.

I was very advanced, in a way. I decided I was going to become vegetarian at the age of 11. I wasn't a great reader and writer, but I loved the radio and watching the news. I was ahead of my time when it came to current affairs, and I could debate with the best of them. When it came to political awareness, I was way ahead of my mother and father. I remember the Biafran War. Most people just knew that there were people called Biafrans who were starving, whereas I could explain how the war started, and people would be baffled by this. I'd listen to the World Service at night – I'd get this little radio and tune in.

I went to various secondary schools. My family started to disintegrate then and me and my mother were moving all around the country. I've never met another person that's been to as many schools as me, and in as many different places – including London, Birmingham, Manchester, Stourbridge and Dudley.

There's one book that I still have from then, one that I stole when I was about 12. I've actually gone back to the library where I stole it from and they told me I can keep it! It's *The Philosophies and Opinions of Marcus Garvey*. Garvey is said to be the founder of pan-Africanism. He was writing in the 1920s and 1930s, at a time when people wanted to start bleaching their faces to look whiter. Garvey was saying that people should be proud to be black, and that black people should be doctors and writers, not just housemaids and field workers. I could pick out bits of this book and my friends would read it to me too. As a child, I didn't read novels and I didn't read poetry, although I loved hearing it.

I've always wanted to do poetry. It's my favourite form of expression. I've always been a good rhymer. When I was young we had competitions in which someone would choose a word and I would have to make up a poem around it. I'd usually win! And as a kid I never thought about doing novels, they were too long and drawn out. I liked music, but you had to get a band together and learn how to play, and in our school we didn't have music lessons. I loved using words and it was just natural for me. Before I even knew that what I was doing was poetry, I just loved doing it. I used to call it 'playing with words'. I can't remember a time when I wasn't doing it. I started by performing around the house, and then I'd perform after church on the way home, and I'd say, 'Listen to this!' Then I went on to performing inside the church. And as I grew up, I played in the community centre. At one time the National Front came over and I was asked to get involved with a counter demonstration, entertaining the troops. And from there, I was performing on television!

It's interesting that one of the very first things I ever wrote – when I was very young – is something I still perform to this day. Although now I have it as more of a set poem. It's 'I Love Me Mother and Me Mother Loves Me'. It's published in my *Dread Affair* collection:

> I love me mother and me mother loves me
> We come so far from over the sea
> I love me mother and me mother loves me
> Some people call her Valerie
> I love me mother and me mother loves me
> She really makes some nice chapatti

In those days I used to improvise around that. And then later on it became:

> I love me mother and me mother loves me
> We come so far from over the sea
> We hear that the streets were paved with gold
> Sometime it hot some time it cold
> I love me mother and me mother loves me
> We try to live in harmony
> Well you can call her Valerie
> But to me she is my mummy . . .

Although my family and everyone around me knew that I loved poetry, they all said to me on various occasions, 'It's nice that you love words and you love acting and performing in front of people, but it's hard enough getting a job. How can you – as a young black man in this country – expect to become a writer? They don't want to hear our poems. Just try and get a job. You can still do your poems, but get a job.' They meant well. You see, there weren't black writers in this country at that time. And in a way, they were trying to protect me. I can understand now why they did it. At school, one teacher actually said that I was a 'born failure'. The first real encouragement I ever got was from friends. I'd do a poem for them and they'd say, 'Yeah man, that's good.'

My first paying gig was when I was about thirteen. I got a fiver for playing in a youth club. I couldn't believe that I'd got payed for it. And at the next gig I got a tenner! At this point I didn't write any of my poems down. I had my whole set in my head. I didn't need to sit down and learn them, I just found it a natural thing to do – to write them in my head and then remember them.

In my late teens, when I was in prison for burglary, I didn't do any writing at all. What I did do was a lot of thinking, and it did help my poetry later. A lot of people ask me, 'Where are the prison poems?' But there aren't any. There's one poem in *The Dread Affair* called 'Two Years One Time' which is all about being in prison, but I wrote that afterwards.

My first collection was called *Pen Rhythm*. That was done by a small community publisher called Page One Books. I was twenty when it came out. With my second collection, *Dread Affair*, Arena approached me. I didn't know anything about publishing then. Arena gave me a year or so to produce the book. But I had years' worth of poems anyway, so I went home that night and wrote them all down. I took them in next day, and they were really shocked! What I've learnt since is that you can't just write down performance poems. That's why I don't like my *Dread Affair* collection all that much, because they're still performance poems, and haven't been tailored to work on the page. To be honest, I'm never really completely happy with any of my books because the words are trapped on the page.

How did I get to write for children? Well, I've always performed in schools, and I'd been performing pretty much the same poetry as I would for adults. Anyway, I strongly believe that with some of the best poetry you can't tell if it's meant for children or adults. And I just used to write poems for people. Teachers used to say to me that there would be certain poems of mine that they wanted their class to read, but they'd have to photocopy them out of my adult books. The teachers couldn't use the books in class because of the swear words in some of the other poems. These teachers were saying to me that they thought it would be a good idea if I could do a collection just for kids – as kids do like to hold and own their own books. Puffin approached me a few times to do a collection for them and each time I said no, and that I write poems – not poems for either adults or children. I was really adamant about this. But eventually I was convinced, but I said to the editor that I wouldn't compromise on the issues I wrote about. So what I've done is taken the attitude I have in my adult's poetry and applied it to my children's poetry.

This may not be the correct thing to say in an interview about children's books, but if someone said to me that they'd got some information to give me, and that I could take this information in by either reading a book or watching a documentary,

I'd take the film documentary. I'm much better at taking in information that way rather than reading. I'm not a great reader. I love reading, but I'm very slow at it. It took me years to learn how to read and write, and when I did finally learn it was only to find out that I was dyslexic. Even now I'm not a great reader. I have loads of books, and I'm given loads of books, but I get round to reading them very slowly. Now I love reading poetry books. I love Shelley. And at the moment I'm reading Keats. A younger me would have been disgusted by me reading white, middle-class poets – but that was until I came across Shelley and realised what a revolutionary he was. I can't get into Wordsworth. I like the French poet Rimbaud. I read a lot of African poetry – there's a collection I like called *The Penguin Book of South African Verse* edited by Stephen Gray. But I also really like poems in local newspapers – like a poem by a housewife about how much she hates doing the washing up or something – just poems by people who aren't known as poets.

2 WRITING: ROUTINES AND REFLECTIONS

Most of the time I write in my office. It's an upstairs front room in my house. It has two computers, a fax and a huge fan for when it gets hot. I have lots of box files of scripts, contracts, reviews and accounts. I really believe in keeping all my business things in order. I know exactly where to find everything. I'm very organised.

I sometimes feel that I'm writing all the time, that I'm always collecting ideas, whatever I'm doing. Once, somebody asked this playwright if they'd finished their play, to which he said, 'Yes. It's all finished. All I've got to do now is write it down.' I feel like that. I once wrote a radio play during a flight to America. It was an eight-hour flight, but the play only took me four hours to write. But really, I didn't write it in four hours, I'd been collecting and thinking about ideas for the play for months and months beforehand. There's a difference between creating a poem and writing a poem. I create poems anywhere and everywhere – like when I'm jogging – but the actual writing happens here in the office.

It doesn't seem that I spend that much of my time writing. Because I'm a performer, I go away and do my touring and then I come back and usually switch off. I've decided that I'm not going to work, work, work all the time and have no fun. I believe that spending time not writing is as important as writing. So I like to come away from being creative for a while and then I can come back to it with a fresh mind.

People often ask me what dub poetry is. Well, I'm just drafting something for *The Oxford Book of Poetry*. They've got a section on me in there, and they've asked me to write about dub and dub poetry and rapping. This is what I wrote this morning, it's the first draft:

> *Dub*. An instrumental version of a reggae musical recording where the music is driven by a heavy mix of drum and bass sounds, with the piano and guitar sounds being heavily filtered through compressors and echo chambers.

> *Dub poet*. A style of poetry that is performed to a soundtrack of dub music. Many practitioners also perform this style of poetry without music. When performed without music, a performer will deliver the words with the same musical rhythms associated with reggae and sometimes burst into song. This style of poetry is also noted for its political and social commentary.

> *Rap*. The performance of a rhythmic monologue over a pre-recorded instrumental backing. Rap developed in the dance halls and clubs of North America as a way of exciting the crowds and allowing the rapper to show off their ability to rhyme. Now recognised as a legitimate branch of popular music. Many of the performers are now referred to as 'rap poets' who are just as concerned with the lyrical contents of the poem as well as their rhyming skills.

There's a Jamaican professor in some American university that said he recognised what us dub poets do, but that it's a very difficult thing to teach because the language we use is so different. And sometimes we even spell words incorrectly or differently. This Jamaican professor tries to do everything by the book. He wants to change 'Dis' to 'This' and 'De' to 'The' and 'Fe' to 'For' and things like that. In one of Michael Smith's poems there's the word 'Larrrrrd'. That's in real Caribbean speak. If my mum's in pain she'll go 'Larrrrrd'. It's a really guttural sound. And there's no other way of writing it but 'Larrrrrd'. This poem by Michael Smith was published posthumously. And it was actually the publisher that wrote it down and spelt that word as L-a-r-r-r-r-d. You see, it's an oral thing that just can't be captured on the page. It's difficult, if not impossible at times to translate oral poetry onto the page because they're two very different things. And that's partly why it's really hard for oral poets to get recognised, except by live audiences.

The way I spell is actually the way it sounds. Dyslexic kids love my poetry because of this. There's a guy down my road who had a lot of problems at school with reading because of his dyslexia. Apparently, when he discovered *Talking Turkeys* he'd go to school hugging the book. He identified with it because he spelt 'This' and 'That' the same way as I do – 'Dis' and 'Dat'. I get letters from people like the Dyslexia Association saying that it's good to see an established poet writing in this way, and that it shows that your ability to read or spell has nothing to do with intelligence.

What's poetry good for? It's good for capturing big emotions in a small, concise way, or for taking little teeny things and stretching them out. It's good because Ted Hughes can do it, Bob Geldof can do it, Benjamin Zephaniah can do it – but also Mr Brown at the allotment can do it. It's the most democratic art form you can get. All you need is a pen and a piece of paper, and when it comes to oral poetry, you don't even need a pen and paper. When someone comes to me and says that they're a poet, then they're a poet. I don't know if they're a genius, a mad person or what. If they've written a couple of lines, if they've had some imaginative thoughts, then they're a poet. I often tell people that publishing poetry is not the be-all and end-all. I tell them to perform it, because audiences will tell you what's good and what's bad. It's a very simple philosophy, and it's always rung true for me until this day. Another thing that poetry's good for is spreading the message of peace, love and unity.

People often ask me about my rhyming. I like my rhyme and rhythm. I sometimes do things like alliteration, but I don't do it consciously. I remember a 12-year-old kid once came up to me and said, 'I loved the alliteration in that poem.' And I said, 'What's that?' He had to tell me because I didn't know what it was! I so often do things without realising I'm doing them. I tend not to be too concerned or to actively think about these things. I say the thing, and if it works, it works. Though I do try not to repeat myself too much, I realise that with rhyme you can do that if you're not careful. When people send me their poems for advice, sometimes I'll spot people who use easy, obvious words for a rhyme. You see, I don't like rhyming a word like 'revolution' with something as obvious as 'solution'. I go for rhymes that you can't see coming, rhymes that are unexpected. Even though I love rhyming I always say that people who do a lot of it should practise some free verse and that they shouldn't get stuck with rhyme. I also say that people should use their own voice in their poetry.

Roger McGough was compering this gig I was performing at. Before I came on, he introduced me to the audience as a 'rhyming dictionary'! Until then, I didn't even know there was such a thing! I never use one now when I'm writing. It interrupts the flow of the writing too much – having to stop and pick up the book and read through it. Anyway, I don't need one!

Why do I write? – because I want to change the world. I'm not a politician or anything, so I realise that maybe I can just change people's minds, and get them to think and look at things differently. I've seen people with a lot of wealth and I've seen how arrogant they can be and how they don't care about the poor or people with disabilities or whatever. And because of their wealth they're paranoid, and they don't trust anyone. That's not happiness. This may sound all very worthy, but my ambition – as much as possible – is to help those that are not privileged or rich. And that may mean helping to raise money to buy wells for kids in Sudan, or it may mean fighting with a group of kids in London to keep a library open. I've spent a lot of my time doing petitions and this type of work because my ambition is to make the world a better place. My poetry might not change the world, but it can change people, individuals – and those individuals might change the world. I know of one person who used to be a racist. He told me he was changed by my poetry – and that he fell out with the rest of his family because they were still racists.

The interesting thing that a lot kids say – and it's sad that they're saying this – is that many children's writers tend to be ex-teachers who write about jelly and funny animals. And these kids can tell that I'm more interested in writing about animals going to slaughter or writing about being bullied in the playground. Kids often feel that there's this adult going, 'Now, boys and girls, *these* are my children's poems!' Come on! They feel they're being patronised. In this area, 12-year-old kids are getting pregnant and are getting into drugs, and they can't relate to that kind of poetry. And I know that a lot of kids come out with their parents to my gigs of their own free will. Part of it, I feel, is because I've never lost touch with kids.

I hate being with people of my age who start talking about 'the kids of today' and how things were when they were young, and how that you could leave the front door open. It's almost as if they didn't have a childhood. And how can you generalise about kids anyway?

It's difficult to say exactly what the difference is between my children's and adult's poetry, and now some of my poems are even published for both. With my children's poetry the language is slightly different in that I can be more playful, and I like that. Also, when you're being political in children's poetry, I think you have to be more clever, you can't just sloganise. I have to use my imagination more. For example, instead of writing something like 'A Beetle Called Derek', I could have just written a poem saying 'Save the rainforest. We need it. What is happening to mankind?' But instead, I did something much more imaginative – I tell the story of how Derek starts off in life, that she has her environment taken away from her and that in the end she dies and faces extinction. These are sad poems, but they're real life. What I like about writing for children is that I can be serious and playful, all at the same time. I would say that children are now my most important audience.

As a poet and a performer, I get asked to do many different things. I'm currently on David Blunkett's education committee. One of the things I've been trying to do is to emphasise how important creativity is. If you've got a nation of high achievers, of brainy people who've got no imagination, it would be a very boring world, and there'd be no poetry or art of any kind. It would also be a nation that would be very stressed. There's a neurologist on the committee who says that the human brain needs to be creative. She believes that scientists and philosophers produce their best work when they're being creative. If they just take what they've learnt and think only in a linear way, then they won't get very far. It's a scientist that can think laterally and creatively that will break boundaries. The neurologist also says that what poets do naturally is juxtapositions – bringing two different things together – and that's what scientists need to do too, to come out of their own discipline and by looking at something else they can put two things together and make important connections. Creativity needs to be encouraged. A real hero of mine is Stephen Hawking – he's a scientist, but he has a really spiritual side to him.

3 GROWING A POEM

Most of my poems start in my head with a rhythm:

> I *love* me mother and me *mother* loves me

It can be just that for a while. Then I might go on:

> We *come* so far from *over* the sea.

And I'll pace up and down the room as I'm saying it, and sometimes I'm actually kind of dancing. I think a lot of oral poets do that. I remember hearing a story about Dylan Thomas building a shed at the bottom of his garden. It was his daughter telling the story, and she said she could hear him in there at night chanting his poems out.

For me, one of the most important things about poems is *how* they're said. When they roll off my tongue nicely, that's when I know that they're ready for writing down. Sometimes I just create the whole thing in my head. But it really varies. One thing I don't want is a technique – I like to do it all different ways. I've got a recording studio downstairs and sometimes I'll write in there and perform to a drum machine rhythm. Other times, I'll record a poem onto a little tape recorder or dictaphone. But if I'm doing free verse, I'll do it on paper.

I keep notes of ideas as they come to me. Here's something I haven't worked on yet, so I don't know what will become of this, but I think it will become more of a song:

> I want to go to Glastonbury

And here's another thing:

> I don't need an identity crisis to be creative

There's so much talk about black people and their identity crisis. I've never really had one. Maybe it's because I read Marcus Garvey early, I don't know. I saw something on the television about black writers being concerned with identity – but it's not true – and I just wrote it down. I'm not sure how it will go – but it will probably be free verse as opposed to a rhyming thing. It will happen on the page and it will go something like:

> I don't need an identity crisis to be creative
> I don't need to be a tortured soul
> I know who I am
> I look in the mirror everyday and I see me
> I don't have an identity crisis

When I work on the page I write it out really rough and then I type it out immediately. Then I'll see whether I like it or not. What I do next is to perform it, and I'll actually say to the audience, 'This is brand new. I don't know if you're going to like it or not.' I'll see by their responses what they think of it. Some poems will end up being scrapped. When I've had some half-hearted responses to new work, I can usually tell why, and I'll know that I've used the wrong ending or I should have put another verse at the end, or that I need to change a certain word or whatever.

Here's a new one I've got here. It's called 'Benny's Wheels'.

> Benny in his wheelchair was the fastest kid in town
> They had to get sleeping police to try and slow him down
> His wheelchair was a mover as fast as any car
> He went 30 mph and he went very far
>
> Benny and his wheelchair were very much admired
> He went to school and returned home without feeling tired
> His wheelchair was unusual it had to be admitted
> Because he had a Formula One Racing Engine fitted
>
> This wheelchair had a stereo to blast out funky beats
> All the neighbourhood got dancing when he drove down their street
> And Benny had a girlfriend he visited at nights
> So his wheelchair was fitted with extra strong headlights
>
> He wins every egg and spoon race and he's never dropped an egg
> He won an Olympic Gold one year in Winnipeg
> His seat is quick reclining just in case he needs a nap
> And he's fitted a microphone in case he wants to rap
>
> When he revs up the engine the earth beneath does shake
> This is not the kind of engine any engineer can make
> It goes from 0–30 in the time it takes to blink
> And when Benny gets thirsty it provides a tasty drink
>
> To go it needs no petrol it likes to stay in use
> All it needs to go is Formula One-type orange juice
> It smells like chocolate roses when it's letting off its steam
> And if it's overheating Benny's wheelchair likes ice cream
>
> One day Benny's teacher offered Benny lots of cash
> If he would take life easier and stop speeding round the class

But Benny didn't like the deal, he took nothing at all
And on that very day he drove his teacher up the wall

Benny in his wheelchair was the fastest kid in town
His Formula One-type wheelchair simply did not hang around
He was the champion of champions that boy just loved to thrill
But the problem is he always leaves his parents standing still

I wrote this lately and I've performed it a couple of times, but reading it off the page. I don't normally do that. I had to read it because I was performing it two days after I wrote it. It was new and fresh and I didn't want to make a mistake. But what I found was that I was concentrating so much on my reading that it didn't work. One time when I was doing it, I just put the piece of paper to one side and did it from memory – which meant that I could do some actions as well. And once I'd done that, it just took on a life of its own. But it's very rare that I read at a performance. I never used to have to learn a poem, but as time goes on I have to. And if I write the poem in my head, I won't have to learn it. Now here's one that I wrote in my head recently. I just thought of this image of a pair of trousers running away:

'Wot a Pair'

I was walking down Y-Front Street
and me trousers ran away
I was feeling incomplete
but still my trousers would not stay
When I found where they had gone
The pair addressed me rather blunt
And they told me they were sick
of being put on back to front
I told them I would treat them good
and wear them back to back
I promised them protection
from a friend who was a mac
But me trousers did not believe
a single word I had to say
My underpants were laughing
when my trousers ran away.

Something like that, I don't know why, just came in an instant, and I just remembered it. Kids love me performing this one because it's kind of rude! As I said, I don't have a formula for writing or one way of doing things. This last one just came into my head, whereas with 'Benny's Wheels' I had to sit down and write it, and then I had to say it out loud to make sure it worked.

'Civil Lies'
(from the *Talking Turkeys* collection)

Dear Teacher,

When I was born in Ethiopia
Life began,
As I sailed down the Nile civilization began,
When I stopped to think universities were built,
When I set sail
Asians and true Americans sailed with me.

When we traded nations were built,
We did not have animals,
Animals lived with us,
We had so much time
Thirteen months made our year,
We created social services
And cities that still stand.

So teacher do not say
Columbus discovered me
Check the great things I was doing
Before I suffered slavery.

Yours truly,

Mr Africa

In history lessons at school you'd hear that so-and-so went over and discovered the Victoria Falls, or that so-and-so discovered black people in Africa. And I remember sitting in the class thinking, I was discovered? What was I before? Why does my history start when the white man discovered me?

It's funny, because I was supposed to be terrible at history at school. But I learnt the alternative version of history – the working-class and black version of history. When my teachers were trying to tell me all about kings and queens and battles and dates, I was getting into things like the Tolpuddle Martyrs. I used to hate all that kings and queens stuff – it never meant anything to me. I was fascinated with things like the Chartist Movement. To think it was led by a black man, William Cuffay, at a time when black people were considered by the authorities to be savages in Africa. That kind of history really excited me, but I wasn't getting it at school.

This poem just came to me as a letter from the word go. I definitely didn't want to rhyme with this one – partly because it's a letter and also I didn't want to be restricted by a rhyme. And I didn't want to play any tricks with words and I also wanted the freedom you get with free verse. This is the first draft. It's never changed – not one single word! I didn't start this one off in my head, because as soon as I got the idea, I wrote it down. I just said to myself, let me imagine that I'm going to write a letter to my teacher. I wrote it really quickly and honestly and because it's free verse I wasn't struggling to find any rhymes. Most of all, I wanted to make sure that every line counted. That's what I started from. And as I set out I knew that I wanted to begin the poem in ancient Ethiopia and to end in the present.

As I said, what I wanted to do with this poem was to think, what would I say if I was being really honest with my teacher?

> Dear Teacher,
> When I was born in Ethiopia
> Life began,

As far as we know, Ethiopia is where the oldest human beings lived.

> As I sailed down the Nile civilization began,

So, as I started to move out of Ethiopia, humans started to organise themselves and to create order.

> When I stopped to think universities were built,

And we started to create places for learning. It's interesting that in ancient Egypt there were universities where people came from all over the world to study. And it was like the Oxford or Cambridge of its time. Some cults believe that Jesus went to one of these places and studied there.

> When I set sail
> Asians and true Americans sailed with me.

And when I say 'Americans', I mean the original Americans. Personally, I've always believed America to be like an occupied territory. Sometimes when I refer to white Americans I call them 'European Americans'. We say 'African American', 'Chinese American' – so why not 'European American'?

> When we traded nations were built,

There was a lot of trade between nations before capitalism and slavery came about. Because of my interest in martial arts I know that in China they've taken a lot of movements from animals that never lived in China. When tradespeople travelled from China to Africa, they saw various animals fighting and they'd come back and adopt the various styles. There are frescoes in the ancient temples in China showing black people, Chinese people, Asian people and European people all trading together.

> We did not have animals,
> Animals lived with us,

That was the point I was making earlier – that we don't own animals, they live alongside us.

> We had so much time
> Thirteen months made our year,

This line really threw my publisher! They asked me, 'What do you mean – *thirteen* months made our year?' You see, there are thirteen months in the Ethiopian calendar. Lots of civilisations had this system. It was the Westerners that enforced the twelve-month calendar upon them. Ethiopia is one of the only African countries that was not colonised. Mussolini went in there for a short time, but he got kicked out quite quickly. Now, the country uses two calendars – Western and Ethiopian.

> We created social services
> And cities that still stand.

Before I wrote the poem I'd been reading that in early times, countries like Egypt and Zimbabwe had social security systems, systems to help the disabled. These systems may not have been run by computers, but they did have back-up services to help the poor and to get doctors to the sick. And there were even sewage systems in ancient Egypt. So we originated many things in Africa long before the Europeans supposedly 'invented' them.

> So teacher do not say
> Colombus discovered me
> Check the great things I was doing
> Before I suffered slavery.

We always say that slavery was one of the biggest blows to us. If you ask Chinese people what God looks like, they'll describe a Chinese-looking God. If you ask a European person what God looks like, they'll describe a European-looking God. If you ask a black person what God looks like, the majority of black people – especially those from the Caribbean – will say a European-looking God. If you ask me what my language is, or my real culture, I'd say I don't know – it's been completely beaten out of me. That's why Afro-Caribbeans have names like 'John' or 'Frank' – not African names – because we've had our culture completely taken from us.

Those of us who are descendants of slaves – we've been the most economically disavantaged, and have become the under-achievers in school. Africans are now doing better than Caribbean kids at school. Asians are doing better than Caribbean kids at school. Slavery really devastated us. We can't use it as an excuse for everything, but it's taken us a long time to recover. So that's what that line is about – 'Check the great things I was doing / Before I suffered slavery'.

> Yours truly,
> Mr Africa

The only thing I do remember struggling with was how to finish it. When I wrote 'Mr Africa', I thought that I might change it later, but I left it. And the title – the wordplay of 'civil lies' – came to me at the very end, once I'd finished writing the poem.

I've never performed this. It's very much a page poem. I've had kids stop me in the street and ask me to read it to them! A lot of black kids take pride in it – and they feel the same way that I felt at school about getting only white, European history. They tell me that they want to take this poem and show it to their racist teachers.

'Civil Lies' comes from *Talking Turkeys*. Some of the poems for this collection I already had and I was performing them before I'd even started to work on the book for Puffin. These poems included 'Body Talk', 'Poems from the Last Person on Earth', and 'Talking Turkeys' itself. In fact, 'Poems from the Last Person on Earth' comes from a television programme I used to do called 'A Beetle Called Derek', which is yet another poem in this collection! Of all the short and slightly surreal poems I wrote for the book, I really like this one:

'Part Wan'

I wonder how babies are made
All babies
Homosapien babies,
Donkey babies,
Bird babies.
Animals kiss
An den what
Babies.
Dere mus be more to it.

It took about six months to write all the new poems for the book. The graphics were done by a design team known as The Point. They do all the artwork and then they come back to me and ask for my responses, as I have overall say with the design. I really like what they did with both *Talking Turkeys* and *Funky Chickens*.

4 VISITS TO SCHOOLS

When I visit schools I do performances, but never workshops. People ask me to do workshops all the time, but I don't do them. The last thing I want to seem like is a teacher. I love teachers, I think they do one of the greatest jobs in the country, but when I come into a school I want the kids to see that it's a poet, not another teacher coming in. I talk about my work and I invite questions – and that's as much of a workshop as I'll do. I won't say, 'Right then boys and girls, get out your pens and paper.' Because I can't sit down and go, 'Right, now I'm going to be inspired' – I can't expect children to do the same thing for me.

What I try and do – and teachers tell me that this works – is that I get the kids to enjoy the performance, so that they hopefully go away having been inspired. Then the teacher can say, 'What did you learn from that?' and can develop some work after I've gone. And usually I get a bunch of poems by the kids sent on to me after a visit. In fact, I get quite a few letters from kids. I've had many letters about Danny, my cat that died. They tell me about their pets that have also died too. I try to respond to everybody.

If I'm in school for a day, I'll take my track suit with me so that I can go and play football or basketball with the kids in the dinner hour. I rope in with them, as I really don't want to be seen as another teacher – I want them to relate to me. And I visit both primary and secondary schools – all ages. Obviously, performing to infants is very different to performing to teenagers, but I'll perform to any age.

I had one teenager – a 15-year-old – with me for work experience recently. He's a good musician, and he wants to work in the music business. He'd been excluded from school, he had no interest in education, and he struggled with his reading and writing. One day, I'd been telling him about people in the music industry that had got ripped off because they couldn't read their contracts. This just struck a chord with him and he completely turned around – he wanted to go back to school and to learn to read and write because he could see that there was a purpose in it. He's now got a year left in school, and he's talking of going on to sixth form college.

I've done an anthology called *Is Different Wrong? – Poems about Racism by Young People of Newham*. It's published by Newham Council and it's a collection of poems by local London kids. 1997 was the European Year Against Racism and the local borough had some money for poets to go into schools in Newham. So we visited various schools and got kids thinking about the issue of race – all the positive and negative things about it. Then we asked the kids to write and submit their own poems on this issue. I edited all the poems. When the anthology was published we made sure that it was getting into shops and that everyone featured got their royalties, so that they felt that they were being properly published. Once we'd done the anthology, we had this big poetry party at a school. We got all the kids together and we all performed, and we had a great time! Here's the title poem from the collection:

'Is different wrong?'

They stare at me
They glare at me
They sneer at me

They swear at me
Because I am different
Is different wrong?

They say I have a different colour
They say I have a different religion

They say I'm different
They say I'm not one of them
But is different wrong?

(Bina Sudra, Sarah Bonnell School)

When kids read my poems I'll tell them not to read them in a Jamaican accent, and to do them in their own voice. A lot of teachers have said to me that when they've been reading my work in class they've been struggling with how to pronounce it, and one of their kids will get up and say 'I can do that!' and they will! You see, if kids are listening to rap and dub, they are going to be able to do it better than their teachers. I've heard scouse and cockney kids do it in their own accents, and it works really well.

I find that in the schools I visit out in the sticks there'll often be about thirty copies of my books – one for every kid. But I'll go to a school in Newham, and there'll just be one book in the library. The kids will know me in Newham – they'll have seen me on television or have heard my records, but they're not reading that much.

What's the greatest compliment I've ever had? It was something that happened to me just lately. I was doing a performance – it was a gig for adults. There was this little kid at the front of the stage, and he was saying my poems along with me, word for word. Afterwards, he came up to me and said, 'I'm your best fan in the world.' He told me that he'd entered a poetry reading competition at school. He'd read my poem 'Talking Turkeys' and he'd won First prize. His mother came up to me later, she touched my hand and said, 'You saved his life.' Sadly, I didn't get to talk to her any more, but I could see that she meant what she said.

5 PERFORMING POETRY

I'm very much at home when I'm performing. People who know me tell me that I just go on stage and open up! I'm never nervous performing – except when I have to introduce someone or when I'm playing with a band. I take each poem as it comes and I try and capture the emotion of what I was thinking when I started writing it. If it's a funny poem, I'll try and capture that playfulness. And if it's a serious poem, I'll try and capture that particular emotion.

I have a different set list for each performance. But you can be guaranteed that when I perform, I'll do them in a different order. I get vibes from the audience, and do poems accordingly. Sometimes I'll do ones that are not even on the list, they just come to mind. I do most of the set from memory. 'Danny the Cat' from *Talking Turkeys* is one poem that I've never learnt, it's never stuck in my head. I won't have the book on stage with me, but if someone in the audience has a copy, I'll borrow it! A favourite poem to perform is 'Like Michael Jackson' from *School's Out*. I love doing all the actions with it – all the stuff which is not on the page. And kids just love it!

There are some poems which have two versions – one for the page and one to be performed. 'Going Lotto' from *Funky Chickens* is one of them. I'll use the last verse as an example:

> I think I've won the lottery
> My goodness greatness me
> I must get some security
> And protect my prize money,

> But don't go telling everybody
> Think before you speak
> I get this feeling regularly
> I thought the same last week.

When I perform this one, I change the line before last to 'I get this feeling all the time' as 'I get this feeling regularly' doesn't roll off the tongue enough. It's too clumsy. With other poems, I might have a chorus that keeps coming back when I do it in performance, but it will only be written once on the page. And live, it gives the kids something to chant along to.

I've probably got something like thirty or so unpublished poems in my head – poems that I perform but haven't written down. I can think of about five that my publisher has been trying to get me to write down for ages. But I haven't done it, because I don't think they'd work on the page very well – they're meant to be performed.

The other day I was watching my mother preaching in church, and I realised that subconsciously I took a lot from her, in that she's been a big inspiration in the way I perform. She's fond of using repetition in her performances. I've always thought that it's good to have a hook that the audience can latch on to. And it's something they do in church a lot. They'll take a phrase or a line and repeat it and improvise around it. And my mother will look at the audience. She really goes for eye contact. And as she's talking, she'll play with the dynamics of her voice – by making her voice ever so soft, and then she'll bring it up loud. There's no doubt that she has influenced me a great deal.

I never work out any movements or choreography to my poems, because I know that when I do go out and do a poem it would be different from my rehearsal. Sometimes I know in my head what movements I'm going to do, but I don't know how much space I'm going to take up until I go out and do it. I adapt my movements according to the area I've got to perform in. Sometimes I'll walk through the audience, but I never plan it as I never know if there's going to be enough room to do it. But with my Michael Jackson poem I now have more of a set routine, the moments where I point to my nose or do certain movements.

For three years, I stopped performing in Britain, and so many black people said, 'We need your voice. All we've got is comedians and musicians.' That was one of the reasons that made me come back. I don't profess to be a spokesperson for the black community, but it does need as many voices it can, to get heard. And I'm just one of them.

My audiences are now very wide. I love my mix of audience. At times I think I know my audience well, but then I'm surprised by the people that write to me or turn up at my gigs. My audiences will include women in their sixties and seventies – as a result of the work I do on Radio 4 – but I get younger people as well, and people from all different walks of life. I've got some vicars' wives and rectors' wives that write to me, and anarchists too, all kinds of people. I do a lot of work for the British Council when I go abroad – and I'll go to somewhere like Zimbabwe and the Middle East and I'll meet people who know my work inside out. I'm always being surprised.

I see poetry as this big tree that has many branches. You can get introduced to the tree by climbing up one of the branches, but it doesn't mean to say that you can't explore other parts of the tree. I got onto the tree via oral poetry, but I've gone on to love all kinds – from nonsense verse to classical poetry like Shelley– and I love them all equally.

There are now lots of performance poets playing live all over the country – in West Indian centres in Cardiff, in Glasgow, in Birmingham and in London. But oral poetry, performance poetry, doesn't have the same status as written poetry and people forget that the oral actually came first. Publishers are missing out on it. I think it's their loss. A lot of people say we should get it recorded, and have it in print – but at least it's happening, at least it's being performed. And I'm really proud to be part of the oral tradition.

SELECTED CURRENT TITLES

Benjamin Zephaniah writes poetry for children and for adults. Below are listed his children's titles:

Talking Turkeys (Puffin)
Funky Chickens (Puffin)
Poems in the anthology – *The Utterly Brilliant Book of Poetry* (Puffin)
School's Out (AK Press)
Face – novel – (Bloomsbury – August 1999)

Cassettes

Funky Turkeys (Audio Book and Music Company)
adult fun for Kids (Benjamin Zephaniah Associates)

An introduction to . . . Ian Beck

WHAT TYPE OF BOOKS DO YOU WRITE? Picture books.

WHAT ARE YOUR BOOKS ABOUT? Many of them are little adventure stories involving safe scares and risks for either children or teddy bears. If it's a story involving children, the adventure will happen without grown-ups. These books include *Emily and the Golden Acorn* and *Tom and the Island of Dinosaurs*. The teddy bear stories include *Home Before Dark* and *Lost in the Snow*. I also do retellings and collections of nursery stories and rhymes, fairy tales and classic texts.

BORN: 17 August 1947 in Hove, Sussex.

EDUCATION: I went to Portland Road Infants and Junior School in Hove. I failed 11+ and went to the local Secondary Modern school – The Knoll School for Boys. From there I went to Brighton College of Art.

LIVES: Twickenham.

PREVIOUS OCCUPATIONS: When I first moved to London in the late 1960s I worked part-time for Harrods in their toy department. I was doing freelance illustrating at the same time, and eventually that took over.

FAMILY/PETS: I am married to Emma and we have three children – Edmund, Laurence and Lily. No pets at present.

HOBBIES: I don't have hobbies! I'm passionately devoted to certain composers and music and architecture. I'm also Honorary Secretary of the Artworkers' Guild.

MOST TREASURED POSSESSION: I put people before possessions.

AWARDS: *Parents* magazine Gold Picture Book of the Year Award for *Home Before Dark* (1998).

LANGUAGES TRANSLATED INTO: Most European languages – including a Gaelic edition of *The Ugly Duckling* – and Japanese.

FAVOURITE PLACE: Home.

FAVOURITE BOOKS: Adults: *Le Grande Meaulnes* by Alain Fournier – it's my desert island book and was a formative influence on me; *Pale Fire* by Vladimir Nabokov; other writers I like are Elizabeth Taylor and Anne Tyler.

FAVOURITE LINES OF POETRY: John Keats – 'On First Looking into Chapman's *Homer*':

Much have I travelled in realms of gold,
  And many goodly states and kingdoms seen;
  Round many western islands have I been
Which Bard in fealty to Apollo hold.
Oft of wide expanse had I been told
  That deep-browed Homer ruled as his demesne;
  Yet did I never breathe its pure serene
Till I heard Chapman speak out loud and bold:
Then felt I like some watcher of the skies
  When a new planet swims into his ken;
Or like stout Cortez when with eagle eyes
  He stared at the Pacific – and all his men
Looked at each other with a wild surmise –
  Silent, upon a peak in Darien.

FAVOURITE MUSIC: Almost exclusively I like twentieth-century music – Ravel, Poulenc, Stravinsky, Les Six, Prokofiev, Walton, Malcolm Arnold. I play music all the time when I'm working.

FAVOURITE FILMS: Truffaut's *Jules et Jim*; French cinema generally; Disney's *Pinocchio* – it's an Expressionist masterpiece; cartoons of the 'golden age' 1930–1960.

FAVOURITE ARTISTS/ART: I'm influenced and inspired by so many styles and painters: Japanese prints; chapbook illustrations – hand-coloured books of the early nineteenth century; the English illustrator Harold Jones; the English painters Eric Ravilious, Paul Nash and Edward Bawden; the Tiepolos – father and sons – they inform my colour palette a great deal; and as an art student I was into American illustrators of the 1960s – James Spanfeller, Barry Zaid and Edward Gorey.

WHAT WERE YOU LIKE AT THE AGE OF 11? I drew a lot. I'd just discovered Classical music. I used to come back from the cinema and re-enact films for my parents.

ENJOYS VISITING SCHOOLS BECAUSE: I find it very revealing to keep in mind the audience that I'm working for.

IF YOU WEREN'T A WRITER: I'm very passionate about films and cinema and telling stories in films – and I'd be interested in writing screenplays.

WHICH FOUR WORDS DESCRIBE YOU BEST? According to Emma, my wife, 'Humorous, hard working, enthusiastic and untemperamental.'

WHAT WOULD YOU LIKE TO HAPPEN IN THE TWENTY-FIRST CENTURY? A craft revival.

WHAT, FOR YOU, ARE SEMINAL CHILDREN'S PICTURE BOOKS? *This Year,*

Next Year by Harold Jones; Edward Ardizzone's *Tim* stories; the *Babar* books by Jean de Brunhoff and Maurice Sendak's *Where the Wild Things Are.* When I first looked at *Where the Wild Things Are,* before I had children, I didn't understand the way the text worked. When I read it to my first son when he was little, the book yielded its magic. It really is a seminal text, and the beginning of the modern age of picture books.

WHICH OF YOUR BOOKS WOULD YOU LIKE TO BE REMEMBERED FOR? *Ian Beck's Picture Book.*

IF YOU COULD ILLUSTRATE ANY CHILDREN'S TEXT FROM ANY PERIOD WHICH WOULD IT BE? A nursery version of Lewis Carroll's *Alice in Wonderland.*

I HOW THE READER BECAME AN ILLUSTRATOR/WRITER

We had very few books in our house, and we weren't a literate household at all. My elder sister had a few books, amongst which was Hans Andersen's *Fairy Tales.* It was a very cheap edition, probably published by Ward Lock. The paper was very light and thick, and it was almost like cardboard. The illustration on the wrapper was of 'The Constant Tin Soldier' on his newspaper boat in a sewer, and there was a rat looking at him. I used to look at that book a lot as a very small child. That haunting image of 'The Constant Tin Soldier' and his little boat – I can still see it in my mind now.

I used to sit on my maternal grandmother's knee at the age of three and four. Even when I could read I would get her to read to me the *Thomas the Tank Engine* books. I loved those bright little pictures – the narrow landscape shapes and the bright sunlit uplands of that little world. And I could read before I went to school. I became a great library user. In sequence, I hired all of Hugh Lofting's *Dr Doolittle* books. Later, I was very keen on *Just William* and the *Molesworth* books.

I grew up in a working-class household. My father was a milkman and my mother was a housewife. My parents, being good, working-class people, would never say to me, 'Darling, that's wonderful', and magnetise my picture to the fridge, as happens today. Art was a mess that was to be cleared away – 'Clear that mess up before your father gets home!' my mother would say. This is not a complaint against my parents, but I was never bought any paper – so I would draw in biro on the backs of wallpaper rolls or in the margins or endpapers of books – anything! I was drawing constantly.

It was when I saw the film of *The Time Machine* in 1960 that I began to get a kick from literature, and to form an understanding of good storytelling. I saved up 5 shillings and bought the Ian Seraillier Windmill Readers hardback edition of the story. It was thrilling to read. From there I read all of H.G. Wells's science fiction stories. At the same time, when I was about thirteen, I discovered the *Molesworth* collection by Geoffrey Williams – with titles such as *Down with Skool* and *Whizz for Atoms.* I found their subversive humour hilariously funny. I loved the drawings by Ronald Searle. I used to copy them in fountain pen.

Ian Beck's childhood drawings in *Things New and Old* (Nelson)

In parallel to this, I would have been noticing the drawings in the *Radio Times* by Anthony Gross, Edward Ardizzone and Eric Frazer. They were all my heroes. And it was at this age that I was taken to an exhibition in the Portsmouth Guild Hall of artwork from the *Radio Times*. It must have been a touring show. They had all the original illustrations that appeared in the magazine – the black and white pen drawings, the kinds of things I tried to do with my little dip pen at home with Indian ink. I was very excited by the exhibition and I wrote soon after to the magazine. I imagined there was such a thing as a job at the *Radio Times* in an office, drawing all these pictures, and I thought that I could apply for this job! I didn't know there were such things as freelance artists. But they wrote me a polite reply saying, 'If you want to do drawings for the *Radio Times* you must go to art college.'

With encouragement from my headmaster, Mr Turner, I wrote a letter to the local art school, and I went and did Saturday morning painting classes there. That was a revelation for me. From being in a secondary modern school where boys beat you up, here was a place where kindly people were doing etchings and lithographs on a Saturday morning. You'd be painting in a room with real art students – older people who came in and were busy doing their stuff. And what's more, they were doing it all day. It seemed like paradise to me. So I applied to go there full-time. My father sadly died when I was fourteen, and so we were very poor. But my headmaster persuaded my mother that I should be allowed to go on to art school after my GCEs.

I was a natural illustrator in a way, as texts interested me more than objectively drawing a bowl of fruit. I wanted to draw atmosphere and to make things up and I

Ian Beck's childhood drawings in inside back cover of *Things New and Old*

used to get frustrated by having to draw things like flints. At art school we had one tutor named Norman Clark. He said something that was a chance remark, but it gave me a little seed that lodged in my mind. He told us that prior to the then current movement in objective drawing, our subjects would not have been drawing flints but our impressions of coming into college on a rainy day. And I thought, that's what I want to do! For I was more interested in subjectivity and interiors and the imaginative re-creation of experience from the head to the page.

One of the main things I got from the course was the idea that the kind of figure you make up from your head or that you do from memory could carry more conviction and more truth than something drawn from a photograph or direct from life. If you look at an Ardizzone figure, for instance, he's remembered how people stand when they're in a certain state. The drawing comes from studying but also remembering and then re-creating so you get the essence of the figure in the picture. And his characters *act* truthfully – it's the *acting* which is important in his pictures.

The college had very influential tutors, who were all children's book illustrators – Raymond Briggs, John Vernon Lord, Justin Todd and John Lawrence. Raymond Briggs was a great teacher. He was very good at pointing out unregarded things. He'd bring in the *Evening Standard*, point to a cheap comic strip – and say 'Look at that head. It's *really* well drawn.' He was good at that.

When I left college I had no sense of career or direction. I just wanted to get freelance work and earn a living. I moved to London and lived with a girlfriend's parents, who were very kind to me. I worked at Harrods on Monday and Friday, and for the rest of the week I did illustrating work. I spent a lot of time doing work for magazines and advertising.

In the early 70s things started to happen. I had a new agent and I was sharing a studio in Covent Garden with other freelance artists. It was at that time I did the sleeve for Elton John's *Goodbye Yellow Brick Road* and the cook's diary for Habitat. And I was also going to evening classes in writing. I was a frustrated writer. Part of me wasn't fulfilled by doing just drawings.

Down the line a few years, I was still doing commercial work, but by now my teenage ambition had been realised and I was doing illustrations for the *Radio Times*. A designer at Oxford University Press had seen my work in the magazine and asked me to submit a sample. This was a year after the birth of my first child and I'd just started to get into modern children's books. David Fickling, who was then at Oxford, liked my sample and asked me to do the illustrations for a whole book. That was *Round and Round the Garden* – a collection of play rhymes – which came out in 1983. The book was immediately successful, and *Oranges and Lemons* followed soon after.

All the commercial work I'd done previously had given me technical and practical experience in how to make a picture work. All this suddenly came into practice in a new form, in a picture book. In *Round and Round the Garden* my own style began to emerge – that kind of chapbook look, my use of colour – all that – and I've been refining it ever since. My first solo effort, doing both text and pictures, was *Little Miss Muffet*. It was with that book that I learnt all about the structure and rhythms of a picture book, which you can only learn by doing it.

I had previously given very little thought to doing books – let alone children's books – although a lot of the commercial work I'd been doing was influenced by nursery styles, and had a nostalgic, childhood feel about it. Having done my first children's book, it was so pleasurable that I want to do more. Apart from occasional commercial work, I wouldn't do anything else now. Picture books are so satisfying, they fill every need I have to express myself. Telling the story and drawing the picture together is the best of all. But to go from being an artist to being an author of one's own books was quite a leap. I never thought I could write a story, and that people like me did books.

2 ILLUSTRATING: ROUTINES AND REFLECTIONS

I work in the front room of my very ordinary suburban, three-bedroom house. I sit in the back part of the room – much as my late father-in-law, Reynold Stone, did. I'm often invaded by my children and the television is frequently on, but I don't mind. I listen to music all the time when I'm working – either writing prose or illustrating. To me, distraction and racket and confusion are the grit that makes the pearl, as it were. My daughter, Lily, will often be watching cartoons while I'm in here working. It doesn't worry me at all.

I've developed a strict daily routine. I get up at 6.30 and I'll read the paper and the post. I often work through from 9.00 till 11.00 in the evening. And I get a lot done from 8.00 till 11.00 in the evenings. But the day will be punctuated with lunch, time with the children, meetings with publishers and many telephone calls. And once a week I do a drawing for the *Daily Express* magazine. Routine is good for getting work done in time, but I'm usually late with deadlines!

I write with a good fine ball-point on a fine-line pad. I'm not fetishistic about writing materials but I am with art materials. I always use the same equipment. This includes Saunders Water Colour Not Paper 140 lb or 90 lb – even though it's not a brilliant white, it has the right surface, as it takes the pen and paint in equal measure. I use Winsor and Newton water-colour paints, and sometimes Schminker. I always use traditional water-colour paints, never inks.

I have a Rotring pen – and I use either a .4 or a .3 nib. I wobble the nib about to get the kind of line I like. I use Rotring as I can't bear the inconsistency of a dip pen. I don't like the quality of the Rotring line so I force the line to do what I want it to do, though it's rather laborious. I also draw in a curious method where I put the colour on first and then draw the line last because I want the strength of colour to be there before I start putting the line on. If you put a lot of strong colour over a line drawing, the line drawing disappears.

For me, a picture book is like a mini-drama. You're dramatising your story, or your idea behind the story, and everything must conspire to that end. For example, at one point in *Lost in the Snow*, over a sequence of pictures, the pictures gradually get greyer and colder over a double page until the bear is rescued. And then suddenly the next page is red. It's an emotional burst. You're manipulating the reader, the audience – however subliminally or blatantly – with your choice of colour, positioning and scale of figures. I incorporate all these techniques, all the tricks of book design to help dramatise the story. And the audience features highly in my work – as I plan a picture I think, how is this communicating to them? How do I tell them about this? How do I draw their attention to that part of the narrative?

Working out a picture book is almost like planning out a little film. My editor, David Fickling, and I often talk about my work in filmic terms. When we were doing *The Teddy Robber*, for instance, there was an image of the boy climbing up some steps. David said he wanted to see a high angle shot like in a Hitchcock film for this image – he wanted it to be from above looking down. And in some respects, a picture book is very close to a film storyboard.

With my picture books, there are 32 pages on average – 32 pages to tell the narrative. And there'll be a combination of single pages, double spreads, pictures that bleed off the page and pictures that are contained on the page. I use the bleed-off page as a dramatic climax. And I like breaking the borders of pictures to show the artificiality, to say 'This is a drawing, don't forget' – and it makes the subject more three-dimensional as well. Some artists bleed all their pictures, but I like the dynamics of using borders and having little pictures as well as big pictures, and also different angles of perspective, all kinds of things to dramatise the story. I don't think there are set rules for using these techniques. It's instinctive.

The composition and design of each picture is paramount because you have to lead the eye through to the most important part of the picture. I always work all my drawings out on detail or tracing paper first. I experiment with them for a long time and each drawing will go through hundreds of stages. I never draw directly onto paper, and I never draw in a quick, gestural kind of way – I draw in an elaborate, laboured fashion. That's the only way I can do it. I work a bit like a printing machine in that I do all the blues at once. I might work it up like when you print layers of colour, one on top of the other, and the line goes on last like the black plate.

I like to think that when people look at my drawings they can see how they were done, and that there's no airbrushing obscurities – it's all just colour and line. I'm not hiding behind a lot of craft, but I take a craftsman-like attitude doing them. I'm not trying to say, 'Aren't I clever? These are very difficult to do.' Some artists do that, they expose their virtuosities.

When I'm writing a text I'll write it in longhand first and then put it on the word processor and then develop it more. I always start in an exercise book with a pen if I'm writing down text ideas. The text and pictures are so interwoven in my picture books that I'll draw scribbly rough drawings alongside the text. I might start with a central image of an idea for a story and then backtrack from that.

There's no set system for deciding what information or details should be represented in either text or picture. It's instinctive. If you're drawing a picture of a straightforward, quotidian scene – such as an old man reading a note – then you might want to layer some other details in so that when you go back to the picture you can see things that you didn't notice before. But you wouldn't do this with a picture of an exploding volcano, for instance. I don't have set theories or hard and fast rules about the roles of text and picture – but clearly, pictures can do things that text can't and vice versa. And somehow, the gaps between the two can be filled by either.

I try not to do research. I like to rely on memory. Some illustrators work from photographs, whereas I prefer to work things out in my head and on paper. But, say I'm doing a specific period, as I am with *Cinderella* at the moment, and which requires the clothing to be right, then I'll look at fashion pictures of the period.

With some books, a little light bulb goes on in my head and an idea starts ticking over in my mind, whereas other books are suggested by an editor. An example of the latter was when Jill Slotover – who was then my editor at Transworld – said she thought I ought to do my own picture book of *Peter and the Wolf*. Other ideas for books can come from spending time with my children. The idea for *Home Before Dark* came from when my daughter Lily and I were returning from a walk and we found an abandoned toy – a woollen tortoise – on a gate post. It was a wet autumn afternoon, rather grey, leaves underfoot. Lily was very upset at the sight of this toy and I told her that the tortoise could probably get back home on its own. Then the little light bulb came on and I thought – here's a story about a dropped toy that makes its own way home but no one knows he's gone. So I went home and made a note of the idea. I do make notes of ideas as a rule, but a good idea will stay anyway.

An idea never arrives perfectly formed. It has to be built upon. It will arrive as a nudge saying, 'You think about that.' And your instinct just tells you that this idea is worth thinking about. Sometimes, two things join together to make an idea – as with *Emily and the Golden Acorn*. I had one idea, which was of a tree falling in a storm. The other idea came when I was washing up in the kitchen and my two boys and their friends were up the tree in the garden. My youngest, Laurence, had a plastic cutlass, and little wellington boots tucked into his trousers. There were ropes up in the tree and it looked like they were in a pirate ship. Then I thought, supposing the tree sailed away? And that was the light bulb moment. So, the two ideas – the tree in the storm and the tree as a pirate ship sailing away – just locked together.

Lily, my daughter, has been a great inspiration – particularly when she was pre-literate, at about 18 months. I would watch her beadily, seeing what she was interested in when she was reading a picture book, and what she noticed, and what excited her. The whole of *Picture Book* came out of me watching Lily looking at books and her noticing the backgrounds in pictures. I wanted to do a book that featured all the things she'd observed in books that had been secondary to the story – such as shadows and clouds. For me, doing picture books is all about getting back to that child-like sense of wonder, and Lily gives me that child's-eye view.

Some books I'll begin but never finish. This happens all the time. It happened with the sequel to *The Teddy Robber*. It can be frustrating. I'll start doing the rough illustrations but won't be able to take it any further as the core idea is not strong enough.

For every picture book I do, I'll make at least one dummy book version. My methodology is such that I'll produce small, half-size drawings – very quickly in pencil – and then have them enlarged on a photocopier and then I'll colour them in. I then assemble each page into a dummy book which I take along to the editors to give them an idea of the look, the feel and the layout of the whole thing. The editors' input is absolutely vital at that stage.

As regards editors, I do enjoy working with David Fickling. David has been instrumental in my career as an illustrator. He actively encouraged me to come up with my own story ideas for picture books. David has a keen visual eye, and he knows what he doesn't want. He's an 'encourager', and, being a good editor, he brings out the best in you rather than imposing himself on the material. He's not afraid to say when things aren't working. For a young person, he's had a tremendous influence on children's publishing. To be taken up by him was the best bit of luck I've had in my whole career. Jill Slotover at Transworld was very good too, and an excellent encourager of artists. My two main editors now are David Fickling at Scholastic and Penny Walker at Transworld. But I must mention Annie Eaton at Transworld who has also been very influential.

There's a quote from the illustrator Edward Ardizzone that has stayed with me throughout my career and it's 'the rightness of the pose'. Say that the text goes, 'He cowered in the corner with fear.' Then immediately you're looking for a mental picture of how that person cowers in a corner in this way, the pose that he adopts. And you try and put that down on the page. Another illustrator might get a friend to pose and then take a photograph and work from that. Ardizzone's idea was that you synthesise the image in your mind – you create a little theatre in your mind of the action. You experiment like this and take the best pose. It's a kind of synthesising the essence of cowering with fear. As an illustrator, you're like a theatre director, and you put your characters through their paces, saying 'Look frightened' or 'Look happy', or 'Do you jump with your arms in the air when you're happy?' You try your best to take these images from your mind's eye and to scribble them down and then develop the image until it's right, and solid on the page. You have more freedom this way, but it takes more work, more lines to get it right. This way it's as if your hand and your mind take over, and when you've got it, the emotion just comes off the page.

book

From *Ian Beck's Picture Book*

Illustration by Edward Ardizzone from *Tim and Charlotte*

How would I describe my illustration style? I aim for something that is strong yet wistful. Strong – in that I like architecturally designed pictures and things that are quite solid within the picture. And wistfulness – in the evocation of childhood itself, or the time of day in a picture, making the reader wish that they were in that place at that time. My style seems such an amalgam of all the things that have influenced me.

I find it very revealing to keep in mind the audience that I'm working for. One's own children will naturally be prejudiced towards your work – their responses can only be subjective. When you're reading aloud to a group of children who don't know you it can be very telling – a false note or an awkward piece of phrasing in the story will leap out at you. And it's pleasurable for me to get good feedback to my work – to the stories and the illustrations. I sometimes take along work in progress to schools, and the children's responses will be most informative and revealing, as was the case with *Tom and the Island of Dinosaurs*. With that book, the children's feedback had a significant effect on how I developed the book.

The most touching compliment I've ever been paid was in a letter from some parents telling me that their daughter had died, and that their youngest child had had great difficulty coming to terms with it. The parents had used *Emily and the Golden Acorn* as a bridge to help that child overcome bereavement – because of its

From Ian Beck's *Emily and the Golden Acorn*

theme of rebirth and renewal. And they had planted an oak tree in memory of their daughter. Obviously, I didn't intend that book to have any such effect, but you can't tell what uses your narratives will be put to out in the world. Things can have resonances you can never imagine.

3 GROWING A BOOK

Peter and the Wolf

As I explained earlier, it was Jill Slotover that suggested I do this book. Jill knew right from the start that she wanted a cassette version of the story as well, with narration and the original music. The cassette, she felt, would enable a child to follow the musical elements too. But Jill wanted the musical instruments – violins, flutes, french horns, etc. – that are featured in the narration to be represented subtly in the borders surrounding the text.

I didn't have quite the finished book in my head immediately, but I knew from the outset how *Peter* might be tackled – that is, in a Russian, folksy way. I thought of the Russian painter Bilibin, and his use of colour and folk-pattern borders and period costumes and settings.

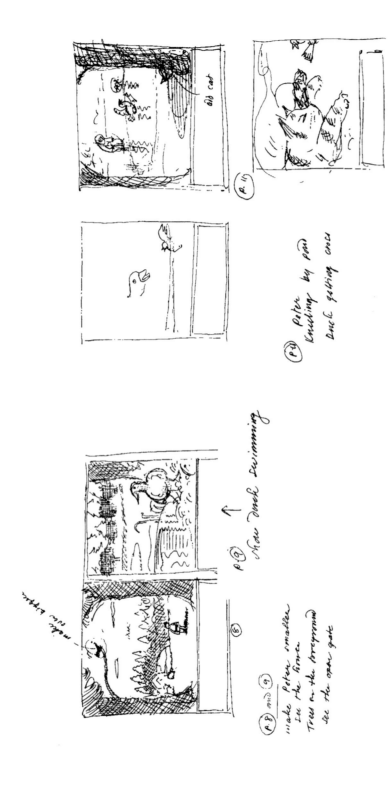

Storyboard artwork for *Peter and the Wolf*

Rough artwork for the procession in *Peter and the Wolf*

The story, however, took a lot of working out. The narrative is not designed for a 32-page picture book. There are many incidents in the full narrative, and I had to select the main events. And it was quite a job shoehorning the story into the shape and length of a picture book. I found that it was important from a practical point of view to use a lot of single pages rather than double spreads. Again, I used the bled double spread for the big dramatic impact – for when the wolf first comes out of the wood.

The text went through two or so drafts. I used different versions for reference – a book that Johnny Morris had done as well as various recorded versions that I have. From these I got the gist of the narrative, and retold it in my own words. I had to get the logistics of the text just right, so that the text and the pictures and the music work together in sync at all times.

The colour scheme was suggested by the setting, Russia, so there was a lot of dark green fir forests, silver birch branches and snow. I put Peter in a red tunic so that he would stand out from all these other colours. There's a lot of red and green and

yellow ochre in the book. And with the double spread of the wolf I made his tongue red – the only bright colour in the whole picture – while the rest of it is light-blue shadows and green and grey and white.

I wanted the first single page to portray the setting of the little house by the forest, so I had to write some text that would work before the music started and the narrative begins. And I used a high point perspective in a few of the pictures for logistical reasons. With the picture of the bird flying up into the tree it's so that we can see all of the characters at once. Another high point perspective comes later when the wolf is chasing the duck. If this picture was at ground level, you'd have the duck maybe in the foreground and the wolf would be obscured behind the duck – and you need to see the clarity of one chasing the other. Later, the wolf is prowling around the tree and you need to see this scene from the vulnerable bird's point of view, from up above. And also in this picture there's Peter climbing over the wall – so there's a lot of information you've got to get across in one spread. The high point perspective will allow you to do this. But

Imagine the triumphant procession ... Peter at the front,
then the hunters leading the wolf, then Grandfather.
And, right at the end, the cat. Grandfather shook his
head. 'Ah it's all very well ... but what if Peter *hadn't*
caught the wolf? What then, eh?'

Final artwork for the procession in *Peter and the Wolf*

Above them flew the little bird, singing happily, 'My, what brave fellows we are, Peter and I. Look what we've caught!'

ultimately, your choice of perspective is governed by what is happening in the text, the narrative.

There has to be 'dead space' in a picture such as the one of Peter climbing the wall so that there's room for the text itself. You have to organise the spread in advance so that you don't cover up anything important with text.

At the very end of the story, the duck is inside the wolf's belly. So I thought, why not include a drawing of this? And I think children are actually rather fascinated by the fact that the duck is *inside* the wolf! On the very last page I've done pictures of the instruments featured in the music. However, throughout the book the musical element is quite unobtrusive, and in this way, it can be read as an independent picture book or as a visual accompaniment to the cassette.

The whole project took the best part of a year. I did many, many rough drawings at the beginning on detail paper in scribbly pencil, which often looked nothing like the final drawings. I might do a single pose ten or so times to get it right. The procession at the end of the book was very complicated to work out – I had to figure out how a man pulls a wolf, and invent how it's done. It's a *very* difficult thing. It comes from practice. It's the sort of advice that I give to art students – that they should try and tackle knotty illustrative problems, such as how does a man pull a wolf along or how does an angel tickle a wolf? I'll suggest they do this without reference to anything, and to work it through in their head first before they commit it to paper.

It was suggested that I myself do the recording of the narration as I have some experience of singing and performing. The version of the music we used was a Naxos recording done by a Czech orchestra, which was recorded with just the music and without the narration. I recorded my own narration in a recording studio where, using modern technology, they juxtaposed my voice with the music.

Tom and the Island of Dinosaurs

This book began with my two boys – then aged nine and seven – both having mountain bikes for Christmas. They were practising cycling up and down the tow path by the Thames, near here. I was watching them and thinking how important bikes are to children at that age, and that it would be good if I could incorporate a bike into a story somehow. Developing this, I thought I could write an adventure story with a bike as a prop to make the adventure happen – and that the boy in this story would adapt his bike so that it could fly.

The flying bike became central to my initial vision of *Tom and the Island of Dinosaurs* – but at that point it was called 'Jack and the Island of Monsters'. And I thought if Jack's flying off somewhere he needs to rescue someone. I then thought that I could start the story with a message in a bottle coming through the sea, and that Jack would eventually find it on the beach. And in order that Jack could carry out this rescue he would adapt his bike. With this book I was certainly influenced by Ardizzone's *Tim* stories – in which Tim goes off and has an adventure untrammelled by parental concern.

These are some of the notes I made to myself at this early stage:

Rescues dinosaur and brings him home.
Dinosaur is mentioned in the note and has found a new home.
Jack helps his father, the lighthouse keeper.
He's a real boy.
He falls asleep thinking of rescuing dinosaurs.
He thinks about Katie and the dinosaur a lot.
He falls asleep worrying about rescue.

– but much of this I didn't use for the final book.

I started doing a version of the story and got it up to dummy book stage. This took about two to three months. Then I took the book to a meeting with some children. The children were slightly older than the age range the book was aimed at and they were very intelligent. I showed them the dummy book and they enjoyed it up to a certain point, but they were unhappy about the idea of the flying bicycle. They felt it lacked logic and they said that you couldn't get a bicycle to fly. They wouldn't accept that particular fantasy element. The monsters living on the island were fine, but not a flying bicycle – that was going too far. It was like when Tenniel said to Lewis Carroll that he was prepared to draw many things that Carroll suggested, but doing a wasp in a wig was going too far.

So I realised there was a flaw in the narrative. My publisher, Philippa Dickinson, helped me to shape and re-work the story because I was now getting quite stuck. I'd put a lot of energy into the first idea and had a half-formed second idea, but it was getting muddled. It needed shortening and tightening and to be much more coherent – and that's what a good editor can do. So I re-thought, and had the idea that the boy would live by the sea in a lighthouse with his grandfather. Exploring this idea, I thought there would be a rescue balloon, which was used in emergencies in the lighthouse. Then I did a second dummy book – which was called 'Jack and the Island of Dinosaurs' – and which made the monsters more specific.

I called the boy 'Tom' eventually because I discovered there was an existing book about a boy called Jack living in a lighthouse with his grandfather by Michael Foreman. I had to change his name and the book's title right at the last minute.

I'll now go through the finished book of *Tom and the Island of Dinosaurs* and I'll discuss each of the pictures in some detail.

First, in the middle of the title page there is a little oval picture in the style of Bilibin. Bilibin was a Russian illustrator, who, like me, was inspired by Japanese prints. The picture shows a bottle in the sea at night, so really the story begins here, on the title page. The dedication and copyright page shows another picture of the bottle in the sea, but it's now daytime, and now we can see that there's a message inside the bottle. Then the story begins:

There once was a boy called Tom, who lived with his grandfather in an old lighthouse at the edge of the sea.

It's a very simple statement – and much crisper and less wordy than my earlier versions. On this page there's a picture of the lighthouse, the rocks and the sea, and there are little vignettes of Tom and his grandfather at the top – which is a very quick way of getting a lot of information across.

Rough artwork for *Tom and the Island of Dinosaurs*

Rough artwork for *Tom and the Island of Dinosaurs*

On the next page there's the first double spread of the book. Right at the top of the left-hand page is a long, narrow, landscape-shaped picture showing a ship at sea and the lighthouse shining through the dark.

Between them, Tom and his grandfather took care of the lighthouse.

On stormy days and moonless nights, they would light the lamp to show passing ships where the rocks were.

The picture below is the same as the one on the previous page except the first is at night-time and is stormy, and the second is in the daytime and the sea is now calm. Opposite is a single-page picture which shows Tom's grandfather fishing, telling tales to young Tom.

On sunny days, they would go fishing together. Tom's grandfather would tell him wonderful stories of faraway lands and sea monsters.

In the picture the clouds are being blown across the sky and they're roughly making the shape of a brontosaurus. It's a hint of things to come. Turning over, at the top of the page there's a single oval picture of Tom gazing out of the window of the lighthouse, looking a bit wistful. I wanted the frame to be oval as the lighthouse is a tall, vertical structure, and to represent the picture in a square would have looked odd. And by having the edges slightly fading out, it doesn't look too boxed in.

Tom loved his grandfather and the lighthouse very much, but sometimes he longed to sail the wide, grey seas in search of adventure.

Below, there's a vignette of the bottle that we've seen at the beginning of the book. The bottle has finally landed ashore and is now covered in seaweed.

One day, Tom saw something glinting among the wet pebbles on the seashore. It was an old bottle, chipped and covered with seaweed, with a message inside.

On the facing page is the message laid out on the beach. I deliberately created the message in a child-like style:

Help! I'm shipwrecked on a faraway island. There are dinosaurs here and a smoking volcano. Please come before it's too late. Help! Thank You from Katy.

The next page has another illustration in an oval, and has Tom showing the note to his grandfather. In this picture I've included Tom's interest in dinosaurs, but instead of explicitly mentioning this interest in the text, I've subtly alluded to his interest in the picture – by putting some silhouette drawings of dinosaurs on the wall, and by putting a toy wind-up dinosaur on the floor. And on grandfather's chair is a flower pattern, and these flowers are the favourite meal of the dinosaurs that we shall meet later on in the story. All these details are further pre-echoes or hints of what is to come.

Tom rushed home with the message.
'Oh, poor girl!' said his grandfather.
'She's in terrible trouble.' He looked worried.
'But what can we do? We can't leave the lighthouse. If a storm blows up we'll have to light the lamp.'
'Don't worry, Grandfather,' said Tom. 'I'll rescue her.'

And here Tom is actually pointing to himself. That's the acting – the thing I was discussing earlier, with a figure doing the very thing it should be doing. Tom's pointing to himself as he says 'I'll rescue her.' It goes back to Ardizzone's idea of 'the rightness of the pose'.

Then we have a strip section, which gets a lot of information into one page. It's Tom racing downstairs, fetching his 'special emergency box', and then rushing upstairs with it.

Tom raced downstairs to fetch the special emergency box. He pushed and pulled and heaved it up the narrow steps to the balcony. He pulled the ripcord. With a rush of wind, the sides of the box collapsed and an enormous balloon filled with air.

You can see the beginnings of the balloon forming on the last picture. As we turn over, there's the first double spread of the book, which is none the less contained within a frame. Tom is waving goodbye to his grandfather.

> Tom jumped into the basket. His grandfather gave him a snack for the journey and wished him luck.
> 'Be careful,' he said, as he let the tether go.

We can see the tether in Tom's hand – he's just broken free from constraint, as it were, and he's going off on his big adventure. We turn over to the first bled double spread – the colour goes right to the edge of the picture and beyond. Here we see Tom in the balloon, he's crossed the Channel, and flying over what may possibly be a French town at night. There are one or two lights on in the houses. The moon is shining in the sky. It's just a poetic evocation of a night-time balloon ride. I bled this spread because I wanted the reader to drift into the picture, so that the reader is floating with Tom.

Then we turn to a series of strips which progress slowly from cold to warm across the spread – from the blue of the sky over the mountains to the red and yellow of the sky over the sea:

> He flew past snow-covered mountains, across wild, dark green forests, through rainstorms and over waterfalls. At times, the balloon dipped down to touch the waves. Later, it drifted across a great city at dawn, and then, as the sun rose, flew on far, far away.

I use these strips as a way of getting a lot of information across in two pages. It's a comic strip technique of covering a long period of time in a short space. It's also a way of using space economically. Next, there's another bled spread – Tom in his balloon basket looking down.

> At last Tom could see the island below him. A ship lay wrecked on the rocks, but there was no sign of Katy or the dinosaurs. Great belches of smoke and fire rose from the volcano.

> He let the balloon drift down through the swirling smoke and fixed the anchor to a tree. He climbed down and began to look for Katy.

Now we turn over to yet another bled spread, with a strange perspective from up above. Katy is in a palm tree and Tom is looking up at her. The whole business of landing the balloon is not shown, only described in the text on the previous page.

> Just then, he heard someone calling him. It was Katy! She was perched high up in a tree. 'Quick!' Tom shouted. 'We've got to get out of here. The volcano is about to erupt!'
> 'We can't go yet,' said Katy. 'Come and look at this . . .'

The next page is also a bled spread – of Tom and Katy in the tree and the dinosaurs eating their favourite flowers.

> 'Those are the last dinosaurs in the whole world,' said Katy. 'If we leave them here, they will be killed when the volcano erupts. We've got to save them.'
> 'But how?' asked Tom.
> 'Those dinosaurs are too big for my balloon!'
> Luckily, Katy had a plan.

During one draft of the story, I had just one dinosaur left. But I realised it was more important to rescue a whole family than an individual. It made more emotional sense too.

Next Katy takes the lead because I wanted both the boy and the girl protagonists to be proactive. And here is another series of strips, echoing the previous set.

> First they collected armfuls of enormous flowers. Katy knew that the dinosaurs loved to eat the flowers. Then they made huge nets from the rigging on Katy's wrecked ship. Tom hung them from the basket of his balloon. All the time the explosions from the volcano got louder and louder. They laid a trail of flowers for the dinosaurs to follow.

Then there is a contained double spread. Katy is dropping the flowers onto the water and the dinosaurs are swimming to safety.

> At the water's edge, Katy clambered up into the balloon's basket and threw handfuls of flowers on to the water. The dinosaurs followed, swimming. The plan had worked! The seas turned black around them and hot rocks hissed down as . . .

We know what's going to happen next, and we turn over and – bang! We're onto another bleed again – with a large volcano eruption, which was great fun to do.

> The volcano erupted! They had got away in the nick of time!

When you're designing a spread you must leave a space clear for the text to be printed on it. If you've got a whole picture like this on this page, you must leave a light colour. For this very reason I created this light patch of sea to contain the text.

> Just as the smallest dinosaur was getting too tired to swim, they reached a beautiful island. Then it was time for Tom and Katy to start the long journey home. They said goodbye to the dinosaurs and set off in the red balloon.

In contrast, the next page – of the dinosaurs safe on their new island – has a smaller, calmer picture and is framed. Next comes the final, little drama to finish off the story – with Katy and Tom being lost. And finally the lighthouse guides them home. It's like that Chekhov quote on the so-called well-made play – 'If there's a gun on the wall in Act One, it will go off in Act Three!' So, I've used the fact that

He flew past snow-covered mountains,

across wild, dark green forests,

through rainstorms and over waterfalls.

Final artwork for *Tom and the Island of Dinosaurs*

At times, the balloon dipped down to touch the waves.

Later, it drifted across a great city at dawn,

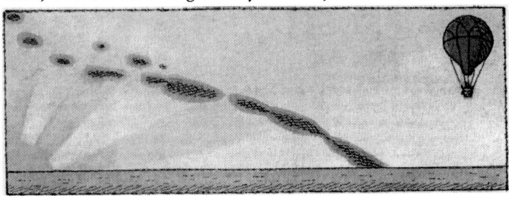

Tom lives in a lighthouse, not only because it's a nice, fun, exotic thing for a boy to live in, but also because it literally draws him homeward at the end of the story. I was quite pleased when I thought of that ending – it seemed to make both emotional and dramatic sense.

> But the journey home was not easy. Winds howled round the basket. Rain lashed over them. The moon vanished. There was nothing but icy blackness.

The penultimate picture is an emotional release. It's a double spread bled to the edges – of Tom and Katy coming out of the clouds, and with grandfather waving at them from below.

> Just as Tom never thought he would see his grandfather again, a bright light pierced the swirling black clouds. 'It's the lighthouse!' he cried. And as they flew closer, Tom could see his grandfather on the balcony, watching out for him to come home.

We end up with a little oval, womb-like vignette of Tom and Katy safely returned home to grandfather. It's drawn in warm colours – pinks, mauves and yellows. It looks all cosy and safe – and has a 'going to bed' ending.

> Safe at last, and wrapped in blankets, Tom and Katy drank hot cocoa in front of the fire. Grandfather listened as they told him the wonderful story of the shipwreck, the volcano and rescuing the last dinosaurs.

The book took about a year and a half to do and it was a long struggle! But it seems to be popular when I read it out in schools now. Children seem to enjoy the adventure of going off in a balloon. Often as a child I would lie in bed and pretend that my bed was the basket of a balloon and I'd fly off somewhere. Perhaps that's where this story really began.

4 ILLUSTRATING TEXT

A rapport or communication between writer and illustrator can happen entirely on the page. I don't even have to meet a writer I'm illustrating for. When you illustrate another's text you need to be a good reader. It's absolutely fundamental. So many people read text without understanding sometimes. I've known my own children complain when they've been looking at a book and an illustration hasn't picked up on something obvious. Perhaps the text has said 'The sun is shining' and yet the illustration didn't pick up on this, and there wasn't a sun, or the sense of the sun in some shadows. Illustrations are part of literature and should not be independent. Illustration is about understanding and interpreting text.

Examples of picture books I've enjoyed where a writer's text and an illustrator's pictures have worked together well would include *We're Going on a Bear Hunt* by Michael Rosen and Helen Oxenbury. And I think Nick Sharratt and Jacqueline Wilson also complement each other perfectly – they're so connected that you now think of one with the other. It's a marriage made in heaven. Nick's pictures are child-friendly in the sense that – and this is in no way an insult to Nick, but a great compliment – a child will look at his work and think 'I can do a drawing like that.' He's a brilliant artist, but he's not drawing in the conventional draughtsmanship sense; he's illustrating in a naïve and accessible manner. I'm a strong believer in accessibility. Nick allows the reader to bring something of their own to the picture as well. Ardizzone worked in the same way too.

SELECTED CURRENT TITLES

Emily and the Golden Acorn (Doubleday)
Tom and the Island of Dinosaurs (Doubleday)
The Teddy Robber (Picture Corgi)
Peter and the Wolf – and music/narration cassette (Doubleday)
The Owl and the Pussycat (Doubleday)
Ian Beck's Picture Book (Scholastic)
Home Before Dark (Scholastic)
Lost in the Snow (Scholastic)
The Ugly Duckling (Orchard)
Round and Round the Garden – with Sarah Williams (OUP)
Oranges and Lemons – with Karen King (OUP)
The Oxford Nursery Book (OUP)
The Oxford Nursery Story Book (OUP)
Little Angel – with Geraldine McGaughrean (Orchard)
The Orchard Book of Fairy Tales – with Rose Impey (Orchard)

An introduction to . . . Neil Ardley

WHAT TYPE OF BOOKS DO YOU WRITE? I write information and activity books, mainly for children. These are general books intended for the home – not textbooks or curriculum books – but they do get used in schools.

WHAT ARE YOUR BOOKS ABOUT? Most of my books are on science and technology, such as *The New Way Things Work* or *101 Great Science Experiments*, but I've also written on music, with *The Eyewitness Guide to Music* and *A Young Person's Guide to Music*, and on nature, especially birds.

BORN: Wallington, Surrey, 26 May 1937.

EDUCATION: Wallington County Grammar School; Bristol University – B.Sc. in Chemistry with Maths and Economics.

LIVES: London.

PREVIOUS OCCUPATIONS: I have been an assistant in a patent agency and an editor for World Book Encyclopedia.

OTHER CAREER: Professional musician – composing, arranging and performing big band jazz and, more recently, electronic jazz. My compositions include *Kaleidoscope of Rainbows* (1975) and *Harmony of the Spheres* (1978).

FAMILY/PETS: I am married to Bridget, and we have a daughter, Jane, who is doing her Ph.D. thesis in Tibetan religion and politics at Keele University. We also have two cats – Tashi and Ruby.

HOBBIES: Walking.

AWARDS: Science Book Prize and the TES Information Book Award for *The Way Things Work* (1989) – shared with David Macaulay.

LANGUAGES TRANSLATED INTO: My Dorling Kindersley books are translated into every language imaginable!

FAVOURITE MUSICIANS: Stravinsky and Miles Davis.

FAVOURITE SCIENTIST: Michael Faraday, an early nineteenth-century British scientist known mainly for epoch-making discoveries in electricity.

FAVOURITE FILM: *Fanny and Alexander* by Ingmar Bergman. It's a masterpiece!

FAVOURITE BOOK: *Middlemarch* by George Eliot.

FAVOURITE BOOK YOU HAVE WRITTEN AND WHY: *The Way Things Work* with David Macaulay – it explains everything so clearly and with such humour, relevance and imagination. This was a watershed book for me.

WHAT WERE YOU LIKE AT THE AGE OF 11? Bumptious!

ENJOYS DOING SCIENCE WORKSHOPS WITH CHILDREN BECAUSE: I like being with children and I get enjoyment from their reactions to my experiments.

WHAT DO YOU ENJOY ABOUT WRITING? Mainly it's the craft of putting across information and finding a good way of doing it.

AMBITIONS: Most of them have been achieved!

WHAT IS YOUR FAVOURITE COMPLIMENT? Barbara Thompson, a marvellous musician I've worked with for 35 years, once said that I am a man who is generous with his knowledge.

WHAT WOULD YOU LIKE TO HAPPEN IN THE TWENTY-FIRST CENTURY? Global harmony with the retention of cultural traditions and differences.

WEBSITE: http://members.aol.com/neilardley

1 HOW THE READER BECAME A WRITER

I remember being given *Alice in Wonderland* during the war. I was probably about six or seven. I can remember the illustrations of that edition even now. It was, perhaps, the first book I really loved. And I had *Gulliver's Travels* by Jonathan Swift, which I enjoyed. And I also read *Doctor Doolittle* and the *Biggles* books, Enid Blyton's *Famous Five* series and Arthur Ransome's *Swallows and Amazons*. As for non-fiction, I remember *Arthur Mee's Children's Encyclopedia* – and I devoured that! I took volume after volume out of the library. I enjoyed reading that encyclopedia as much as I did fiction. I must have been eight or nine then, and I read a lot at that age.

I can still recall my first chemistry lesson at my grammar school when I was about eleven. Mr Dickinson, the teacher, came into the class and put a conical pile of orange red powder on the lab desk, got out a match and set fire to it. This was a substance called ammonium dichromate, which is combustible. The powder bubbled up like a volcano – with red hot lava coming down its sides and smoke billowing out. And then the whole thing transformed itself into a pile of green ash. I was amazed at this! I thought, this can't be school! He captured us, showing us what chemistry could be like – the activity of it, the colours and the smells. That was the moment that really clicked with me. And Mr Dickinson was a very inspiring teacher.

As a teenager I loved science fiction. I was fascinated with the idea of people going into space, which, of course, hadn't been done then. First, I was into H.G. Wells – *The Time Machine* and *The War of the Worlds* – and then I moved on to Arthur C. Clarke, and as a young adult, Isaac Asimov. I've found Asimov's non-fiction writing very inspiring. His *Biographical Encyclopedia of Science and Technology* from 1975 is a superb work of reference. In addition, he did a science dictionary that explained scientific terms in everyday words. Asimov wrote superbly, with great clarity, and he always made the subject interesting – telling you everything you need to know, but not too much! As an inspiration for non-fiction scientific writing, he is probably my greatest influence.

In 1960, after I finished my science degree at Bristol University, I worked for two years as an assistant in a patent agency, handling the documents for chemical inventions such as plastics and things like that. Next I went to work as an editor with World Book Encyclopedia, which was the foremost children's encyclopedia in the world. In those days, there were very few people in children's information book publishing with a science background, such as myself.

World Book were an American publisher, and at that time they were establishing themselves in London to set up an international edition. All of the new editors such as myself went on the World Book training course. You had to edit all these articles on different subjects – from Assyria and Babylonia to sugar, all sorts of things. Then your work was assessed. There was a set World Book house style which you had to assimilate before you could go on to work on a book. And we had an in-house style document that was about 100 pages long and it defined everything we needed to be aware of with respect to grammar, punctuation, layout, language, structure and content.

The whole of my writing career stems from that time. It was a brilliant start, I couldn't have asked for better. Working for World Book was very important for me and my writing career generally. With them I learnt how to write clearly and concisely for children and how to organise information in a book. That project lasted for four years – in which I learnt children's information book publishing, literally from A to Z.

Soon after that, I went to work as an editor for Hamlyn for two years. And then in 1968 I went freelance in order that I could also give time to my musical career. So instead of moving up the executive ladder of publishing, I became a freelance editor and that just gradually changed into being a freelance writer in the 1970s. So I've been freelance for 30 years now – in which time I've written exactly 100 books.

Now I write exclusively for Dorling Kindersley, but in the past I've written for other publishers – Franklin Watts, Macmillan and others – and mainly on science and music. But when I first started I did a lot of books on birds and nature. My first proper book was *How Birds Behave* for Hamlyn. Slowly I moved into science and technology books, with the odd music text now and then. The first book I wrote for Dorling Kindersley was a computer manual – *The ZX Spectrum + User Guide*. It sold a million copies because Sinclair – the computer manufacturer – sold a million computers!

2 WRITING: ROUTINES AND REFLECTIONS

I do all my writing in a converted bedroom upstairs and I usually work 9.30–5.30 p.m., five days a week. I used to write on a typewriter – I taught myself in the early 1970s. I went on to a word processor in about 1983. It made a huge difference, for my productivity went up by about a third. I can't write by hand now – it takes too long!

Computers are convenient – I can chop and change easily, and now I'm able to e-mail my work to my editor. That's terrific. What I don't like about them is that you don't necessarily have to think out what you're writing about when you start. In the old days at the typewriter, or even writing longhand, you had to sit down and work the whole thing out in your head or in note form before you began, and it worked well. With a word processor you don't have to do that, and you can end up with a paragraph that is awkward because you haven't thought it through. And it can be difficult to get it right, because you haven't organised it or thought about it in advance. Even with computers, some forward planning is useful.

The books that I write always originate with the publisher. I've tried originating books with editors, but I've got nowhere – because things have to fit in with publishers' marketing concepts and everything. So my work has always been commissioned.

Before I begin a book I'll know almost all the information that will be going into it – I have to. I couldn't write it otherwise. With something like *A Young Person's Guide to Music* I'll use dictionaries and encyclopedias to make sure I haven't forgotten any composers or to research various dates. I use Groves' multi-volume music encyclopedia. These days I also use the Internet for research. With *The New Way Things Work* I've used the Internet a great deal, and so has the Dorling Kindersley in-house researcher, Robert Graham. Robert did a lot of research for me with that book.

My usual routine for research is to look in my own collection of books, then I'll possibly try the Internet or the library and then, if all else fails, I'll phone up some specialists. With *The New Way Things Work*, Dorling Kindersley put me on to various scientific specialists. And to keep up with new technological innovations, I always read *New Scientist* magazine and *The Guardian On Line* every week.

All of the experiments that go into my books – books such as *How Things Work* or *101 Great Science Experiments* – I do them here, in my kitchen! First of all, I'll think of various experiments – let's say to do with light. I'll know the various elements that I want to include, such as mirrors and lenses, and then I'll have to think up ways of doing the experiments that utilise everyday materials – materials that are immediately to hand. And once I've tried them out at home I'll go and demonstrate the experiments to the editorial team at Dorling Kindersley in London. And then they get to work on them. Sometimes the editors will say 'Can you think again?' – which can often be the best advice, as there may well be a better way of doing the experiment.

Ultimately, the experiments *have* to work – you can't publish a book giving children experiments to do that don't actually work! For the final stage, the experiments are developed so that they work well and look good and then Dorling Kindersley will take them into a school. The children, from diverse ethnic groups, are dressed in neutral clothes and are photographed for the book while they are doing the experiments themselves. It's a brilliant way of doing it!

The ability to pitch a book at the right level is essential. You get that through years of experience. It becomes instinctive. If you don't get it right, your editor will – or should. And at our editorial meetings, even if we are not explicitly talking about what young 'Johnny' or 'Susan' would make of this information or that experiment, the level of the readership is implicitly there, all the time.

18 Measure the rain

Rain falls from the clouds, which contain millions of tiny water droplets. These come together, forming rain drops that fall to the ground. Make a simple rain gauge to measure "rainfall". This is the amount of rain that falls over a certain time.

You will need:

Ruler and marker pen

Measuring jug

Small clear plastic bottle

Large clear plastic bottle

Scissors

1 Cut off the tops of both bottles, using the scissors. Make sure the edges are straight.

2 Fill the jug to the 50 ml mark. Pour the water into the small bottle. Mark the level.

3 Repeat step 2 several times, so that you have a series of marks on the side of the bottle.

Empty the bottle after measuring the rainfall. Put it back in the same place.

4 Empty the small bottle. Place it inside the large bottle. Put the top of the large bottle upside-down over the small bottle. It forms a funnel.

5 Stand the bottles outside on a table or a wall to catch the rain. Record the water level in the small bottle each morning. This is the daily rainfall.

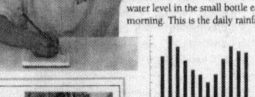

Chart showing the rainfall for 12 months

Weather station
Each day, scientists called meteorologists take detailed measurements to help them keep track of the weather and forecast how it will change. They record the amount of rainfall, the highest and lowest temperatures, the humidity, the speed and direction of the wind, and the air pressure.

6 Add up the rainfall for each week or each month. Then make a chart to show how much rain falls over several weeks, months, or even a whole year.

From *101 Great Science Experiments* by Neil Ardley

3 GROWING A BOOK

The Way Things Work

In 1985, Alan Buckingham, editor at Dorling Kindersley, asked me to prepare a general synopsis for a book on machines that the American writer/illustrator David Macaulay was going to do, and with the idea of a possible collaboration. Their original approach was to have a book on machines that groups them together according to their uses – such as machines in the home, various modes of transport, machines on the farm, and so on. I said that this was not a good approach because if you want to know how machines work, then first you have to understand the principles of science that govern them. And I therefore suggested that the book be organised by the principles of science, rather than by the machines' uses. At first, this didn't go down very well. But it's true – you have to know about gears, levers, electricity, light and so on if you are to understand how machines operate. But I'm pleased to say that eventually my idea was taken!

We decided from the start that the book would be 400 pages long. Now usually, the structure of a book would also be mapped out from the beginning, but the structure for this one evolved. We just started with my typewritten synopsis, in which I'd detailed all the various machines I wanted to cover, which were grouped according to their scientific principles. And Dorling Kindersley gave us the freedom to keep going until we found the right structure and formula for the book.

For a year, Alan Buckingham, David Macaulay and I worked on ways of presenting all the research information that was building up on the various machines. At the meetings, I would brief David on each of the scientific areas and the workings of the machines we were covering. David would then send me sketches from the States, and I would return them with my responses. But we could not find a good way of presenting the information.

Then suddenly David discovered the idea of the mammoth. He'd been toying with an illustration of a mammoth having its tusks straightened! And from there he got the idea of the mammoth stories – in which a woolly mammoth is subjected to various indignities, and with the narratives illustrating a particular principle of science. Once we had the mammoth idea, the structure was clear and we were on our way, but the project then took another two years. So the whole book took three years in total.

In addition, David came up with the idea that the mammoth stories are recounted by an inventor, and what you get throughout the book are extracts from the inventor's notebooks – which are sketches and stories. And these are overlaid with tea cup stains! When David was doing the illustrations he actually got a teacup and immersed it in coffee and ground it into the artwork to give it a used and antiquated look! The whole thing is in a beautiful yellowy-brown.

David's approach is quite unique. Take the page with the zipper, for example – the zipper is magnified and has lots of little people pulling the bits and pieces along! It's a 'Gulliver'-type zipper! It has a wonderful three-dimensional look. There are so many funny elements that David Macaulay injected into the book to really enrich it.

Overall, my role was to decide upon the contents of the book in terms of the machines and scientific principles we would cover, to organise the structure and to

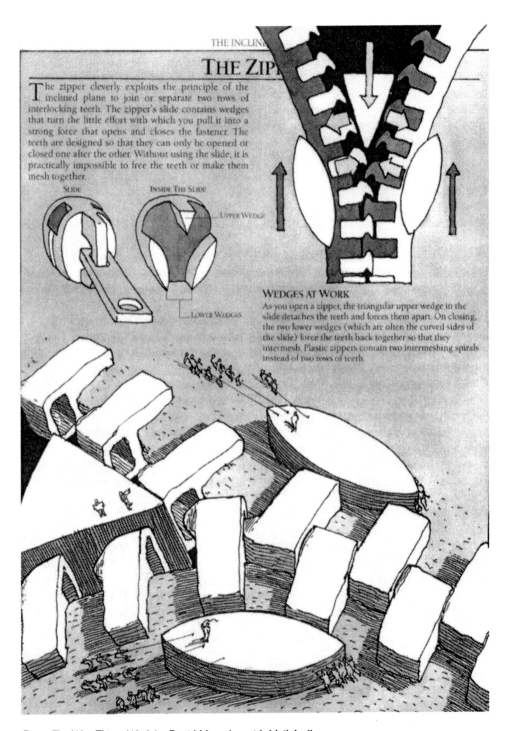

THE INCLINE

THE ZIPPER

The zipper cleverly exploits the principle of the inclined plane to join or separate two rows of interlocking teeth. The zipper's slide contains wedges that turn the little effort with which you pull it into a strong force that opens and closes the fastener. The teeth are designed so that they can only be opened or closed one after the other. Without using the slide, it is practically impossible to free the teeth or make them mesh together.

SLIDE

INSIDE THE SLIDE

UPPER WEDGE

LOWER WEDGES

WEDGES AT WORK

As you open a zipper, the triangular upper wedge in the slide detaches the teeth and forces them apart. On closing, the two lower wedges (which are often the curved sides of the slide) force the teeth back together so that they intermesh. Plastic zippers contain two intermeshing spirals instead of two rows of teeth.

From *The Way Things Work* by David Macaulay with Neil Ardley write all the technical text explaining the principles and the machines. David Macaulay's role – in addition to defining the overall approach, the most vital ingredient in the book's success – was to produce all the illustrations and to write the stories. The editor for the book was David Burnie – who is now a writer on natural history. He kept the project together, and he rewrote various parts for me when we were working flat out towards the final deadline.

What the book offers is a hierarchy of information, on macro and micro levels. On the macro level there are the four main parts of the book, divided into the fundamental scientific principles:

Part 1 – The Mechanics of Movement
Part 2 – Harnessing the Elements
Part 3 – Working with Waves
Part 4 – Electricity & Automation

From there, you have the micro – made up of the individual sections on scientific principles, which themselves are comprised of various individual machines. Within Part 1, there are individual sections on The Inclined Plane, Levers, The Wheel and Axle, Gears and Belts and so on.

On the first level of each individual section is David Macaulay's mammoth story exemplifying a scientific principle. Next, and below David's story, there is the technical explanation of the principle with diagrams. And after that, on the following pages, there are the machines themselves. Each page or double-page spread will start with an introduction which is followed by different levels of subsidiary texts, annotations and captions and labels, all of which become increasingly sophisticated. If you read the whole lot, you'll find out exactly how, say, a plough or zipper works – but you may not want to know that much, and the story or another part may be enough for you. This dividing up of the knowledge, this type of structure, will satisfy the varying needs that people have with an information book – whether they are skimming through or researching something. Organising the information in this way – and making the right decision as to which information will go into the introduction, which will go into the subsidiary text or annotation, a caption or a label – is absolutely vital.

My sections of technical text would each have gone through two or three drafts. I was governed by the fact that each small section had to be of a certain length, and I was working to an upper limit of about 300–400 words over a double page. What I aimed to do in the explanations of scientific principles was to relate my own text to the mammoth story, to create an interplay between the two. This is taken from p.14, The Principle of the Inclined Plane:

> The laws of physics decree –

'Decree' – that's a nice word!

> that raising an object, such as a mammoth-stunning boulder, to a particular height requires a certain amount of work.

That sounds lively – 'mammoth-stunning boulder'!

> *These same laws also decree that no way can ever be found to reduce that amount. The ramp makes life easier, not by altering the amount of work that is needed, but by altering the way in which the work is done.*

Here, as always, I wanted my prose to be easy to read and understand, and for the text to be interesting and relevant. Because of the vocabulary, which is perhaps rather hard, this book is not for very young children, but it would be interesting for anyone of 11 upwards.

This text relates to the very first story in the book which is called 'The Inclined Plane: On Capturing a Mammoth'. In a very humorous manner, the story illustrates the very basic principle on force, distance and work. Beneath David's mammoth narrative and illustration is my text, which gives a scientific explanation of the principle of the inclined plane.

From here, the following pages cover the machines that employ the principle of the inclined plane – such as locks and keys, cutting machines of all kinds, the plough and the zipper. So you get these lovely conjunctions of machines with very different uses, that all fundamentally work in the very same way. I think this element is one of the book's great strengths.

We are now working on the revised tenth anniversary edition called *The New Way Things Work* – and the title has a double meaning, as not only is the book to be a new edition but there is a new chapter to be included that covers the new way in which things work (i.e., digital technology, as in computers, cash machines and digital cameras). This section – which also features the mammoth, but now in a big story made up of several episodes – is entitled 'The Digital Domain'. This too follows the same macro/micro structure and has a hierarchy of information levels. We've also had to rework some of the original book as some of the machines are now out of date – for example, the mechanical parking meter is being replaced by the bicycle brakes and the firefighters' ladder. And the book is also available in CD-ROM format.

Eyewitness Guide No. 12: Music

I worked on this book – also for Dorling Kindersley – immediately after *The Way Things Work*. I'd already done a music encyclopedia for Hamlyn, so when I began this book I knew enough about music generally to put it together. In all – as I'll go on to explain – this book was a collaboration betweeen myself, the designer and the two editors. This book is the twelfth in a phenomenally successful series, and it was produced over a period of three or four months, in the summer of 1988. Once we got going, the team worked on it non-stop.

The plan that we have for a book like this is a flow chart, which the publisher will produce. Effectively, this flow chart is an outline of the whole book with thumb-nail sketches for each page. From this, you can see how the book visually progresses from one page or double page to the next. The chart is the designer's responsibility. Getting this right is paramount – the reader is presented with a whole series of

THE INCLINED PLANE

ON CAPTURING A MAMMOTH

*I*n the spring of that year, I was invited to the land of the much sought-after woolly mammoth, a land dotted by the now familiar high wooden towers of the mammoth captors. In ancient times the mammoth had been hunted simply for its meat. But its subsequent usefulness in industry and growing popularity as a pet had brought about the development of a more sophisticated and less terminal means of apprehension.

Each unsuspecting beast was lured to the base of a tower from which a boulder of reasonable dimensions was then dropped from a humanitarian height onto its thick skull. Once stunned, a mammoth could easily be lead to the paddock where an ice pack and fresh swamp grass would quickly overcome hurt feelings and innate distrust.

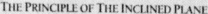

THE PRINCIPLE OF THE INCLINED PLANE

The laws of physics decree that raising an object, such as a mammoth-stunning boulder, to a particular height requires a certain amount of work. Those same laws also decree that no way can ever be found to reduce that amount. The ramp makes life easier not by altering the amount of work that is needed, but by altering the way in which the work is done.

Work has two aspects to it: the effort that you put in, and the distance over which you maintain the effort. If the effort increases, the distance must decrease, and vice versa.

This is easiest to understand by looking at two extremes. Climbing a hill by the steepest route requires the most effort, but the distance that you have to cover is shortest. Climbing up the gentlest slope requires the least effort, but the distance is greatest. The work you do is the same in either case, and equals the effort (the force you exert) multiplied by the distance over which you maintain the effort.

So what you gain in effort, you pay in distance. This is a basic rule that is obeyed by many mechanical devices, and it is the reason why the ramp works: it reduces the effort needed to raise an object by increasing the distance that it moves.

The ramp is an example of an inclined plane. The principle behind the inclined plane was made use of in ancient times. Ramps enabled the Egyptians to build their pyramids and temples. Since then, the inclined plane has been put to work in a whole host of devices from locks and cutters to ploughs and zippers, as well as in all the many machines that make use of the screw.

From *The Way Things Work* by David Macaulay with Neil Ardley

While the process was more or less successful, it had a couple of major drawbacks. The biggest problem was that of simply getting a heavy boulder to the right height. This required an almost Herculean effort, and Hercules was not due to be born for several centuries yet. The second problem was that the mammoth, once hit, would invariably crash into the tower, either hurling his captors to the ground, or at least seriously damaging the structure.

After making a few calculations, I informed my hosts that both problems could be solved simultaneously by building earth ramps rather than wooden towers. The inherent sturdiness of the ramp would make it virtually indestructible should a mammoth fall against it. And now, rather than trying to hoist the boulder straight up, it could be rolled gradually to the required height, therefore needing far less effort.

At first, the simplicity of my solution was greeted with understandable scepticism. "What do we do with the towers?" they asked. I made a few more calculations and then suggested commercial and retail development on the lower levels and luxury apartments above.

HOW EFFORT AND DISTANCE ARE LINKED

The sloping face of this ramp is twice as long as its vertical face. The effort that is needed to move a load up the sloping face is therefore half that needed to raise it up the vertical face.

HALF EFFORT

FULL EFFORT

SLOPING FACE

VERTICAL FACE

THE WEDGE

In most of the machines that make use of the inclined plane, it appears in the form of a wedge. A door wedge is a simple application; you push the sharp end of the wedge under the door and it moves in to jam the door open.

The wedge acts as a moving inclined plane. Instead of having an object move up an inclined plane, the plane itself can move to raise the object. As the plane moves a greater distance than the object, it raises the object with a greater force. The door wedge works in this way. As it jams under the door, the wedge raises the door slightly and exerts a strong force on it. The door in turn forces the wedge hard against the floor, and friction (see pp. 86-7) with the floor makes the wedge grip the floor so that it holds the door open.

pictures, illustrations and text, and they've all got to work together and make a big impact. Personally, I very much enjoy working under these restrictions – making the text the best that it can be for a specific space to fit the best pictures or photographs that can be used. And as with this book, I do like to be part of a project from the start, because this way I can get involved with organising the design and structure of the information.

The *Eyewitness Guide No. 12: Music* exemplifies the Dorling Kindersley approach of using photographs on a white background, using airbrush shadows to give the photographs depth as well as surrounding them with introductory text, captions, annotations and labels. When we did this in 1988 it was pretty revolutionary! But they've done lots more books like it since.

The stages the book went through were as follows. First I wrote a synopsis, showing how we could fit the whole subject into 64 pages with double-page spreads throughout. This meant 29 working spreads in all, into which I had to divide all the different types of musical instruments, including ethnic instruments too. I grouped them according to the standard ways that instruments work – moving from wind instruments through to stringed instruments, percussion instruments and on to electrical instruments at the end.

At the beginning I didn't know exactly what instruments would go on each spread as it depended upon which ones would be available for us to photograph. We had two main sources – the Musicology Department of the Horniman Museum, London, and the Ethnomusicology Department at the Pitt Rivers Museum in Oxford. I went with the designer to talk to the curators at both museums, and they were most helpful. I was taken around, and I was given complete lists of the instruments they had. The curators also gave me some background information on the instruments – such as how the instruments are played, some history behind them, as well as how the instruments produce their sounds.

Then I rewrote my synopsis, detailing the instruments I had chosen to include on each spread. In the meantime, the designer worked on a rough layout. These were then approved by the editor.

The next stage was the photography. At both museums, the curators made arrangements for the instruments to be taken out of their cases for the day. The photographer set up a portable photographic studio. This contained a huge, white formica board that had the same dimensions as the double-page spread. Onto the board he projected a grid, showing the layout of the page where all the headings, text and captions could go, and the instruments were placed in the positions at which they would appear on the spread, leaving space for additional illustrations and other photos. This was a very lengthy process – shifting the instruments around the board to give us space for everything else, and to give the spread balance. Each spread took about three hours. We took some Polaroids to check that everything was right, and then we would take the final photographs. I'm sure this sort of work is done on computer now.

Most of the spreads were done in the way I've just explained, for example, the 'Pipes and Flutes' spread which shows various kinds of flutes – from lovely ethnic flutes, and pan pipes, to the lovely Chinese Dragon flute and these early bone whistles which are 40,000 years old. These are probably the earliest instruments in the world. The other way a spread was done can be seen on the 'Electrifying Music' pages. We bought a cheap electric guitar, took it to pieces and put all the parts down onto the board! This way, you can really see how it works. Again, the designer and I would have previously worked out the spread design. The last stage required me to write all the text and all the captions to fit around the instruments and other illustrations. By then I would have known exactly what I wanted to say and how much space I would have to do it in.

With the 'Creating a Guitar' spread we went to a guitar maker and took photos of an instrument as it was being constructed. We did the same for the 'Making a Violin' page. And while the photographer was busy at work, this gave me a chance to talk at length to the violin maker and to ask about the whole process – what woods were used and the various stages involved. I made copious notes, and much of what he told me informed my text.

I was very conscious that the introductions should really be lively, colourful and informative. On the 'Pipes and Flutes' page it begins:

> *The breathy, intimate sound of pipes and flutes gives them a haunting quality. Perhaps this is why they have long been associated with magic – as in Mozart's opera* The Magic Flute, *and the legend of the Pied-Piper of Hamelin* . . .

Here I'm trying to put across the quality of sound that comes from the instrument and the connotations that the sound has in people's minds. And the introduction to the 'Blazing Brass' page begins:

> *Modern brass instruments in full cry, notably serried ranks of trumpets and trombones, can create a blaze of sound. This is not due just to the amount of effort that goes into blowing them, although purple faces may well accompany a thrilling fanfare* . . .

I would say that the text itself is pitched at readers of eleven upwards.

There were very few drafts of my text with this book. I knew exactly what I was going to put in each section because I'd been involved right from the beginning of the project. So by the time I got to write the text I was just bursting to put it down on paper!

4 WORKING WITH EDITORS

I can't emphasise too much the importance of a good editor. The role of an editor is to read your work objectively, for as a writer you can produce things that, while not exactly wrong, are ambiguous or unclear. Editors will clarify all those parts of your writing, and point out all the problem areas that you aren't aware of, because you're too close to it. A good editor will give you a lot of help and support, and be open and candid in discussions. I like to feel I can discuss anything. As an information book writer, you work very closely with the editor. It has to be a partnership.

It will be the publisher that will come up with the initial concept for a book or a series of books and the editor will develop it alongside the writer. So we'll sit down and say, 'How are we going to do it?'

Creating a guitar

THE ACOUSTIC GUITAR IS FOREVER LINKED with Spain, so much so that it is often called the Spanish guitar. Flamenco, the folk music of Spain, is renowned for its exciting guitar music as well as its energetic dancing. The instrument, with its body shaped like a figure eight, probably came to Spain from North Africa, and may be descended from lutes like the 'ud (p. 36). By the 17th century, the guitar was being played all over Europe. Today acoustic and electric guitars (pp. 58 - 59) have spread throughout the world, and dominate popular music and much folk music in America and Europe.

This portrayal of a 19th-century Spanish guitar player shows the instrument in its present form.

Top block joins the neck to the body

CLASSICAL GUITAR
This is the traditional form of the guitar, also known as the Spanish guitar. It has six strings, usually made of nylon, and a wide neck. The design dates back to the mid-19th century, when it was perfected by a Spanish carpenter called Antonio de Torres Jurado, often known simply as Torres. Guitars played in popular music usually have a fingerplate fixed to the body to protect it.

Soundboard with struts for strength

Mould

Wooden linings are glued along top and bottom edges of ribs

MAKING THE SOUNDBOARD
The most important part of the guitar is the soundboard - the upper part of the body underneath the strings. It is made of two pieces of pine, spruce, cedar, or redwood that are glued together and then cut and shaped, or it may be made from layers of plywood. To strengthen the soundboard, struts are glued across the inside in a pattern that is crucial to the tone of the guitar. The sides, or ribs, of the guitar are made of two strips of rosewood, walnut, mahogany, maple, or sycamore. The strips are heated and shaped in a mould. Wooden blocks and linings are fixed to the inside of the ribs to make good joints for the soundboard and other parts.

Flat-top guitar with fingerplate

Classical guitar

From *Eyewitness Guide No. 12: Music* by Neil Ardley

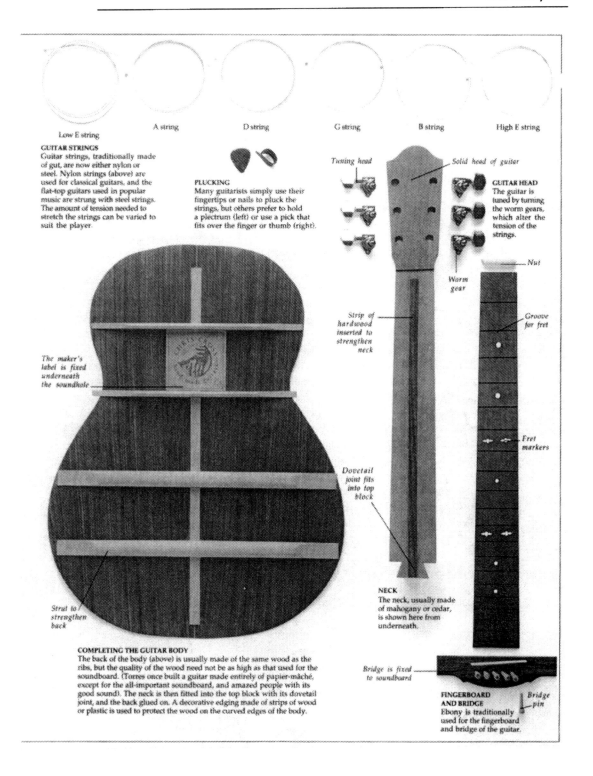

Low E string   A string   D string   G string   B string   High E string

GUITAR STRINGS
Guitar strings, traditionally made of gut, are now either nylon or steel. Nylon strings (above) are used for classical guitars, and the flat-top guitars used in popular music are strung with steel strings. The amount of tension needed to stretch the strings can be varied to suit the player.

PLUCKING
Many guitarists simply use their fingertips or nails to pluck the strings, but others prefer to hold a plectrum (left) or use a pick that fits over the finger or thumb (right).

Tuning head

Solid head of guitar

GUITAR HEAD
The guitar is tuned by turning the worm gears, which alter the tension of the strings.

Nut

Worm gear

Groove for fret

Strip of hardwood inserted to strengthen neck

The maker's label is fixed underneath the soundhole

Dovetail joint fits into top block

Fret markers

Strut to strengthen back

NECK
The neck, usually made of mahogany or cedar, is shown here from underneath.

COMPLETING THE GUITAR BODY
The back of the body (above) is usually made of the same wood as the ribs, but the quality of the wood need not be as high as that used for the soundboard. (Torres once built a guitar made entirely of papier-mâché, except for the all-important soundboard, and amazed people with its good sound). The neck is then fitted into the top block with its dovetail joint, and the back glued on. A decorative edging made of strips of wood or plastic is used to protect the wood on the curved edges of the body.

Bridge is fixed to soundboard

Bridge pin

FINGERBOARD AND BRIDGE
Ebony is traditionally used for the fingerboard and bridge of the guitar.

Very few of my editors have a science background, which is generally a good thing, because when they read my text they look at it with the same amount of knowledge as a reader, and come to it in the same way. I think it's preferable for an editor to have little knowledge of the subject, otherwise they're not really able to do the task in an objective manner. Though with some books we will have consultants. With my *Dictionary of Science* there were a couple of science consultants involved, and they went through the book with a fine-tooth comb to pick out any errors.

Some of my best writing has been done when an editor has rejected my work and has asked me to think again because it's not good enough. With *How Things Work* two of the editors, Mukul Patel and Paul Docherty, were tremendous in that although they would reject my ideas at times, they would always make positive suggestions about the way they could be improved. And sure enough, I would rework things, and second time around it would be better. That kind of frankness from an editor is invaluable. In *How Things Work*, my original design for a micro-phone – which appears on pp.140/141 – was going to be the standard thing of the tin-can telephone where you have two tins and a piece of string. This was rejected because it had appeared in nearly every other science book – which I had to agree with! And anyway, it doesn't always work very well. So then I thought hard and invented a way of making a microphone using everyday materials – magnets, rubber bands and so on – one that could be plugged into a stereo and could record your voice. And I went and demonstrated it to the editors and it worked!

Sue Unstead, whom I first worked with at Franklin Watts, and now at Dorling Kindersley, has been my most influential editor. Sue is meticulous with grammar and continuity and everything else. With the first series I was working on – *The World of Tomorrow* – I went to see Sue, and laid out before her on her desk was something I had written. It had a lot of blue pencil on it. She pointed at the blue pencil and said, 'I think this is what you meant to write.' What a wonderful way to put it! She taught me a lot. Things had changed by the early 1980s and I think I must have slipped, because I wasn't writing all that well. Sue took me in hand and really showed me how to write with interest, but above all to use lively, exciting language and to involve the reader the whole time. Sue reinforced that for me – to find a way to write that would both educate people as well as entertain them.

SELECTED CURRENT TITLES

All titles published by Dorling Kindersley

Dictionary of Science
Exploring the Internet (to be published late 1999)
How Things Work (Eyewitness Science Guide)
My Science (series)
101 Great Science Experiments
Eyewitness Guide No. 12: Music
A Young Person's Guide to Music (with music by Poul Ruders)

With David Macaulay:
The Way Things Work
The New Way Things Work

CD-ROM – with David Macaulay:
The Way Things Work
The New Way Things Work

An introduction to . . . Terry Deary

WHAT TYPE OF BOOKS DO YOU WRITE? I set out to try and avoid writing types of books. I set out to create my new types that push back the boundaries of what's possible. So, I write fiction, non-fiction and a strange blend called 'faction'. I write a lot of history books – such as *Horrible Histories* and *Tudor Terrors* – because they're popular. I'm starting on science as my next challenge with *The Spark Files* – making science entertaining and accessible to young people and children.

WHAT ARE YOUR BOOKS ABOUT? My history books are not about history, and that's what makes them different from other history books. They're not about dates, times, battles, kings and queens. They're about people.

BORN: 3 January 1946 in Hendon, Sunderland.

EDUCATION: Fullwell Primary school up to 11, then I passed 11+ and went to Monkwearmouth Grammar School. After a year with the electricity board, I trained to be a teacher. I've got a teacher's certificate, but I haven't got a degree!

LIVES: Burnhope – an old pit village in County Durham.

PREVIOUS OCCUPATIONS: Professional actor; theatre director; education officer in a large theatre company; advisory drama teacher; manager of a museum and art gallery.

FAMILY/PETS: I've been married to Jenny for the last 23 years. We have a daughter, Sarah, coming up to her nineteenth birthday. My wife and daughter have horses, sheep, geese and a dog called Moss.

HOBBIES: Work mainly, but every couple of days I go out running to try and keep fit. I support Sunderland FC and I like watching black-and-white films on television.

MOST TREASURED POSSESSION: Nothing! You come into this life with nothing and you leave with nothing.

AWARDS: For a local history book I got a couple of awards, but I can't remember what they are.

LANGUAGES TRANSLATED INTO: Sixteen in total, from the East (China and Thailand) to the West (Brazil and USA), and Europe in between.

FAVOURITE PLACE: There's no point getting attached to places any more than possessions.

FAVOURITE BOOKS: Children's – by far and away my favourite is L. Frank Baum's *The Wizard of Oz*. It's a very cleverly written book because it has two quite distinct levels: one, it's an adventure story; two, it's about people discovering themselves and overcoming their problems. Philip Pullman's *Clockwork* I admire tremendously. I also very much like Morris Gleitzman's *Water Wings* – it's very brave yet very entertaining to read. Adult's – *The Napoleon of Notting Hill* by G.K. Chesterton which I read at 16 and was stunned by it – it's the way he could take words and use irony and paradox. It was a revelation when I read that book. It was a great influence on me. Also, the works of Sir Walter Scott.

FAVOURITE LINES OF POETRY: From Shakespeare's *Macbeth*:

> To-morrow, and to-morrow, and to-morrow,
> Creeps in this petty pace from day to day,
> To the last syllable of recorded time;
> And all our yesterdays have lighted fools
> The way to dusty death. Out, out brief candle!
> Life's but a walking shadow, a poor player,
> That struts and frets his hour upon the stage,
> And then is heard no more; it is a tale
> Told by an idiot, full of sound and fury,
> Signifying nothing.

It's very clever – it likens life to a play and it's about nihilism and many other things.

FAVOURITE MUSIC: Tom Paxton's 'The Last Thing on My Mind' and 'Can't Help But Wonder Where I'm Bound'. I'm just getting into Classical music. At the moment I'm listening a lot to Haydn's Trumpet Concerto. Classical music is the only thing I can have on when I write.

FAVOURITE FILM: *Casablanca* – it's a story of one man up against the world, and he beats not just the establishment but the Nazi party too. Rick is my hero.

WHAT WERE YOU LIKE AT THE AGE OF 11? The seeds of my adult personality were coming through. I was starting to become anti-establishment.

WHY DO YOU WRITE? Because I don't have a boss. It's the only job I know that I can do where nobody tells me what to do.

IF YOU WEREN'T A WRITER: I'd be a monk in Tibet and have no possessions and remove myself from the world.

AMBITIONS: I have no ambitions.

WHICH THREE WORDS DESCRIBE YOU BEST? Some kinda man.

WHAT WOULD YOU LIKE TO HAPPEN IN THE TWENTY-FIRST CENTURY? An end to privilege where people achieve because of who they are and what they are born to. An end to the establishment.

WHICH CHARACTER FROM HISTORY WOULD YOU MOST LIKE TO BE?

William Shakespeare – because he's a tradesman's son who went to a grammar school and became an actor and from his acting developed his writing skills. I'm a tradesman's son who went to a grammar school and became an actor and from his acting developed his writing skills. I can identify with him – he's not part of the establishment yet he managed to please both the peasants and the establishment. Beyond this, he took the English language into a new dimension. He was a creative genius; he's someone I aspire to be like.

WHAT IS THE BEST COMPLIMENT A CHILD READER HAS EVER PAID YOUR WORK? 'I don't like books, but I read yours.' That's absolutely magic. I've had that comment a lot, and it's usually boys, boys who are reluctant readers. I've had parents thank me because their sons wouldn't pick up books before, but they've become avid readers and have gone on to read other people's books too. I think that's wonderful.

WHICH OF YOUR BOOKS WOULD YOU LIKE TO BE REMEMBERED FOR? None of them. I don't want to be remembered for anything. I want people to leave me behind.

I HOW THE READER BECAME A WRITER

Up to the age of 11, I had two books. They were Enid Blyton's *The Island of Adventure* and *The Ladybird Book of British Birds*. Enid Blyton taught me that characters in books *have* to have gone to public school, they *have* to be middle class and they *have* to go away for their holidays. None of which I did. I was reading as an alien looking in on another world, and I enjoyed it tremendously. When I grew up I learnt how politically incorrect Enid Blyton was and I was rather shocked that I'd liked her books.

Last year, I was given a copy of Enid Blyton's *The Island of Adventure* by a bookshop. I was thrilled because it was the same edition that I read as a child. And I re-read it and I was delighted. Enid Blyton was a wonderful craftswoman. I admire her enormously now. Politically, she's terribly incorrect, but she's a product of her age and upbringing. But technically, she actually knew how to write. So maybe my limited childhood reading wasn't too bad. And with *The Ladybird Book of British Birds* I learnt that information books can be interesting.

We weren't read stories in class. We were given test books so that the class of 52, or as least as many as possible, would get through the 11+ and go on to grammar school. And we weren't allowed to write in primary school. I remember our first day. We were given set formats, and we had a test. The test consisted of 'As good as . . .' and 'As stiff as a . . .' So if we're talking about teaching creative writing, I had the most bizarre education imaginable.

In secondary school I was introduced to Thomas Hardy and Shakespeare. At the age of 13, Thomas Hardy was incomprehensible to me. But by then I had joined the library and I was able to borrow adventure books and to read more widely for myself. I have to say that the most important thing for me at the end of a school day was to change into my tennis shoes, get down to the recreation park and play football with the lads until it got so dark you couldn't play any more. That was what mattered. And that's what education is about. Teachers can only give you facts. True education is about building relationships with people and authority. The greatest value of school is that it gives you a framework to build relationships.

Most writers can remember the moment when they find out they can write. Mine was so embarrassing. It happened at the age of 13. A teacher asked us to write an essay entitled 'My Hobby'. My hobby was trainspotting, and what I *could* have done was write, 'My hobby is trainspotting. Every Saturday I take the train to Newcastle station and collect train numbers.' But I didn't. I began by saying, 'The train stopped on the bridge and I looked down into the murky waters of the Tyne below.' I was wrapping myself in a writer's style that I'd picked up from reading various books. Everyone else in the class got between 10–13 out of 20 for their essays. I got 17½. And I thought, 'This is easy!' So I carried on doing it. My disadvantage was that writing came to me so easily that I never valued it.

I did my 'O' and 'A' levels and passed comfortably. I had a miserable time working for a year before going to college, where I studied drama. I learnt about dramaturgy and about structures of plays – the ways in which plays are not just collections of words, like a wall is not just a collection of bricks, it has three dimensions. Everyone who is not a writer can put a brick on top of a brick and build a wall. But it's nothing, it's bland. A writer, like an architect, can see the structure and can build in three dimensions. And that's what I learnt by studying dramaturgy. I saw the way other people could do it. I understood it almost instinctively.

After teaching Juniors for a year and a half, and then teaching Secondary Drama for a year or so, I saw a job advertised for an actor-teacher to work in Wales in Theatre In Education (TIE). TIE was very new in 1972. I applied for the job and I got it, much to my amazement. The plays we had to perform around schools were either (a) self-written or (b) when we did community theatre, they were very badly written established plays. I found that I was able to look at these plays and see what was wrong with them. It was usually structural. The dialogue was fine, but the play didn't hang together. Again, I had this perception of structure which I was able to bring to this and improve the plays we were doing. It seemed to evolve over a year or two that people in the company would ask me to write our next play. It never occurred to me that this was difficult or even a skill.

I often lie about my first book. It was not *The Custard Kid*. The truth is often a messy thing. My first real book came about as a result of doing TIE work. As the others in the company went off for their summer holidays, they turned to me and said, 'Terry, when we come back we want a Western.' And why? So they could talk in American accents all the time and get away with it! And I looked at the convention and it was John Wayne, 'A man's gotta do what a man's gotta do!'

So I thought, how do you turn that convention on its head? You don't have a tough hero, you have a cowardly hero. And then I thought, how does John Wayne resolve conflicts? And this is going back to narrative structure. John Wayne does it by being faster on the draw or harder with his fists than the bad guy. The resolution is always a violent one. Also, John Wayne always wears a white cowboy hat, and the bad guy a black one. This was all terribly boring, so I thought I'm not going to have black and white hats, I'll have a hero in a grey hat. Also, he'll do wrong, but he'll do wrong because of the situation he finds himself in. And this is what I try to do with genres all the time now – to turn them inside out and on their heads.

The other element involved was the cast. Nigel Bennett, one of our actors, was a natural for a cowardly cowboy – I couldn't call him Billy the Kid, that was too conventional, so being a 'cowardy custard' he became The Custard Kid. Kath in the company couldn't be Calamity Jane, so she became Calamity Kate. Then one of those happy circumstances – a serendipity – happened. I discovered that both of these characters had the initials 'CK' – and that gave me my plot. The characters would have identical bags with the same initials on them, and they would get mixed up.

Next, the Custard Kid gets accused of stealing Kate's bag because he's a *weak* person, not because he's a *bad* person, and he reacts by trying to fight his way out of the situation and gets into worse trouble. The audience are the jury – they've witnessed the events and they have to sit through the Kid's trial. And this was a TIE play – so it gave us an opportunity to look at issues such as justice. The Custard Kid did the crime, but *why* did he do it? And there was no clear-cut right or wrong answer. We toured this play for six weeks. We even swopped characters – we'd pull the characters' names out of a hat, so sometimes I'd be the Custard Kid. When it was my turn, my colleagues would arrange it so that I was found guilty and my punishment would be a hanging!

The play was a lot of fun, and it was educational because there was a lot to think about. And that really set the tone for a lot of what my writing is now – which, first of all, is to engage the audience. You grab them, you hold them, you make them laugh, and when they're laughing you smack them between the eyes with something to think about.

I left the theatre company to become a theatre director, and the next bit of the story is just as hard to believe as the rest. I went to a small library to get a book to read. I'd read most of the books I wanted to read, so I thought, what I'll do is start at 0.001 in the classification system and read my way around to 9.999! And there at 0.001 was *How to be a Writer and Get Published*. Serendipity again. So I picked it up and read it and it gave me two useful bits of information. One was write – W-R-I-T-E – don't just talk about it, do it! The second was to choose something with which you are familiar and comfortable. I'd done TIE, and nobody had written a book about TIE, so I did. I collected together my scripts and I turned them into a book called *Teaching Through Theatre*.

After a year, the book was published by Samuel French but it was such a narrow market and it was not like how I imagined a book to be. I remembered back to my days as a Junior teacher, when I used to start every morning with a story. I had trouble finding good stories to read. *Charlotte's Web* by E.B. White was brilliant. But other stuff was heavy going – even Clive King's *Stig of the Dump*. So I thought, why don't I use my experience as a teacher and go into that market and write stories for children? And I thought of *The Custard Kid*, and how, after six wonderful weeks of laughter and craziness, there was nothing left of the play except memories. I realised what I needed to do was to take a story like *The Custard Kid* and turn it into a children's novel and then it would be preserved.

Unfortunately, I didn't research my market. In 1975 people were not publishing funny stories for children. Books were far more serious and worthy. My book was too wacky, even though it did have a serious message underneath. *The Custard Kid* was rejected 23 times. But one editor at A&C Black saw a potential new market, and said that he'd publish it if I made a few changes. Being so young and naïve, I didn't realise what a breakthrough this was. It took quite a brave editor to say, 'There isn't a market for this, we'll create it.' And they found another author, Jeremy Strong, and we used to write a book each a year for them. After a while, these books became a series, Black's *Crackers*.

Then I started working in secondary schools and came across Reginald Maddock's *The Pit*. As a result, I began writing social realism – books about ordinary kids in ordinary comprehensive schools. These books were for reluctant readers for a Longman series called *Knockouts*. And I churned one of those out a year. It was dead easy because I found I could just switch on a different style, but more than that, I now discovered I had a range of styles.

I probably wrote about fifteen Black and Longman books and then I started to look for new markets, which came in a most unexpected direction. Scholastic had begun to grow but they had no great editorial base whatsoever. They bought in American books called Point and sold them in vast quantities in this country, but they had few original imprints. One of the things they did was to buy one of my Black books – *Ghosts of Batwing Castle* – and turned it into a paperback. And so a door just opened a chink.

The next stage in a writer's career is when she or he is approached by a publisher saying, 'Will you write such-and-such for us?' It happened to me when Scholastic asked if I'd do a 'Father Christmas joke book'. People might turn their noses up at this, but it's work. I applied myself to this book and did something unusual with it because it was a challenge. I eventually did two or three of these books. Then Scholastic asked me to do *True Monster Stories* because I say 'Yes' to just about anything! And I thought, well, there are no such things as *true* monster stories, because a monster by definition is a fabulous creature. What I decided the book would be is a collection of stories that people have *said* are true, and that would be the validation for the 'True' in the title – and not that they are true *per se*. I also wanted to allow the readers to make up their own minds. And how could I do that? By giving them facts. I was very conscious that other books that had presented 'true stories' before were journalistic; they weren't stories, they were newspaper articles. I wanted to bring people and characters into these stories.

I have a very clear vision of what has become my *True* series – and it's how people confront traumatic situations, whether it's a monster, a UFO or a disaster. So, the questions I'm interested in are – what did these people do and how did they react? These books may dramatise and invent characters and dialogue, but the basic confrontation is still true. I'm not there to present my readers with answers, I'm there to make them think and to present them with questions. The *True* series has been very successful. Later, I'll go on to talk about how the publisher would start to tell me what books would be successful before they were even written.

Next, the publishers and I then planned to do a history joke book as a follow-up to the Father Christmas joke book. It would include such gems as, 'Where did the French keep their guillotine? In the chopping centre!!' To pad out the awful jokes we had some anecdotes from history, but we decided that the anecdotes were so much more interesting and entertaining than the jokes. And from there, *Horrible*

Histories emerged, and the joke book never happened. We did just two to start off with – *Terrible Tudors* and *The Awesome Egyptians* – as we didn't know if they'd be a success.

Next came *The Rotten Romans* and *The Vile Victorians*. But it was the fifth *Horrible History* that really did it – *The Blitzed Brits*. It came out in 1995, and quite accidentally it coincided with the fiftieth anniversary of VE Day. The bookshops all wanted books for children on World War Two, but there was only *Anne Frank's Diary*, *Carrie's War* and *Goodnight Mr Tom*. There was nothing for the reluctant or casual reader. So, *Horrible Histories* filled a niche and *Blitzed Brits* went immediately to No. 1. On the back of it, people started to buy up the back catalogue and they waited in eager anticipation for more titles. As Philip Pullman says, a writer needs both talent and luck. That was my bit of luck.

2 WRITING: ROUTINES AND REFLECTIONS

When I started writing I was on a teacher's timetable. The only holidays I had were school holidays. Very quickly I got into the idea that you have to fit your writing into the time available. I became very disciplined about this. A 12,000-word book such as my *Lampton Worm* was written literally in two days. I've also sat at the kitchen table and written while my family were off on holiday. And one book I was writing was episodic and I wrote a chapter every night on the bus going home from work. Eventually, when I gave up full-time employment, I decided that I would build an office in my house – especially as I was writing more non-fiction and I needed my research books around me.

So, into the roof of the house I built a room which became my office. It's connected to the outside world with phones, fax and e-mail, so I'm not out of touch with the world – but it's very much a sanctuary. I sit down at my word processor at 8.00–8.30 a.m. every day, clear away the administration, start writing and work through until 5.00 p.m. I work six days a week. Saturday is my one day off. The last time I took a holiday was eighteen years ago.

I agree to write a book every month. The work usually expands to fill the time available, so I can do a book a month comfortably, whatever length. Sometimes I'll do two a month, but that's pushing it a bit. I always write one book at a time. I usually have a year planned ahead. I sit down with my publishers every September and say, 'What do you want from me next year?' And we'll organise what I'll be writing over the next twelve months. I keep my writing fresh by alternating between writing fiction and non-fiction books. And I tend to do my research in here. I buy books and bring them back here and read them. I also use videos and the Internet.

I used to write on a typewriter and it was so much quicker. You couldn't correct on the typewriter, so you didn't bother. Whereas with a computer I tend to fiddle and cut and paste. I never, ever revise. Editors come back to me and say, 'Change this, change that', and with very bad grace I do. When the editor rings me up and says, 'There's nothing I want to change', I cheer! I hate re-writing. If it's not right the first time, it's never going to be right. For writing to be beautiful it's got to be intuitive and it's got to flow. People that start chopping and changing lose the flow.

There is a symmetry in the best writing which comes from seeing it as a unit. I admire – but can't understand – people who take years over writing books. How do they do it?

When I'm writing, I have an imaginary audience. It's someone who is not a particularly fluent reader and doesn't have a large attention span. The vital thing for me is *not* to come over as, 'I'm an adult, I know this and I'm going to tell you. Are you listening?' That is absolute death, and you see it in book after book. What I am is an ignorant person saying, 'You'll never believe what I found out when I read this book. I'm going to share it with you.' That is my author's voice for *Horrible Histories*, anyway. It's this wonder of discovering about human nature : 'You'll never believe how people used to behave. Could you behave like that?' I am a genuine enthusiast, and that comes across. I am *never* an academic, I'm *never* a teacher and I'm not even an adult. I'm a big kid who wants to share this with other kids, big and small.

Writers learn how to write in the same way they learn how to speak. They imitate. And in the same way you develop your own way of speaking and conversing, you develop your own way of writing. But initially, if you want to be a writer, you imitate, like a parrot. Some people have the ability to imitate, like some birds have. A parrot can imitate, but a curlew can't. Writers happen to be the parrots of the human world. There are so many sparrows and starlings and curlews out there who desperately want to be parrots. How do you begin to tell them, 'Sorry, you're either born with it or you're not'? It's a sad fact of life.

I'm aware that writers can be precious people and those sorts of writers don't always like authors who treat writing as a business. There's an aura around being a writer. And I don't like the aura, though some authors do. I've been to conferences where authors have gone on about their editors, and what 'wonderful people' these editors are, and how they are their friends. I've stood up and said, 'Actually, editors are a waste of space. They are mostly middle-class, middle-aged women from the south of England. Except for middle-aged, I'm none of those things. These people can't relate to me and they can't relate to my audience, who are very often working class. Why are these people in the business?' And the writers are gob-smacked. I had another publisher write to my publisher and say 'How can this man go around saying these things, slagging off the very people who are giving him work?' I don't expect what I say to be popular.

I'm very conscious of my author's voice. Some writers are consciously literate in their style. I'm consciously populist or accessible, but some people look down their noses at these qualities. Sometimes I'll go over what I've just written and adjust it so that it's more natural to speak. Though I never sit here at the screen and read it out loud, I do it in my head. I'm very aware of speech cadences. I just love words and often I'll pour myself into an orgy of words, and I'll go over the top with alliteration or assonance. Poetry is often seen as a higher form of prose, but it's just another weapon in the writer's armoury. Poetry should be used in a far more relaxed way. Writers should feel free to slip into poetry whenever they want to. I do, and I feel comfortable with it.

I used to visit schools, but now I do occasional promotional work in bookshops – and I'll only do talks for children from deprived schools who would not normally go into a bookshop. I became very worried that schools wanted me to teach children how to be a writer, and it's not a transferable skill. What really got to me was a boys' private prep school I visited. The teachers told me they had Harold Pinter the year before. What on earth could Harold Pinter say to 7- to 9-year-old boys?! Why was he there? It was so that the school could boast, 'Last year, we had Pinter, and this year we had that Terry Deary chap.' I have no interest in being a trophy. I was getting more requests from private and grant maintained schools than the schools who really needed it, and I'm sorry, I began to resent it.

A published author can write junk just as much as the next person, in fact they often do. Roald Dahl was a brilliant writer, but there's times when you think, how did the editor let him get away with that? And you know the answer, it's because he's Roald Dahl. In *The Witches*, for example, see how the boy gets from Norway back to England. It's because the plot requires it, and it's explained in two lines and it's totally unbelievable. Not many writers would get away with that – an editor would write in the margin of your manuscript, 'Could you please explain this for the reader?'

Having said all that, Dahl is seminal. I couldn't publish *Horrible Histories* if he hadn't written what he did. He made the idea of horror and black comedy in children's books acceptable. As a result of Dahl's work, the public accept horror and humour and irony. Although my books in no way copy Roald Dahl, I am tremendously indebted to him. No author works in a vacuum, every writer works in a social era and context, and different things are acceptable at different times. Certain writers – like Dahl – make things acceptable; they make new genres, like I've done with *Horrible Histories*. And what I want now is somebody to come along and do something better.

When I was a kid of 16, I got into Rosemary Sutcliffe and Henry Treece. They wrote historical novels. Even at that age, as a non-writer, I was conscious of their technique, which was to pack in subsidiary clauses full of historical information. For example: 'The Roman centurion dressed in a toga came to the wooden door studded with iron and stood under the red-tiled porch roof and looked between the Corinthian pillars'; and so it goes on. And you feel you're being preached to. With my *Tudor Terrors*, I wanted to create adventure stories about authentic historical characters who went through authentic historical incidents. Essentially what I'm doing is dramatising historical events.

With each *Tudor Terror* there is an adventure story which is happening during the latter part of Queen Elizabeth's reign, 1602–1603. And the central characters in the novels are the three generations of the Marsden family. The way that the family resolves their own conflicts is by someone in the family saying 'When I was young such-and-such happened.' And thus they're able to explore stories from their past to solve their own problems. So, there are always two stories running in parallel. If readers pick up any historical facts, it's not because I've rammed them down their throats, it's because they're essential to the story, and they colour the actions of the characters. Historical detail is not just a matter of what people ate or wore, it's the attitudes they had as well. Some of my characters question the attitudes of the people around them. Characters in old historical fiction were more like Madame Tussaud's waxworks that were dragged across cardboard cut-out scenery. But my characters are more like actors in costumes – they're flesh and blood.

With all of these *Tudor Terrors*, Orion, the publisher, needed the actual titles before I'd even written the books for marketing purposes. Though I knew who the central characters would be – a king, a prince, a lord, and so on – and that informed my choice of titles: *The Prince of Rags and Patches*, *The King in Blood Red and Gold* and *The Lord of the Dreaming Globe*, etc.

Basically, there are two types of children's books. There are fiction books where you go to learn about life and to be entertained, and there are fact books where you build up some sort of database of information in your head which at sometime in the future you might need. And never the twain shall meet. I want to blend the two in such a way that I create a new type of book, and the *Spark Files* series is an attempt to blend fiction and science. Science, I felt, was a particularly difficult subject to approach because it's not about people, but abstractions. So, first of all, I needed a fictional framework, for which I chose a family. In that family are all the relationships and conflicts that will make the characters zip off each other.

Also, the main characters are young people because they're approaching the scientific problems they encounter in a naïve way – in the same way that I do, as a non-scientist. In these books, the reader will find out about science, but, as I said, within a fictional framework, and it's the story that draws the reader through. You can experience these books any way you like. You can read the book and do all the scientific experiments as you go along, or you can just enjoy the story and ignore the science sections. And these experiments are not presented as textbook extracts, and they come in many forms. For example, in one of the books, in granny's attic there's a World War Two magazine in which there's a feature, 'How to make your own spin dryer'. Throughout, the characters in the books find all sorts of experiments in all kinds of unlikely places. Each book has a science theme. The first book is about the sun, the moon and the earth. The second book is about changing materials. The third book is about electricity, and so on.

I've written these books in such a way that the experiments are not just inserted into the plot, they're integral to the story. And also, the experiments can be done with everyday, household materials. I hope that the *Spark Files* series will challenge people to see that fact books don't have to be boring and that fictional books don't have to neglect educational concepts.

3 GROWING A BOOK

Growing *Horrible Histories* – the books and the play

For each *Horrible Histories* there is a designer, an editor, a copy-editor, a historical expert, an illustrator – such as Martin Brown – and myself. And an average *Horrible Histories* book will go through various stages. First, I'll send the manuscript to the editor who'll make her comments and then pass it on to a copy-editor, who will look for details such as spelling and punctuation, and then it will be passed on to an expert. And then, when they've all picked over the bones and I've managed to make as few changes as possible, a final draft will be sent to an illustrator such as Martin Brown. And then Martin will send me his roughs. Very occasionally, I'll get him to make the odd change – but Martin spends days and days getting his facts right. He's very thorough.

Martin's a genius. He's an Australian and his sense of humour is totally compatible with what I'm trying to do. It's a great marriage of text and picture. I've

1   A French soldier at the battle of Waterloo had his arm shattered by a British cannonball. He used the other arm to tear off the damaged one then threw it up in the air. "Long live Emperor Napoleon till the death!" he cried. (No wonder the French lost if most of their soldiers were fairly armless chaps).

2   The British were just as cool when it came to having limbs blown off. Lord Uxbridge was sitting next to the British commander, the Duke of Wellington, when a shell blew Uxbridge's leg off. The conversation that followed is probably the most famous war story of all time. Uxbridge turned to the Duke and said, "By God, sir, I've lost my leg!" Wellington took a look and said, "By God, sir, I believe you have!" (Of course it would have been funnier if the Duke had said, "Hop it, Uxbridge!" or "You'll save a bit on boot polish in future.")

3   The French set off to invade Ireland and looked for the Irish rebels to support them. But the French ships were defeated by the British navy and the Irish rebel leader, Wolf Tone, was captured. Wolf was sentenced to be hanged but when his jailers arrived to take him to the scaffold they found him covered in blood. The rebel leader had tried to cut his throat with a penknife, missed the artery and cut his windpipe instead. The Brits didn't want him to die like that – they wanted to hang him! So they gave him a week to recover. Wolf's doctor told him, "If you try to speak you will die." The rebel smiled and said, "That's the best news you could have given me!" Then he died!

4   Historians say that Napoleon's biggest mistake was to attack Russia in winter. His army were beaten by the bitter cold and the snow. But it isn't that simple. The problems started in the summer as he marched through Poland. It wasn't the cold that caused the problems but the heat. The water in Poland's wells was warm and stagnant and began to grow a poisonous scum. As Napoleon's army reached the River Niemann they began to develop typhus – the men suffered a high temperature, pink blotches on the skin and a blue tinge to the face. (Sort of early Rainbow Warriors.) The French set off with 450,000 men but only 95,000 reached Moscow. Only 10,000 returned to France to be fit enough to fight again. The French lost more to the green scum making blue faces than they did to the white snow.

[handwritten margin note: The French may have believed that the typhus was caused by foul water but it is actually transmitted by lice.]

5   Napoleon went into a French shop and asked for a map of the area so he could plan an attack. The shopkeeper asked him, "Do you want a local map or do you want a general map?" Napoleon replied, "What a stupid question to ask! I'm a general so I must have a general map, of course!"

Answer

Numbers 1 to 4 are horrible ... but true. Number 5 is also true, *but* the stupid general was not Napoleon. It was an old Prussian general who made this potty remark in 1870.

[handwritten lines, partly illegible]

Manuscript page for 'Rowdy Revolutions'

been so lucky in getting a quality illustrator like Martin who's in total sympathy and harmony with me. He adds so much to a book. And we've probably only met five times! At first, Martin wrote 100 per cent of the cartoons in the *Horrible Histories* that we did together. I would write the text and Martin would do the illustrations. After a while, I got the hang of the cartoons, and I started to write them too. The books we've done together have definitely matured as we've gone along. At times I'll look at a cartoon now and I won't remember who wrote it. Martin says his job is to read the text and to think of jokes as he goes along. And he says that sometimes he enjoys reading the text so much he forgets that he's supposed to be illustrating – which is a lovely thing to say.

My research methods vary. I use researchers because there's a vast amount of material out there, and I can't read it all, especially with the tight deadlines I work to. So I pay researchers – not so much to give me their specialist expertise but more to act as extra pairs of eyes for me. One of my researchers has been a researcher for Open University, and I also use librarians and teachers. For the World War Two *Horrible Histories* which I'm writing this month, I'm using a military historian. The problem is tuning my researchers into what I need. The example I always think of is when I was doing *The Dreadful Diary*. I needed a bizarre happening for every day of the year. A researcher came back to me and said, 'On 5 December 1895, the first person was stopped for speeding in a motor car.' This is quite quaint, though not that illuminating, but it rang a bell in my mind. So I went to my own sources which said, 'On December 5, a policeman was sitting having his breakfast when a car went past his window very fast. He jumped on his bicycle and cycled five miles until he caught up with the car and fined the driver a shilling.' Now *that's* a great story! That's a *Horrible Histories* story. *That's* what I've got to train my researchers to look for. And while they're doing that, I'm reading general background pieces. I'll be absorbing the very latest research because *Horrible Histories* have research that is as modern and contemporary as I can make it. As I'm researching, one question I constantly ask of myself is, 'What feeling do I get for this period?'

The secret of *Horrible Histories* is that they don't have a format. What my imitators have done is to look at a format and say, 'Oh, these are all the compartments, let's just pour in the information.' As a result, they're as dull as a textbook. Every *Horrible Histories* is different because I come to every book fresh and ignorant. It's always an adventure for me. The reason they succeed is that I don't have a set method. My formula is not to have a formula. When I've got a loose idea of what I want to write, I begin writing, and I don't know what it's going to be until it's written. And once it's written, it's done. I do not overplan – even in fiction – and certainly not in non-fiction. I've got the whole book in my head and it just pours out. Afterwards, I forget everything I've written.

The different media I use in the *Horrible Histories* – the diaries, the letters and so on – are simply a way of allowing a story to be told from the point of view of individual people. In *Even More Terrible Tudors*, there's a story about a young executioner who'd never executed anybody in his life. His first job was to behead Countess Pole. He missed her the first time he took a swipe at her and had to keep chopping. Now the interest for me wasn't from an onlooker's perspective, it was the executioner's, so I told the story from his point of view: 'Dear Mum, I'm here in the Tower of London and you'll never believe what happened to me . . . ' I'm trying to get away from the objective, and to get my readers to experience history subjectively, so that they become that executioner. Generally, I want children to think about how people in certain moments of history felt and also for them to consider what these people were experiencing.

I never set out to write either a definitive or an alternative history to a country or a period, and the dates I provide serve to give a context. I had one criticism lately from a young reader saying that I don't give important information, only things such as a king dying on the toilet. What I set out to do is to demythologise the idea of royalty, and the idea of a king dying on a toilet does that. That kid might not appreciate why that is useful information, and that it was put there for a specific purpose. These books are anti-establishment and aim to counterbalance the anti-septic view of history that people just fought and died. They fought *and* suffered *and* died. This suffering is so often missed out – and without it, history becomes very bland and unreal. It's the same with newspaper reports. Stalin said that if one person dies it's a tragedy, yet if a million people die it's a statistic. He's right. All the time I want to look at the people, the personal, the individuals that make up that million. History is never boring when you look at it on the individual level. In these *Horrible Histories* I'm asking, 'Why do people behave the way they do?' And, ultimately, 'Why do *I* behave the way I do?'

I've just finished a *Horrible Histories* play. It's called *Mad Millennium* and it covers British history of the last thousand years. The first performance will be 5 June 1999 and it's being premiered at the Sherman Theatre, Cardiff. The director is a friend of mine, Philip Clark. The play could have been a bit of light entertainment, taking the funniest stories from history, but I didn't want to do that. I didn't want a pantomime or an end-of-the-pier piece of theatre. What I've done is to take the *Horrible Histories* concept and to write a play about a group of people discovering themselves through history.

The setting for the play is a classroom. Seven kids come into the classroom and they have tensions and relationships amongst themselves. There's one character you don't meet until the end called Master Mind, who's the history teacher. He leaves messages on the blackboard and on tape: 'This is the work you have to do before I get back and test you . . . ' He's very much the traditional teacher. Then in comes Miss Game, the drama teacher, who says, 'Don't worry, we'll look at history through drama.' And so they begin to re-enact scenes from history with her. And it becomes apparent that the characters of the people in the classroom are reflected in the historical characters they play. The bully in the classroom is called Henry, and he plays Henry VIII. The wimp in the classroom is called Edward, and he plays Edward II. And in turn, each of the seven kids become a key historical figure.

The play is also a musical and it's interactive, in that the audience get involved as well. As the play develops, the more the relationships between the characters in the classroom develop, and they eventually become more tolerant of each other. At the very end, Master Mind turns up, and he's hideous. The children put him in an electric chair and fire questions at him. And because it's a *Horrible History*, the questions are about interpretations of history – they're not about facts. And so Master Mind gets them all wrong and he's zapped into unconsciousness. When the kids take Master Mind's mask off, it's really Miss Game, because history is about what both of these teachers represent – it can be about facts but it's also about enjoyment and interpretation. Adults will come away from the play thinking, 'Wow, the layers of meaning in that!' It may sound boring and profound, but actually it's fun and very fast moving!

Bloody Scotland

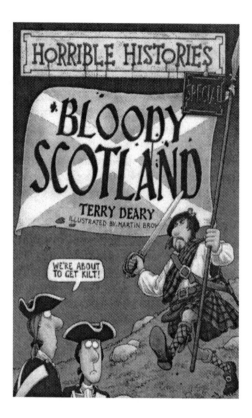

This is a very rare book in that the initial idea didn't come from me or the publishers, but from the readers. I was sitting here at my desk one day when a fax came through from the publisher saying, 'I know you never visit schools, but there's this school in Scotland called Buckie High School and they love your books and they're doing a whole week of activities based on your books. They're cooking according to your recipes and they're dressing according to the pictures. Can you pop in there?' It was so flattering that I broke my rule and I went. I had a great time. They entertained me wonderfully.

While I was at the school I was having a conversation with a librarian in the history department, and the inevitable question came up: 'When are you going to write something about Scotland?' Well, I thought, I'm not Scottish. But I've written books about the Tudors, and I'm not a Tudor. So I thought, why not? So the initiative came from the school, my readers.

The school did a lot of research for me. And I went up to Princes Street in Edinburgh and bought a couple of hundred pounds' worth of contemporary books and gave them to my researcher. So I had material coming in from all over. And the sales manager at Scholastic was very pleased about the book, because he's a Scot himself. He said, 'You write it, and we'll put all our marketing behind it to make it a bestseller.'

I was originally going to call the book *Savage Scotland* but I was overruled by the marketing department at Scholastic, who came up with *Bloody Scotland*. They have strong views on what sells, and I trust them. Actually, titles are so important to me that I've been known to go back and alter an epilogue because the title has changed.

The book was tremendously hard to write because with other *Horrible Histories* – such as the Georgians – I've looked at a small period of a hundred years. With *Bloody Scotland*, I was looking at two thousand years or more of a history of a whole country and I had to condense it all. It was quite vast to hold it all in my head at once. But I had wonderful material. I'm not usually proud of what I do, but I was satisfied with that book.

The publishers asked if I'd do a week of publicity in Scotland. I agreed to it, not knowing the uproar that the book would cause. This article appeared in the *Sunday Times*:

Aye Jimmy, it's a grand sport is pulling the legs off a cow!

by Julie Smith

What did Scotsmen do for sport before they had the World Cup squad to cheer? Well, according to a new children's history book, dismembering dead cows was a popular jape at the Invergarry Games of 1820. Winner? The first to twist off all four legs. The book, *Bloody Scotland*, written by Terry Deary (an English man), portrays the Scots as a barbaric nation with ancestors who love nothing better than cruel pastimes. It suggests that Scotland may hold the record for highest numbers of murdered royalty as well as for the number of murderous kings. It describes the bagpipes as sounding like tortured cats –

That's a misquote.

and mocks the Scottish language as drivel . . .

Another misquote. Later it goes –

Richard Finlay, lecturer in Scottish history at Strathclyde University, condemned the book as 'cheap, sensationalist rubbish'.

He hasn't read it.

He said, 'It verged on the racist and could upset children.' It misses out on Scotland's positive achievements. Are these the things we want to teach children – about Scots being murderers and cruel to animals? If you said things like that about Asians, you would be booked . . .

In fact, if they'd read the book they would have seen that the villains in *Bloody Scotland* are actually the English, and the Scots come out of it very well. This article generated a lot of publicity. The local papers wanted a reaction from me, and the Scottish National MP was on the radio saying that the book was a disgrace. He hadn't read it either. It's wonderful that a children's book can make that sort of impact. Publicity like that you cannot buy! And of course, it has sold in its tens of thousands, and it became the number one best selling book in Scotland – adult's or children's.

One of the books that I bought for research was of Scottish customs and sayings. Some of the Scottish sayings are quite funny and banal, like 'A bald head is easily shaved'. The challenging thing was that I wanted to use some of these sayings, but I needed to liven up the presentation of them. So I took these sayings and I split them in two and mismatched them. And they became 'A crow is easily shaved', and, 'A bald head gets no whiter when it's washed'. But when you've worked through this section, you've got a solid fact. If you present people with non-stop facts, even in my author's voice, they get tired. A different and a more inspiring way to get information across to the reader is to have a quiz. This makes the book interactive and encourages the reader to stop and think.

Bloody Scotland took five weeks to write, and the changes I had to make took another two days or so. I had my structure for the book within a week of research-ing and writing. The structure, as with all my books, just appeared in my head. I did this book all in one file in my computer because I like to be able to access everything at one time, and it makes it easy to move passages of text around.

The structure came fairly easily as I was doing the whole country for two thousand years, and so it automatically had a chronological structure. Throughout the book I alternated the chronological sections, such as the Dark Ages, the Middle Ages and so on, with the theme sections, such as 'Weird words' and 'Wild women and crazy cures'. By doing it this way, you don't get the feeling that you're reading a history book. You're breaking up the chronology with the sections on human customs and the way people lived. So they're interspersed. I like that.

There were subjects which I came across repeatedly during my research. One example was the way that women were treated. While I was writing the Celtic era, I found a bit of information on a particular woman, and I put her in the 'Wild women and crazy cures' section. This is where the word processor is so useful. I simply cut and pasted this information across so that I could use it later. Therefore I was writing the chronology of Scotland, but doing other things in parallel. I also kept coming across many stories on horses, so I created a section especially for horses. Likewise, in the manuscript I sent to the publisher I'd included so many stories on Mary Queen of Scots that they said that the book was unbalanced. There was a huge section on Mary in the middle. So we took it out and put it in my next book, *Even More Terrible Tudors* – no problem! And I had to do some other revision, which was to include more twentieth-century history of Scotland.

Martin Brown and I both wrote the captions for this book. Here's an example of how one of my captions for *Bloody Scotland* looked before Martin illustrated it. The verb 'wirry' means to strangle.

Cartoon: Witch (male) is being executed
Witch: I'm a bit wirried about this.
Executioner: I should wirry.
Witness 1:   Life's too short for wirrying.
Witness 2:   Yes, that's what wirries me.

The very final thing in the whole book is a scathing comment in the form of one of Martin's cartoons. It's pure Martin. The text tells that in the 1700s, the Highlanders were thrown off their farms to make way for sheep. In 1997, the same thing happened – the farmers were thrown off their land to make way for grouse. I think that's a powerful comment. And Martin twists it, takes it further and twists the knife by adding that cartoon. It's brilliant.

One of my favourite stories in *Bloody Scotland* is the one of Queen Finella. She was a prehistoric queen, so the story that has come down about her is only legendary. What I decided to do – as it's almost a fairy tale – was retell it in this form. I was switching on another style, but I was subverting it to make the reader see the humour of the story. I particularly enjoy the use of language here.

Once upon a time there was a beautiful queen and her name was Queen Finella.
    Finella was lovely, but she was ever so sad because her son Malcolm had died. She cried and cried, but that did no good. So, in the end, she decided to find out how Malcolm had died. They say she was a little bit of a witch, but a good witch.
    Finella went to her cauldron and stirred the magic brew, chanting . . .

Until this point it's all fairly conventional. Then I start to slowly hint that this 'fairy tale' might not go the way you expect it to, by giving her a slightly ridiculous chant:

Eye of bat and a
Sprinkle of talcum:
Tell me who killed
Poor little Malcolm!

And it's obvious here that the writer is struggling to find a rhyme for 'Malcolm' – so I just stick in talcum!

The pot bubbled and boiled and then it answered . . .

Your Malcolm died,
the poor young thing,
Murdered by a rotten king!
Dry your eyes, good sweet Finella
Old King Ken's the guilty fella

And again, it's very bad poetry, and with a purpose. With the next sentence I went totally overboard with alliteration.

Now the only King Ken that Queen Fin kenned (knew), was cruel King Kenneth in Kincardine, the kingdom next door.

And this is good fun! And what did the editors do? They cut up my sentence to give the reader a translation of the word 'kenned', even though I'd suggested having a footnote. And it just clutters up the text and kills my prose. You see, many editors don't like footnotes.
    I was sent a lot of research material from Buckie High School. They sent me photocopies of books and material from local history archives. I had to work through all this material, but I can skim and I know what I'm looking for. With this book I wanted stories that were so local they wouldn't normally get noticed by a historian. One example I came across is of three German spies during World War Two that were dropped by a plane in the sea in northern Scotland. But that one didn't get in this book – I put it in *True Spy Stories* instead!
    There's also the story of the wives of the fishermen. They had horrible lives – a truly horrible history. And it's not funny. People tend to think my books are funny. They're not – they're ironic, they're often about the hard lives that people had to live. They're about human resilience. They do have humour, but they're much more

than that. In *Bloody Scotland*, there's much about human resilience – from William Wallace, who suffered days of torture, to my favourite story of the two women who refused to say 'God save the king' and so were drowned as a punishment. It's a wonderful story about two women that said 'Up yours' to the establishment. It's a horrible story, and it challenges you to ask yourself what kind of person you are. So, in all, I was looking for stories which are in themselves quite grim and gruesome but which say something about the conditions in which Scottish people lived.

Shakespeare Stories

Scholastic commissioned this book. They said, 'We've got a great idea for a series, it's called *Top Tens*, and we want you to do something like Top Ten legends.' And I said that there were a lot of different legends, so I narrowed it down to Greek legends. I told them that I don't like writing one-off books, that I like to start a series off with at least two books, so you can create an impetus in the market. They asked me what else I could do and I suggested Shakespeare, and they asked if it was possible, so I said no! So for that very reason I did it – I always look for the impossible.

I told them that I wanted to use my own structure for this one. I already had a couple of structures – one was *True Stories* – in which I have alternating stories and 'fact files'. And with *Horrible Histories* I'd retell stories from history but in different media – newspaper articles, diaries, magazines, etc. So I decided to put these two structures together and come up with a new genre.

First, I researched the ten most regularly performed Shakespeare plays over the last 150 years. And I already had lots of material on Shakespeare anyway. One of many books I used was *William Shakespeare – The Extraordinary Life of the Most Successful Writer of all Time* by Andrew Gurr. It's a light book, but it gives Shakespeare's life in well-organised facts.

I sat down and I imagined what would be the best way for each play to be told. *A Midsummer Night's Dream* has a fairy-tale quality, so it should be told as a fairy tale – but from the omniscient character of Puck. That one just wrote itself. When I came to *Hamlet* I realised it was a rather heavy play, and I wanted to narrate the story in the first person; but who would tell it? – there's only Horatio left at the end! And who could he tell it to? He could tell it to a police inspector who's found all these bodies. As it happens, if you include Yorick, there are ten corpses in the play. And that's ten corpses in the play that's number 1 in the Top Ten. And the story itself becomes an Inspector Clouseau-style investigation. And *Taming of the Shrew* I saw as a play about a woman's problem, so why not write it as a problem page from a woman's magazine? And every time I came to a play, the format just seemed to suggest itself.

Romeo and Juliet is a natural for a photo love story. But the publisher bottled out of doing it with photographs. They said that technically, photographs presented them with problems. And unfortunately, it doesn't work so well in the cartoon-style format we used. In real photo love stories, the actors' expressions are always blank, whatever they're supposed to be saying, and that's where the humour comes from.

With *Twelfth Night*, I went for the *Rupert the Bear* format – pictures with speech bubbles and a quatrain underneath. The publisher said that it was difficult to design. I'd conceded with the photo love story for *Romeo and Juliet*, but *Twelfth Night* I got away with. And with *King Lear* I had to re-write much of it as I had originally incorporated a lot of Shakespeare's own language, and the publisher made me cut a lot of it out.

Out of sheer indulgence I did *Macbeth* in iambic pentameter because it's impossible! And my sheer arrogance of using Shakespeare's own poetic form to retell one of his plays. It's unbelievable! Nobody should be allowed to do it. So I did! Once you get into it, you can see how Shakespeare wrote in this form, and after a while you go around talking to people in iambic pentameter! This is the beginning of *The Ballad of Big Mac*, which is my retelling of *Macbeth*:

> The lightning flashed as red as blood across
> The purple morning sky. It lit the little
> Group of shapeless, gruesome figures
> As they huddled round a pot and chanted.

> *Double, double, toil and trouble;*
> *Fire, burn; and, cauldron, bubble.*
> *Cool it with a baboon's blood,*
> *Then the charm is firm and good.*

> The heath was empty as the witches worked
> Their spells. It seemed that every living thing
> Had fled for safety from the moor or lay
> In hiding underneath the dripping rocks.

> Until a man appeared and splashed along
> The lonely, stony path across the moor.
> A man in leather armour with a sword
> That carried scars and stains from recent battles.

> The witches chuckled and gave toothless smiles
> And stirred and stirred and mumbled frantic curses.
> '*By the pricking of my thumbs,*' one screeched,
> '*Something wicked this way comes. Macbeth!*'

I wanted to use iambic pentameter in the way that Shakespeare did when he was mature, which is not to finish on the end of a line. In *Romeo and Juliet* he was quite clumsy – 'How she doth teach the torches to burn bright, it seems she hangs upon the cheek of night' – and he used all these end-stop lines.

What I wanted from my text was that as you read it you could hear the rhythm but that it wouldn't come over in such an obvious and laboured way as, 'Humpty Dumpty sat on a wall'. I wanted it to flow. And that's incredibly difficult to do. At the same time you've got to write it so that the plot actually moves forward. Things have got to happen. First of all, you set the scene, which is the lightning flashing in the sky, because the atmosphere is dictated by the weather. It's a conventional sort of image, and a common way for a theatre director to portray the witches – with lightning flashing. It also shows the disruption in the universe.

I incorporated the witches' charms from the play – which are not in iambic pentameter – and by putting them in italics, the reader is aware that these are Shakespeare's own words. Macbeth enters as early as the third paragraph. Something's got to happen. You can't do a Rosemary Sutcliffe and build up the atmosphere endlessly. So the witches are there, Macbeth's there, and the reader is wondering what is going to happen when they meet. And that's the motive to turn the page. And in the opening twelve lines I've achieved a lot – I've set the place, I've introduced a group of mysterious characters, I've introduced Macbeth, I've begun the plot and I've also done it all in iambic pentameter. And it gets away from the idea that poetry must have rhyming lines – which is something that teachers don't seem to discourage enough. Too much of children's poetry I come across rhymes. Everybody should write in iambic pentameter, because until you do, you don't realise how good Shakespeare is. And hopefully, as a result of reading my version, the reader will say, 'I'd like to try that.'

The plot was fairly simple to reduce in length. Essentially, the play is the story of Adam and Eve. Adam is tempted, and Eve – Lady Macbeth – reinforces the temptation. The witches are the serpent saying, 'There's the apple.' And it's Lady Macbeth who says 'Go on, eat it.' And Macbeth does, and commits a murder and the consequences are that he stirs up various people who eventually kill him. And the victors are the witches. I left out Banquo as he's part of a subplot that looks at Macbeth's guilt in detail, and murdering Duncan is enough of a motive for guilt anyway. I only had so much space, and this subplot was not vital, so I took it out. It's like the casket scene from *The Merchant of Venice* – it's not entirely relevant to the main plot, and what I did in that case was to remove it from the main story, and to turn it into a spoof of the television programme *Blind Date*!

Overall, my aim with this book was to give the readers an experience, to make them feel that wherever they dipped into the book they would get a smack in the face. If they'd read Shakespeare before they would never have seen it quite like that. Having read it, a reader might respond with 'I didn't know he was that enter-taining.' Interspersed between the ten plays are all the anecdotes. My researcher went to Stratford and found out lots of information about things that happened on the stage during performances of the plays. And it is these sorts of details that brings the whole book to life, in one respect.

In addition, I wanted to give the impression that Shakespeare is not a literary writer, and that you can't detach him from the stage for which he was writing.

Shakespeare didn't write plays to be read – he wrote them to be seen on stage. And it's a fact that people went to his plays for very different reasons. They didn't go to the theatre to be told, 'Sit in your seat and be quiet and listen and clap politely.' I wanted to give a whole context to his plays – a social history, a history of the theatre and a history of Shakespeare all interwoven.

I tell the stories in different styles so the reader never gets bored. Some things worked better than others. For example, I think *Hamlet* is pitched at an adult level. And it took me four weeks to write this book in all. But the bad news was that two weeks after I launched the book in Shakespeare's home town of Stratford, the town was flooded. Perhaps I upset the Bard, and his spirit rose up in anger and vengeance saying, 'Who's this bloke from Sunderland trying to rewrite my work?!'

4 SERIES PUBLISHING

Series publishing is a concept like Mills & Boon, whereby a publisher creates something that the public likes, and the public likes what it knows and the public knows what it likes. So publishers package it and present it and the public buy it unread, unrecommended. The public have read others in the series and they know they will enjoy it. This is either (a) good, because it hooks people on to good literature and keeps them coming back for more, or (b) it's disastrous because you get absolute porridge churned out time after time dressed up to look like caviar.

The problem with series publishing is that I sometimes worry that children buy my books and don't read them, they simply want the satisfaction of collecting them. I suspect that happens with *Goosebumps*. I worry when kids come up to me in a bookshop with fourteen pristine books for me to sign. I know which kids really enjoy my books as they come up to me with fourteen tatty copies because they've read them over and over again.

Publishers have a habit of selling books before they're written. This worries me immensely. I wrote a book called *True Monster Stories*. It sold 25,000 copies in the first year. The publisher then asked me to write *True Horror Stories*. They showed me the cover of it, and I hadn't even written it yet. And then they told me they'd sold 6,000 copies. Apparently, they'd subbed in to various bookshops who had liked the title. This is fine, because I was able to write it and I was proud of what I did. With *True Shark Stories*, though, it was a different story. Someone had agreed to write the book for them, but what they did produce was not up to standard. And the publisher had sold the book to the bookshops, who were now waiting for their copies. So, from knowing nothing about sharks, I went from 0 to 22,000 words in eight days. I researched and wrote the entire thing in that time. And I'm very pleased with what I did.

But I do worry about series publishing. It makes publishers and bookshops very rich, but what is it doing for the readers? And what happens when a child has to choose between a *Goosebumps* and a quality non-series book like Anne Fine's *Bill's New Frock*? The child will go for *Goosebumps*, and for the wrong reasons. Single books rarely make an impact in the trade, and the very few exceptions over the last couple of years are things like Melvyn Burgess's *Junk*, J.K. Rowling's *Harry Potter* and Philip Pullman's *Northern Lights*.

I'm proud of my own series books. With the *Horrible Histories*, every book is different. And I'm actually quite pleased with my *True Stories* series. Even though the books all have the same format, they do have integrity.

The problem with creating my own genres is that people copy them. I can do nothing about it. That brings the genre into disrepute. So I have to be continually inventing new ways to be different – such as with my new *Spark Files* series. If they're a success, they'll be copied. If they're a failure, they won't. People sit in editorial offices, look at the top ten bestsellers and cherry-pick, saying, 'We'll have some of those and some of those.' The one thing I don't like about series publishing is that it can discourage originality. *Goosebumps* has been imitated endlessly, and so have my *Horrible Histories*.

SELECTED CURRENT TITLES

Fiction

Tudor Terror Series (Orion) including:
The Prince of Rags and Patches
The King in Blood Red and Gold

The Spark Files (Faber & Faber) including:
Over the Moon
Chop and Change

Shadow Play (André Deutsch)
Diary of a Murder (Ginn)
The Treasure of Crazy Horse (A&C Black)
The Joke Factory (A&C Black)
Ghost Town (A&C Black)

Non-fiction

Horrible Histories (Scholastic) including:
The Vile Victorians
The Twentieth Century
The Rotten Romans
Wicked Words
Bloody Scotland
The Blitzed Brits

Top Ten (Scholastic) including:
Top Ten Shakespeare Stories
Top Ten Greek Legends

The Knowledge – Potty Politics (Scholastic)

True Stories (Scholastic) including:
True Detective Stories
True UFO Stories

Shivers series (Franklin Watts) including:
Mystery
Spooks

By Martin Brown: *Poisonous Postcards*

An introduction to . . . Helen Cresswell

WHAT TYPE OF BOOKS DO YOU WRITE? There are two main categories of novels I write – fantasy and humour. Sometimes the two overlap, as in *The Piemakers*.

WHAT ARE YOUR BOOKS ABOUT? In the fantasies – mysteries, hints, the fluidity of time. In *The Bagthorpes Saga* – the absurdity of modern life seen through the eyes of three generations of a family who are undoubtedly off their trolleys.

BORN: Nottinghamshire, 11 July 1934.

EDUCATION: Nottingham Girls' High School and King's College, London.

LIVES: In a tiny village in Nottinghamshire.

PREVIOUS OCCUPATIONS: Fashion buyer, teacher.

FAMILY/PETS: My elder daughter, Caroline, read English and is now a producer with Central TV and lives in Kenilworth with her partner and their beautiful 2-year-old daughter. My other daughter, Candida, has just finished her Ph.D. at Oxford – in Animal Behaviour – and is taking up a three-year Research Fellowship at Newcastle University. I am inordinately proud of them both! Our Persian cat was the role model for the magical cat in *Bag of Bones*. Our two shaggy dogs, Whiskey and Boris, were the prototypes for the hopeless Zero in *The Bagthorpes Saga*.

HOBBIES: Reading, walking, gardening, collecting antiques.

MOST TREASURED POSSESSION: A water-colour of a Victorian girl by a stream.

LANGUAGES TRANSLATED INTO: Japanese, German, French, Italian, Swedish, Danish, American.

LITERARY AWARDS: Phoenix Award for *The Night-Watchmen* – for an outstanding novel 20 years continuously in print – (USA, 1988); runner up for the Carnegie Medal with *The Piemakers* (1967), *The Night-Watchmen* (1969), *Up the Pier* (1971) and *The Bongleweed* (1973); runner up for Whitbread Award – *The Secret World of Polly Flint* (1982); runner up for Guardian Award – *The Night-Watchmen* (1969).

TELEVISION AWARDS: Writers Guild nomination – *Lizzie Dripping* (1973); BAFTA nominations – *Five Children and It* (1990) and *The Demon Headmaster* (1996); Royal Television Society nomination – *The Demon Headmaster* (1997).

TELEVISION WORK INCLUDES: Books read on BBC's *Jackanory* programme – *The Piemakers, The Night-Watchmen, The Signposters, The Outlanders, Up the Pier, The Wilkses, A Game of Catch*. The first two books of *The Bagthorpes Saga* were adapted by James Andrew Hall into a six-part BBC series. I have written books/dramas side by side with *Lizzie Dripping, The Secret World of Polly Flint, Moondial* and *The Return of the Psammead*. My adaptations include *Five Children and It* (E. Nesbit), *The Phoenix and the Carpet* (E. Nesbit), *The Demon Headmaster* (Gillian Cross – three series) and

The Famous Five (Enid Blyton – seven episodes). I am currently working on the screenplay of a feature film of my novel *Stonestruck* and a 26-part animation of Alison Uttley's *Little Grey Rabbit Stories.*

FAVOURITE BOOKS: Poetry, and anything by Thomas Hardy.

FAVOURITE MUSIC: Bach and Mozart.

FAVOURITE FILMS: *Top Hat, Guys and Dolls.*

FAVOURITE LINES OF POETRY – Emily Dickinson:

> Exultation is the going
> of an inland soul to sea
> Past the houses – past the headlands
> into deep eternity
>
> Bred as we, among the mountains,
> can the sailor understand
> The divine intoxication
> of the first league out from land?

WHICH ONE OF YOUR CHARACTERS WOULD YOU MOST LIKE TO BE? Josh in *The Night-Watchmen.*

WHAT WERE YOU LIKE AT THE AGE OF 11? Myself!

ENJOYED VISITING SCHOOLS BECAUSE: Children cheer me up.

WHY DO YOU WRITE? Because it is a compulsion.

IF YOU WEREN'T A WRITER: I'd be an artist or an actress.

AMBITIONS: I don't honestly think I have one. I like where I'm at.

WHICH FOUR WORDS DESCRIBE YOU BEST? Having consulted with my daughters and friends, they came up with: hopelessly impractical, hypersensitive, funny and deep.

WHAT WOULD YOU LIKE TO HAPPEN IN THE TWENTY-FIRST CENTURY? For my family to blossom and be happy and useful.

WHICH OF YOUR BOOKS WOULD YOU LIKE TO BE REMEMBERED FOR? I have a feeling it will be *The Piemakers, The Night-Watchmen* and *The Bagthorpes Saga,* but my own personal favourite is *The Bongleweed.*

1 HOW THE READER BECAME A WRITER

My mother taught me to read when I was four. I can still see the books – they were called *The Radiant Way*, and they had really pretty pictures. The minute I could read my mother would take me every week to the library and get four books out for me. I can still smell the library, with its parquet flooring. It's the smell of magic to me. As a young reader, the books I really, really loved were Andrew Lang's fairy tales – the Yellow, Blue, Green and Violet and so on.

In those days there weren't children's books like there are now, and we didn't have much money, but my mother did have whole bookshelves of classics – Shakespeare, the complete works of Thomas Hardy and Jane Austen and others. There weren't enough children's books for me to read, so, at a very early age, I was reading Palgrave's poetry anthology *Golden Treasury*. I knew it almost by heart. And one minute I would be reading Enid Blyton and the next minute *Pride and Prejudice*.

It's amazing how my writing started. My mother would come up to my bedroom at some unearthly hour and find me still reading in bed. She'd say, 'Come on, you'll ruin your eyes. Put the light out.' And I'd lie there not wanting to go to sleep. To pass the time, I'd make up little rhymes inside my head. That would have been at the age of five or six. A bit later, I remember thinking to myself that these rhymes were not real poems because they were inside my head, so I started to write them down. Almost everything I wrote through my childhood and adolescence was poetry. It was my great love. I knew I was going to be a writer, and I wanted to be a poet. I remember feeling very worried about this because I realised that all the poets were men, but still I carried on.

My very first published poem was 'The Seagull' in *The Mickey Mouse Club* comic:

> Swooping with a plaintive cry
> O'er the flapping sails on high,
> the seagull, pure and white
> comes flying from a distant height

I can't remember the middle verse. But then it goes:

> And once again he soars on high
> A silver speck on a sunlit sky

a something something on the sea:

> the lovely seagull pure and free.

And I got 10 bob – 50p – for it! I was nine when this was published.

I taught myself to write poetry by imitation. I would read a Keats ode and I would work out the shape of the stanza and the beats of the lines and I would write a poem, say in the style of Keats' 'Ode to the Nightingale' or *The Faerie Queene*. Then I got on to Gerard Manley Hopkins and sprung rhythms, and Dylan Thomas. So, in a way, I was teaching myself by doing the equivalent of five-finger exercises or playing scales. This was my apprenticeship. It got to the point where I nearly thought in iambic pentameters! Poetry was like breathing to me. And if I changed a single word I would write the whole poem out again. Whereas other kids would play with Lego, I played with words. I was very much a book- and word-orientated child. My heroes were Faber & Faber because they did all the best poetry – de la Mare and T.S. Eliot. Though the writers that were seminal for me in my teenage years were Thomas Hardy and Wordsworth.

At school I became the clown, and I made people laugh as a coping strategy. I was very popular. I never let on to other children that I was writing this poetry. But then I got to sixteen and I had poems published in the school magazine and then I won a national poetry competition. So that rather gave it away. The fact of the matter was I had to pretend to be like everybody else, and yet I knew I wasn't. I felt totally different from the rest, so I had this camouflage right back from when I can remember. I felt like a subversive. And I think my poetry actually benefited from being kept under wraps. Even now, my instinct is not to talk about my writing too much, and to be careful who I discuss it with. But basically, I was obsessed with writing from the word go.

Throughout my childhood and teens I had poor health. By twelve, I was my present height, and I developed a spinal disorder and I was in hospital a fair bit. I went to a little private school and was doing French and Latin by the age of seven. By nine I was in the twelve-year-olds' class. And when I got my scholarship to Nottingham Girls' High School, I was still ahead of my year group. And much to my mother's disgust, I wasn't made a prefect when I got to sixteen. My school had got me sussed as anti-establishment and subversive. And that's basically how I've always been.

In my first term at King's College I entered a poetry magazine competition judged by Alfred Noyes with my poem 'Beauty Forsaken'. Guess who won! And as a result, all these arty types who ran the magazine came fawning on me. I've never wanted to belong to anything, particularly a bunch of posers, so I stopped writing for a little while. Later, when I was still at university, I wrote several stories that were broadcast by the Home Service on a programme called *Morning Story*. I also wrote my first children's book which was never published. I've still got it. It has my own water-colour illustrations in it. It's called 'Priscilla and the Sea King'. It's like *Alice in Wonderland* under the sea, and there are lots of funny rhymes in it.

I knew that I was only biding my time until I eventually became a writer. I worked for a while as a fashion buyer in Norwich, and I wrote an adult novel. It was like *Rebecca*, only set in Norwich and on the Broads. That too was never published. Next, I worked for a chap in London who was working on a book – a psycho-analytical study of Van Gogh. Then I taught myself shorthand and typing and ended up as a secretary in the BBC Natural History Department in Bristol. During the office hours – as there was often little to do – I wrote what eventually became my first published children's book, *Sonya-by-the-Shore*. After that, I did some supply teaching in Nottingham. Meanwhile, I sent *Sonya-by-the-Shore* to the Brockhampton Press, a division of Hodder & Stoughton in Leicester. They sent it back saying that unfortunately it didn't fit their list, but that it had great charm and that it would eventually find a publisher. So I decided to get an agent. I looked in *The Writers' and Artists' Yearbook.* and wrote to A.M. Heath. and I've been with them ever since.

Then I wrote *The White Seahorse* and got married and had my first child. This was all in quick succession, and a shock to my system. I'd never even picked a baby up before, and I was very isolated and I had post-natal depression. And it was as though a head of steam was building up. In the evenings, when my husband got home, I would write. I wrote a book called *Where the Wind Blows*. Then came *The Piemakers* and I sent those two together to Faber & Faber. From then on it all just took off and I never did a stroke of work again in my life, except occasionally I would go into schools and help with remedial readers.

At this time I was very isolated. It was only in my early thirties that I began to meet and become friendly with kindred spirits. C.S. Lewis said 'we read in order to know that we are not alone'. In those early days the only place I ever came across ideas and subjects I was interested in was in a book. So I started keeping a Commonplace Book. I copied down quotes and extracts that resonated, to store up my confidence. I still keep it, though it has trailed off to a mere trickle in later years.

2 WRITING: ROUTINES AND REFLECTIONS

I write here, on the floor in my study, leaning my back against the chaise longue. I like to write facing the window. I used to write at my desk, which I bought from Faber & Faber when they moved from Russell Square to Queen Square. I like to think that Eliot or de la Mare would have sat at this desk as they were once directors of the company.

The only time I'll work 9 to 5 is when I'm doing a television script – as you're talking about craftsmanship, about doing a job of work and meeting a deadline. And I like that. You can't be forever creating, and in a way, I feel almost as if I'm written out. I'm not that passionate about saying anything anymore. And as I've got to find some way of spending my day, I might as well do adaptations.

I have pale pink or ivory-coloured pens with sepia ink for writing timeless fantasy. I have bright scarlet pens with black ink for writing *The Bagthorpes* or anything modern. I write all my television scripts in black ink. I write in big blank books which I decorate myself with collages. I'll put pictures and postcards on the cover, things which will have something to do with the themes of the story. I write in longhand in these books, only using the right-hand side of the page. I write very fast and I make very few corrections. In my youth – and on a good day – I would probably write 3–4,000 words. These days, it doesn't come as easy, and I do about 1–2,000 words. If I'm doing an adaptation, it's something like tens of thousands, because I just scribble away.

With most of my books I simply write a title and a sentence, and I set off and the road leads to where it finishes. All my books are like journeys or explorations. Behind my desk I used to have this saying by Leo Rosten pinned up on the wall that went 'When you don't know where a road leads, it sure as hell will take you there.' When I first read that, I thought, that's exactly it! That's what happens when I start on my books – I really don't know what's going to happen; it's quite dangerous, in a way. I often put off starting because it seems a bit scary. Yet at the end of the day, I feel that a story has gone where it's meant to have gone.

I perceive myself as more of an ideas writer. On the whole I don't go in for plots – though I have tended to do so more in the stories written specifically with TV adaptation in mind – *The Secret World of Polly Flint, Moondial*, etc. I make a distinction between plot and story. A plot is just a mechanical thing, whereas a story is organic – it actually grows out of ideas or characters or a combination of ideas and characters. And stories have meaning. A story will resolve itself. Stories connect and people can tune into them. Whereas a plot is almost a mechanical thing.

I also make a distinction between fact and truth. I hold no particular brief for Bertrand Russell, but am bound to say that I'm with him when he says 'It is a dangerous error to confound truth with matter-of-fact. Our life is governed not only by facts, but by hopes; the kind of truthfulness which sees nothing but facts is a prison for the human spirit. To kill fancy in childhood is to make a slave to what exists, a creature tethered to earth and therefore unable to create heaven.'

I am very uninterested in facts and know hardly any. An average ten-year-old could probably beat me at *Trivial Pursuit*. Someone once said, 'The great questions are those an intelligent child asks and, getting no answers, stops asking.' I'm still asking. These are not the 'how' questions but the 'why' questions. And they're probably to do with the nature of 'reality'. I always put that word in inverted commas. I have never quite succeeded in believing in what most people call the 'real world'. I don't see it as particularly real. I go with Blake: 'The imagination is the only real and eternal world, of which our vegetable world is but a pale shadow.' The real landscapes are the inner ones. That, at the bottom, is what most of my fantasies are about.

I become quite defensive about this idea, which is how I felt when I wrote *The Night-Watchmen*. That came about as a result of the general feeling at the time – the mid to late 1960s – that everything had to be based in reality. And that's exactly what *The Night-Watchmen* is about. The night train in the story is a metaphor for the imagination, and it's under threat. The Greeneyes can't bear to think that Josh and Caleb have their own freedom and the ability to escape.

A psychiatrist once told me at a conference that the plant in *The Bongleweed* is also a symbol of the creative imagination. And he's right. For me, above all my other books, *The Bongleweed* expresses this idea of mine most clearly. It's the closest thing I have to a credo. And whereas there are the Greeneyes in *The Night-Watchmen* – the threat to Josh and Caleb – in *The Bongleweed* there are the adults, who want to give the plant a Latin name, and they want to tame it, control it and, ultimately, destroy it. With both *The Bongleweed* and *The Night-Watchmen*, it was only in long retrospect that I could see what these books were all about. I'm not always aware of the meanings of a book as I'm writing it. But I do strongly believe that the real strength of any book is subliminal, that the words are merely a surface, and that all the meanings are unconscious.

From the moment you are born you are building an inner landscape. In my youth, I spent more time in than out. I do worry about children playing computer games and watching cartoons. Computer games and cartoons don't nurture the imagination in the same way that books do. When I used to visit schools, I told the children that if they didn't exercise their imaginations they'd better take care that they're never taken hostage, because the only place you've got to go is inside your head. If there's nothing in there, you're a goner. If you don't feed your imagination, it will shrivel up and die inside you. But the solution is easy – read poems, stories, books, whatever. So basically, that's my only idea – the power of the imagination – which I keep saying over and over again in different ways. I think a lot of writers do that; they cover the same idea, but from different approaches, in different stories.

I never do drafts. The only thing I do drafts of are television scripts. I have never, ever done more than one draft for a book. If you got one of my manuscripts and compared it with the book it would be word for word the same. Though editors will sometimes have to point out things to me such as the Amazon is not in Africa, or occasionally they might ask me to make something a bit clearer. And although I don't do drafts as such, I will spend a long time on certain passages, polishing them as if they were a poem. I did that with *The Bongleweed* in the section where the plant takes over the graveyard. I think of my major fantasies – like *The Piemakers*, *The Night-Watchmen*, *The Bongleweed* – as almost being poetry. Those books were written in the same kind of process. It was as if my poetry skills were still there, even though I hadn't written poetry for a while. In fact, I would say that some of my best descriptive passages are in *The Bongleweed*. This is one of them:

> The flowers were brimful with sunlight, suffused with it so that each individual blossom seemed itself to be a source of faint, glowing light. The heads were alive, they sniffed the wind like pale, fluorescent foxes.

I've always had this habit of using challenging words in my books. The only way that anyone built a vocabulary is by seeing a word in context. And usually, if a word is correctly used in context, you can guess perfectly well what it means, and if you can't, there's always the dictionary. Editors do often tell me to change words, and I'll tell them that I'm leaving it as it is!

Too much literary analysis can be harmful to writing, I think. In fact, all my great friends in life – like Leon Garfield, Richard Kennedy, Cedric Messina – were all self-taught. None of them went to university. As a result, they could actually *think*, and read things and respond – absolutely freshly. If you get brought up through the system – reading F.R. Leavis and the like – reading all these critics, these intermediaries, you would be told how to respond to books. I have no time for that.

As a children's writer, one does have a great responsibility. This isn't the case with writing for adults. And on the whole, adults read only to reinforce their own prejudices and inclinations. If something doesn't fit in with what I think, I don't bother reading it, but if it does, I will. I don't actively think about this responsibility or the morality in my own work. But I'm always on the side of the child in my books, rather than the adults. Adults can be very unreasonable.

I think all writers have this cold, calculating eye – weighing everybody up, deciding whether to make fun of someone or turn them into a villain or whatever. All writers do this. I told my daughters recently that Graham Greene had said that there was a splinter of ice at the heart of every writer. And they hated me saying that. They didn't agree. But I have. At rock bottom, I'm a total loner. And I think I have got a splinter of ice – and I'm really glad it doesn't show. It doesn't mean I don't love my daughters, but I know what he means – as, in a way, everything is grist for the mill. Everything.

One of the best compliments I've ever had was when I was at the Edinburgh Festival one year. I was with the author Chris Powling and he said that he wanted to introduce me to someone who was longing to meet me. And it was Anne Fine. I'd never heard of Anne then, but we started to talk and she told me about the time that her daughter was just going off to Oxford University to read History. They'd been clearing her room out and they'd come across an old diary she'd kept. And then Anne showed me a photocopy of the flyleaf of the diary, and it said,

> This is dedicated to Helen Cresswell, whose books have sped me through my childhood.

I was very moved by that, and it still brings a lump to my throat as I say it.

3 GROWING A BOOK

The Piemakers

Illustration by V.H. Drummond from *The Piemakers* by Helen Cresswell

I saw a story in a newspaper about this village in Yorkshire called Denby, where, over the centuries, if there was some great national event, like the Battle of Waterloo or the Corn Laws, they would bake this enormous steak and kidney pie for all the locals – all thousands of them. And once there had been one that had gone wrong due to the hot weather in August, and instead of eating the pie they had a funeral for it, and they buried it in quicklime and issued black-edged mourning cards to raise money! In this particular year, five royal babies had been born and there was this photograph in the paper of this stainless steel pie dish and it was floating down the river and it had a pop group playing in it! I thought this was absolutely absurd!

I would have liked to have gone up there to have a look, but I couldn't as my first daughter was still a baby then.

I had the title for the book right from the start. It's too obvious to miss. It had to be called *The Piemakers* – and in the newspaper clip it actually referred to the people as 'the piemakers of Denby Dale'. In fact, many of my earlier book titles were similar – with *The Beachcombers*, *The Signposters*, *The Outlanders*, *The Watchers* – because, in a way, I think I was setting out my stall, saying '*this* is what it's about, *The Night-Watchmen*'. I haven't done that so much lately.

I wrote a prologue for the book as I wanted it to be grounded in the real world, even though I knew I'd made the whole thing up. I wanted the reader to be seduced into thinking that this really happened.

In a way, this one took far less time to germinate than some of my other books. Some have taken twenty or thirty years. That autumn, in 1965, I thought that if I couldn't go to see the pie I'd have my own. So I changed the name of the village from Denby to Danby and set off writing it, without any plan. I wrote the title at the top of the page and began. It took about three weeks to write. I wrote it very fast. And there was no polishing with this one – it was just one single draft. It's about the fastest book I've ever written, so fast that it was as if it wrote itself.

I don't really remember that much about writing it, but I do remember loving it – and not just the little girl, Gravella, but also her mother and father, Jem and Arthy. I loved the craftsmanship of Arthy, and the spikiness of Jem – she's a sort of Northern archetype – spiky on the outside but very warm-hearted on the inside. I totally entered into the world as I was writing it. Even now I look at some of the details in the book, like the description of their little front parlour in Chapter 6 – with the curtains that she runs her hands down, and I think, where did that come from? How did I know about that?

> They all rose and Jem led the way through the narrow flag-stoned hall into the parlour. There was always a faint smell of must and pressed rose petals in the parlour that filled Gravella with excitement. Why it should smell of must she could not tell, because Jem dusted it every day of her life, tending it as lovingly as her herb garden itself. The dried rose petals were in little glass bowls scattered about the room 'to keep the air sweet', as Jem said.
>
> Gravella placed one of the oil lamps on the mantelshelf and the other on the table and the room sprang into life. The corners gathered shadows. The brocade cushions gleamed softly, rose and gold. Jem edged Essie round to the tapestry chair by the fireplace from which she would have the best view of the curtains and the cushions which lay neatly along the back of the long settle.
>
> 'Sit yourself down, Essie,' she fussed. 'Gravella'll fetch a spill and put in to the fire and it'll be cosy in no time. Oh! Getting quite dark outside, I see. Don't the evenings draw in? I'd best draw the curtains, or we'll have half the Dale peering in at us.'
>
> She went to the window, and drew the curtains with a grand sweep. They, too, were of brocade, and she secretly stroked her rough fingers down their softness before turning back to face Essie.
>
> 'Ain't they new curtains, Jem?' she said sharply peering forwards.
>
> 'What? Oh, them!' Jem shrugged. 'Newish.'

That whole thing – of Jem loving to have her front parlour as somewhere very special, and then Essie, the sister-in-law, coming over and Jem's pride of possession of her lovely things – I just think that when you're writing, you're not actively thinking any of that, it just arrives. And it's difficult for me to talk about the language I use. I never think about it, even when I'm writing. I also like this passage with Gravella from Chapter 2:

> She had never seen a play, but she knew that there were such things in London, and she always went to see the strolling players when they came with their wagons to the harvest supper.

This next sentence I really love:

> Even after she was supposed to be in bed she would creep up behind a hedge and watch them under the strange blend of moonlight and rushlight, tiptoe on their shadows while the bats rushed past them and the people of Danby Dale stared with pale, upturned faces.

I can just see that moment with the light and the bats. It's so vivid.

I can't remember how I came across the name 'Gravella', but I must have played around with various ideas to come up with that one. You'll notice that my characters are never called anything like 'John' or 'Susan'. They'll be 'Arthy' or 'Jem' or 'Minty' or 'Else'. I used to have a notebook in which I'd collect names, and would sometimes look around graveyards for any good ones! In fact, the names 'Joshua' and 'Caleb' – from *The Night-Watchmen* – I've been told, come from a piece in the Old Testament. I must have read it when I was at school and I must have stored those names away in my mind.

I first sent *The Piemakers* to Dent, and it was turned down by their new editor. The main reason given was that the parents in the book were called Jem and Arthy, not 'Mummy' and 'Daddy'. The editor asked if I would consider rewriting – more from the child's point of view, and also changing their names. And I thought, no! Parents are people too, they have names. I think it was also because at that point in my life I didn't want to be put in this category of being Mrs Somebody and being called 'Mummy'.

When I used to do school visits I would sometimes walk into a school and there would be this amazing artwork done by the children. These were very imaginative and inspired responses from both the teachers and the children. One school responded to a picture book I did called *My Aunt Polly*. On one page of the book, this girl imagines such a thing as a mile and a half long green scarf. And this school had knitted this massive scarf that stretched all the way around their football pitch. Every child from the school had knitted their own segment and had crocheted their name on it. I've still got it in my loft. I thought that was fantastic! Another brilliant school – inspired by *The Piemakers* – held their own pie-making competition. So that was another nice visit for me. I do like it when people come together to produce something, it gives a school a great sense of working as a community, which is very much the sentiment behind *The Piemakers*.

4 WRITING FOR TELEVISION

I do get fed up with this sort of sniffy attitude that says 'books are good, television is bad'. And I know that writers like Malcolm Bradbury have been subjected to this attitude as well – this sense that people feel you're selling yourself a little way down the river, that the filthy lucre's coming into it, and it's not quite as pure as writing books. In fact, English literature is almost purely an oral tradition. Everything – all early poetry, early dramas – from *Beowulf* and the Mystery Plays and through Shakespeare was oral. The novel has a relatively short pedigree in the scale of things. And we mustn't forget that our greatest literary figure was a dramatist. It's absurd to say that any book is better than television. It's like saying reading a Barbara Cartland is better than watching an Alan Bennett monologue or a Dennis Potter play. There are good and bad books and there's good and bad television. The best drama for television has the flow and the rhythm of the best of poetry or prose. And they're not mutually exclusive. A child can consume both and be enriched.

But when it comes down to it, I value the book infinitely above the television in childhood, because the book is the prime way that the child's imagination is stimulated and nurtured. And alongside children's fantasy play, reading is the most fundamental tool in the development of the imagination.

When I do an adaptation I have more or less *carte blanche*. I write the first draft with no outside input at all. Before I begin I will speak with the director/producer about any specific parameters he or she might have – such as can we afford snow, which was an issue with both *The Demon Headmaster* and *The Phoenix and the Carpet* – or possibly controversial areas – I was worried, for instance, about children being sealed into a tower block that was to be set on fire, at the end of *The Demon Headmaster* series. The BBC thought we'd get away with it, and we did – though there was a lot of post-production worry about the possibility of children climbing up rubbish chutes!!

With the first draft of a script I also usually send a couple of pages of notes to the director – about things I want emphasised, such as the use of music or special effects. After the first draft there will usually be a meeting between myself and the producer and director. By then the designer will have seen the scripts too, and may have queries or suggestions. Any difficulties raised will be hammered out now. Once the second draft is done any change will usually be a matter of fine tuning, with the script editor keeping an eagle eye open for any inconsistencies, slips in continuity, and so on. The third draft is usually the last. One outstanding exception to this was the final episode of the second series of *The Demon Headmaster*. This is where Dinah follows her half-lizard double into the underground tunnels. This scene was immensely complicated and was rejigged several times. Detailed diagrams were made and every move by each character was plotted.

When I do adaptations, I'll read the book and soak it up and decide what has got to be removed from the text. Then I sit here and I write so fast I can barely read my own writing! And it will come almost exactly the right length and I don't know how I've done it. I never think about it.

My great hero is Dennis Potter. He never followed any rules. A lot of established writers go to drama writing classes to learn the structures of screenplays – I've never done that. As Anna Home of the BBC says, it's easier to adapt other people's books than your own, because you can't be objective enough with your own work. I can adapt an Enid Blyton book and I'll be able to remove any events or details that are not needed for a screenplay, but with your own novels you can't be ruthless enough to take anything out. But as I'm going on to explain later, my own television dramas are not adaptations in the real sense.

Lizzie Dripping

It was absolute serendipity how I got into writing for television. Nearly all my early fantasies were read on *Jackanory*. *The Piemakers* was read by Wendy Craig, *The Night-Watchmen* by Joseph O'Connor, *The Signposters* by Billy Whitelaw and *Up the Pier* by Hannah Gordon, amongst others. At that time – the early 1970s – the BBC decided they were going to do children's drama. They were going to start by having 25-minute one-off dramas for children. There had never been anything like it before, and there wasn't a pool of talent they could call on. And as I was a children's author, they asked me, to see what I could do.

Then, we'd just moved to this house and had had our second daughter. She was only about a month old, so Anna Home and Angela Beeching of the BBC came up to see me here. Not long after we'd moved up here, when I was putting the washing out on the line, I heard our next door neighbour, Mary Stokes, say to her little girl, Catherine, who was about eleven – 'Now look what you've gone and done, Lizzie Dripping!' And a shiver went straight down my back. I thought, 'That's a name to conjure with!' So I wrote it down, and when Anna and Angela came here I said that I'd got this idea about a girl called Lizzie Dripping. And I saw them exchange glances, and it was almost as if they knew this had to be something. So they commissioned me to write a one-off 25-minute drama about a girl called Lizzie Dripping. So when they'd gone I came into this study, and I don't know what made me write the title, but I just wrote down 'Lizzie Dripping and the Witch'.

Because I didn't know how to write a script I asked the BBC to send me some examples so I would know how to lay it out. And what I did was to write it as a story first and then a screenplay, and that was *Lizzie Dripping and the Witch*. I was then asked to write another scipt, which became *Lizzie Dripping and the Orphans* – and that was the first one to be filmed – which, at that point, was intended as a one-off. That particular one was based on a true story that happened to my elder daughter. And I insisted on doing location shots, as I'd seen other dramas on television where it was very obvious that they'd filmed in the studio. The BBC said that if all the location shots were done here – at my house and in the village – they could afford to do a whole series – and they did. And my daughter Candida ended up playing Lizzie Dripping's baby brother, Toby!

I used voiceover a great deal in *Lizzie Dripping*. I've got a feeling that it was part of the programme's appeal. And it was the first time that it had ever been used on children's television. I did it so that the audience would know what Lizzie was really thinking. The thing about children is that they're operating in a world of adults, and all the while they're picking up signals, and will say to adults what adults *want* them to say. But what children are actually thinking could be something very different indeed. So in the programme you'll hear what Lizzie says to Aunty

Blodwen as well as what's really going on in her mind. And children identify with that situation. Voiceover is the equivalent of the aside in Shakespeare's plays, and it's not nearly as clumsy as an aside. It can be done so subtly on television that you hardly know it's happening.

Moondial

As with *Lizzie Dripping*, I wrote the novel of *Moondial* immediately before I wrote the screenplay for television. I had to do it with *Lizzie Dripping* because I wasn't used to writing dialogue straight onto the page, so I needed the comfort of having written the story out first. And I think that it's a good idea for the initial excitement and narrative drive to write the book first. I still see a book as something set in stone. Once I've got the story in book form it's permanent. When I started writing for television, television was genuinely ephemeral. Nobody had a VCR, and the BBC didn't keep tapes of all their programmes. Many dramas were performed and broadcast live, and not kept. So, there was no way I was going to put all that amount of effort in with nothing permanent to show for it.

It's strange, in that if your subconscious knows that ultimately what you are writing will become a six-part drama – as with *Moondial* – in a quite mysterious way, the book, without any pre-planning, will become a six-part adventure. And as you write the book, you are visualising it, as you would a screenplay. And there is a difference in the way you write a book that you know will become a six-episode drama. The book will have a structure that contains narrative climaxes at the end of every sixth section or so.

Moondial is a cumulative piece, and not as episodic as something like *Lizzie Dripping* or *Five Children and It*. One thing I was aware of as I was writing the book was that there needed to be these specific points in the story where there would be a hook, but there would also have to be an overall sweep to it and yet within that there would be little peaks and troughs.

I wrote a prologue for this book because I wanted to set the atmosphere and also, if I'm going to move into a surreal situation, I like to establish absolute ordinariness first. It's crucial. If you've given a taster – that 'watch out, something's going to happen' – then it's going to hook them in. And the reader will think 'I'll stay with this as any minute now something really weird's going to happen.' With *Moondial*, it's partly written in the second person – using 'you' – to guide the reader into the book:

> It is midnight in that most dark and secret place. If you should chance – and why should you? – to be walking there, you would be blindfolded by the night. You would hear the hooting of a lone owl from the church tower, the scuff of your own steps on the gravel.

What I describe in this prologue is exactly what happened to me when I went to Belton myself. And in this piece I'm trying to let the reader know what it was like. And the television drama has an equivalent of this prologue – a short scene at the very beginning in which the viewer is shown a montage of images of Belton at night.

I would have been thinking about the story of *Moondial* some six months before I wrote anything down. It took that long to ferment. The novel took probably three or four months in total, and the script would have taken about a fortnight – as long as it would take to type it out. It was straightforward to do because it was all there, in the book. I had all the dialogue already, and all the descriptions were simply turned into camera directions. You see, I wasn't adapting anything, because, in a sense, it had already been written for television, as the book was a kind of script in prose form.

The Demon Headmaster (Gillian Cross)

I don't choose the books I adapt, I get chosen for a project. With *The Demon Headmaster*, someone at the BBC would have seen that the book had great potential as a television drama. It's amazing how few modern children's books can be adapted into a six-part series. In fact, the only reason this one achieved it was because we merged the first two books – *The Demon Headmaster* and *The Prime Minister's Brain* – together.

What makes *The Demon Headmaster* ideal for television drama? *The Demon Headmaster* was just a brilliant concept full stop! The idea must have resonated with every child in the land. The hypnotic eyes of the headmaster were eminently televisual – and not expensive! The first book was also highly televisual in that we have a whole school of children in uniform, absolutely atypically, lined up, marched and regimented like troops. Much depended on the casting of the lead. It would have been easy to overplay and the whole thing descend into farce. It was a very fine line to tread. Luckily, we got Terence Hardiman, who can suggest cruelty with a twitch of the mouth, whose smile is deliciously sinister and whose whole body language expressed the headmaster's rigidity and urge to control. Also, the books featured a gang of children – SPLAT – and younger children have always liked gangs. Then we have the introduction of computers – and hey presto – the magic mix!

The way the second two series were done was by a process new to myself but by no means unusual in television, especially when further series of a popular drama are being planned. I initially had misgivings. We kicked off with a 'brain-storming' session at the TV centre, with myself and Gillian, producer, director, assistant director, designer and 'money person'. This, to me, smacked of 'writing by committee' – which happens all too often these days and which I abhor and want no part of. The results are generally dire – what I call a fudge. For one thing, to have a real dramatic drive and sweep a piece needs, at least initially, to be the vision of one person.

However, this did not turn out to be the case. Once ideas had been fed in, Gillian, in record time and in amazing detail, came up with synopses of each episode. I saw that from now on it was very much business as usual. If anything, one had rather greater freedom with detail and dialogue, because these were not already existent in book form. While I was writing the scripts Gillian was independently writing her books. In the end I enjoyed it, and think she did too. We both consulted the brilliant Marilyn Fox, script editor, who would liaise over any difficulties – 'Hyperbrain' and 'The Interface of the Lady', and the complexities of how SPLAT finally beat her by

EPISODE 1

Shot of DEMON HEAD in helicopter hovering over the BRC
It descends through the trees
We see entrance to BRC : sign BIODIVERSITY RESEARCH CENTRE and logo

Shot of village, where we see various houses and cottages with
Bed and Breakfast signs, most with Vacancies.
Centre in to shot of the house that is to be the Huters', where a
SOLD sign is being put in place.
Change this same shot to one from POV surveillance
Then DMON HEAD, smiling. Things are slotting into place....

INT DAY HUNTERS' HOUSE (any convenient location with drawers &
mirror - I know you don't want to use the original house)
HARVEY, who has been studying a book, takes it over to the drawers
and puts it down, then looks at himself in the mirror above.
He deepens his gaze.

      HARVEY
   look into my eyes.....
   You are feeling tired... you are feeling very
   very tired....

LLOYD looks in, grins and disappears

   Your arms and legs are like dead weights...
   (He droops his arms and sags his legs)
   Heavy.... heavy... heavy...
   Your eyelids are heavy...
   Your eyes are closing.... you can hardly keep
   them open....

LLOYD & DINAH now both peer round door and watch

   Sleep.... sleep... (DINAH lets out a stifled
   giggle and he turns and see them)
   Hey! Rotten things! I'd nearly gone then!

Page of script from the BBC TV series *The Demon Headmaster* overload. This took some working out, and had to be presented to young viewers in an easily comprehensible form.

SELECTED CURRENT TITLES

Bag of Bones (Hodder & Stoughton)
The Bongleweed (Oxford University Press)
Book of Mystery Stories (Editor) (Kingfisher)
Lizzie Dripping (Puffin)
Moondial (Puffin)
The Night-Watchmen (to be reissued by Hodder & Stoughton – September 1999)
The Phoenix and the Carpet – novelisation of TV series (Puffin)
The Piemakers (Oxford University Press)
The Snatchers (Hodder & Stoughton)
Stonestruck (Puffin)

The Bagthorpes Saga (Hodder & Stoughton) including:
Ordinary Jack
Absolute Zero
Bagthorpes Unlimited

For younger readers (all Hodder & Stoughton)

A Gift From Winklesea / Whatever Happened in Winklesea
The Little Grey Donkey
The Little Sea Horse
The Seapiper
Sophie and the Sea Wolf

An introduction to . . . Gillian Cross

WHAT TYPE OF BOOKS DO YOU WRITE? Novels – long (such as *Wolf*), medium (such as *The Demon Headmaster*) and short (such as *The Tree House*).

WHAT ARE YOUR BOOKS ABOUT? All sorts of things. I like to do something different every time, but I hope the stories are always full of action and suspense.

BORN: London, 1945.

EDUCATION: Oxford and Sussex Universities – B.A. and D.Phil. degrees in English Literature.

LIVES: Wolston, near Coventry.

FAMILY: I am married and have four children – Jonathan (32), Elizabeth (29), Anthony (15) and Katy (14).

HOBBIES: Orienteering and playing the piano.

PREVIOUS OCCUPATIONS: I have been an assistant to an MP, a child-minder, and I have also worked in a school and a local bakery.

MOST TREASURED POSSESSION: My contact lenses!

AWARDS: Carnegie Medal (1990) for *Wolf* and the Whitbread Children's Novel Award and Smarties Prize (both 1992) for *The Great Elephant Chase*.

LANGUAGES TRANSLATED INTO: European languages as well as Icelandic, Japanese, Korean and Catalan and some Indonesian languages. *Wolf* looks great in Greek – it makes me look like a classical author!

BOOKS TURNED INTO TV DRAMAS: *The Demon Headmaster* series. There is a film script for *The Great Elephant Chase*, but there are currently no plans to make a film of it.

FAVOURITE BOOKS: My favourite things do change! But the books I like at the moment are *The Secret Garden* by Frances Hodgson Burnett, *The Beethoven Medal* by K.M. Peyton, *Waterland* by Graham Swift, as well as the novels of Peter Dickinson and Shakespeare's plays.

FAVOURITE MUSIC: Beethoven's Violin Concerto and John Taverner's choral work *We Shall See Him as He Is*.

FAVOURITE FILMS: *Dead Poets Society*, *The Piano* and *Cyrano de Bergerac*.

WHICH ONE OF YOUR CHARACTERS WOULD YOU MOST LIKE TO BE? Clipper in *Save our School* or Sprog in *The Tree House*.

WHAT WERE YOU LIKE AT THE AGE OF 11? Very bookish, not at all sporty, friendly – but I also liked spending time on my own.

ENJOYS VISITING SCHOOLS BECAUSE: I like it because, in my experience, children are enthusiastic and interested in books.

WHY DO YOU WRITE? I can't see why anybody does anything else!

WHICH WORDS DESCRIBE YOU BEST? People probably see me as talkative, more extrovert than I really am, friendly and happy!

WHAT WOULD YOU LIKE TO HAPPEN IN THE TWENTY-FIRST CENTURY? World peace.

WHICH OF YOUR BOOKS WOULD YOU LIKE TO BE REMEMBERED FOR? I'll be remembered for *The Demon Headmaster* – but I'd choose *Wolf* or *The Great Elephant Chase*.

1 HOW THE READER BECAME A WRITER

I can't remember my very first book, but I do remember that my mother read to us when we were little. She read us *The Heroes* by Charles Kingsley and *The Wind in the Willows* by Kenneth Grahame, and she told us stories as well. She was an English teacher, so she was always recommending books to us. When I was young I always read a mixture of things because my parents had a lot of books. I read Shakespeare and Enid Blyton, poetry and plays, but always fiction. I discovered non-fiction as an adult, as a result of writing and having to research things. I read *The Secret Garden* by Frances Hodgson Burnett a lot too.

I've always written things ever since I can remember. I told stories to my brother from time to time. And I used to tell stories to my friends on the underground train to and from school – a serial story about themselves! And I often wrote beginnings of books – first chapters, and then I tore them up because I thought they weren't any good! Sometimes I wrote the odd play with friends – just informally, the way you do at that age. Except for what I wrote for school, I would never show anyone my writing because I never finished anything! And I think that's important for children, that they keep some of their writing to themselves.

I went to Oxford University and studied English Literature, which I enjoyed very much. Later I went on to Sussex University to do my D.Phil. on G.K. Chesterton, and I also did some freelance teaching there afterwards. My D.Phil. certainly helped with my writing – it taught me about how to think about a long book, how to pace an extended piece of writing, and also to consider structure – although academic writing has a very different structure to fiction. Talking to tutors about my thesis, and being told what areas needed re-working, also prepared me for working with editors.

At that point I realised I didn't want an academic career. My first two children were still quite young then, and it was then that I got involved with the Lewes

Children's Book Group, and we would organise book days, book sales, fund-raising events and storytelling sessions. So I was reading lots of children's books.

One evening, when my husband Martin was out at a meeting, I went into the kitchen and I sat down and read *The Beethoven Medal* by K.M. Peyton – all the way through. When I finished, it was like coming out of the cinema in the daytime, I was a bit dazed. It reminded me what reading was like before I'd been to university, where I had to read in a business-like and analytical kind of way. It had been a long time since I'd read a whole book all the way through for pleasure in that kind of submerged way that you read as a child. And it brought home to me that at the heart of a book should be a good story – and I knew then that that was exactly what I wanted to write. And I even wrote to Kathleen Peyton, and she sent me a lovely letter.

Also around that time somebody said something important to me. I'd told them that everything I wrote sounded so silly, and he said that you must ignore that, it's just your own voice you're hearing, like your own voice on a tape recorder. That was very liberating. So, all these things came together – reading *The Beethoven Medal* and being told not to worry about my voice – and then I got an idea for a book. I bought a pair of ear plugs and I wrote in the evening while Martin was watching the television. So I wrote my first book, and it was really bad – it was chaotic and badly structured. But at least I knew I could get to the end.

I got into a habit of writing books and sending them to publishers for about four or five years. I never got a straight rejection slip from anybody. The editors all wrote me very helpful letters. One children's editor at Gollancz was very nice indeed to me. She shepherded me along and I also went to see her at one point. That kept me going.

When I was writing my fifth book, Martin said that I should be more business-like and draw up a table of all the publishers and what I was sending off where. So I scanned *The Writers' and Artists' Yearbook* for children's publishers, and I made myself a little chart of who they all were, and what my books were. And because of my involvement with the Lewes Children's Book Group, I had a fairly good idea of who published what. I sent off my four books to different publishers and went on writing my fifth. Two of them came back quite speedily, and with nice letters, and two of them didn't come back for months and months. Eventually, I went back to *The Writers' and Artists' Yearbook* which said that after three months, if you have sent the return postage, it is permissible to write and say 'Where is my book?' Like everybody else, I was typing then and I really did need my manuscript back – apart from the etiquette then that you were only supposed to submit to one publisher at a time.

I wrote to Methuen and Oxford University Press and they both responded within a week or so saying that they wanted to publish the books – *The Iron Way* (Oxford University Press) and *The Runaway* (Methuen). So, from having no publishers at all, I had two! And that was great. I showed them the other three books, but they said that I should start a new novel. And that was how I began. But once I'd written a whole book, and I could get to the end, I just knew that was what I wanted to do. I was in the very, very fortunate position when I started of not needing to work and being at a stage in my life where it was okay not to work. But at the back of my mind I think I've always thought that I would write books.

2 WRITING: ROUTINES AND REFLECTIONS

I write in my office, a smallish room behind the kitchen. It has a dining-room table with a rather old computer on top of it, which was once upgraded to a 286! I get up around 7.30 a.m. When Martin, Anthony and Katy have gone I say my prayers and I begin work about 9.15–9.30 a.m. If I'm writing a first draft, I'll aim to write for three hours. If I'm revising – which I really, really like – I'll often work all day.

Although I've written short stories, I only write them if somebody has specifically asked me for one. I like novels because I enjoy working out how the book will all hang together and trying to work out a shape that is satisfying but doesn't falsify things. I do err on the side of neatness, but I try to find a structure that's not too neat. Also, novels are what I like reading. I do like poetry – but being a poet seems to be a time- and life-consuming job. With a few exceptions, I actually don't like reading short stories very much – they annoy me because they're over so quickly! With novels I like the feeling that there's a lot to explore. And I wouldn't know how to do that with a short story; I don't think there would be enough space.

The main quality I aim to achieve in my prose is that it's invisible – I want it not to interfere with the story. I don't want the reader to be conscious of my language – though I think that this approach can make me too conservative and not as daring as I ought to be. I don't want people to read something I've written and think, 'What beautiful prose this is!' I just want them to be thinking about the story.

There are many advantages in writing for children. The main ones, as far as I'm concerned, are that I have immense freedom about form, style and length. The fact that I've written a thriller doesn't mean that I can't then write a comedy or a simple family story. My impression is that adult writers get typecast much more easily. Also, I can't fall into the error of thinking that my readers are the same as I am. Thus, I have to remember that writers need to communicate and can't insist that their readers understand. And the story has to be my prime concern. I can't kid myself that style, or wise words, or clever structures are enough. I know that I have to concentrate on what is the storyteller's prime task.

I think of *Story* as a sequence of events that happen. And the events are important because they express how people are feeling or what goes on inside them or what kind of developments they're going through. But when I'm telling the story it's important to me that those things should actually happen in terms of being events, being things that people actually do. Very often they're not like that in real life. You can have enormous psychic events in real life happening with not a ripple on the outside. Some people write novels like that, but that's not what I like to do. I like to do it so that you have the event being symbolic – I like to think of it as being resounding, these events resonating with the meanings that they have, which doesn't come from an event and saying 'What event will I choose to symbolise such and such?' It comes from telling the story and feeling which things work like that. I don't think of plot and character as separate. My characters express their personalities through the plot, the things that they do. I like to put them in extreme situations which highlight the moral choices they have to make. I think moral choices are important and I think children share that view.

Most of the first draft of a book will be done on the computer, but if I find things too difficult, I'll write longhand. It's easier to write rubbish on the computer, I think!

If I'm writing in longhand, it's more of an effort, so I'm less likely to put down words just for the sake of it – which is easy on the computer. There's a major difference between the writing you do with two hands and with one hand. Maybe it's to do with the left hand connecting with the right brain and vice versa. I've heard other people say that they do different types of writing on computer and by hand. A lot of people who write novels on computer will write poems by hand. When I'm stuck, I'll write by hand, and when I've finished, I'll type it onto the PC.

One piece of advice that has always stuck with me is that in a novel you must have a 'hit on the head' by Chapter 3. In other words, your really big, dramatic event, the thing that draws you into the book, has to have happened by then. Some books don't – they amble on for ages, settling in, and they work well – but I don't know if they work well for children like that. Children will read really big, fat books with complicated stories – but only if they've been convinced early on that it's going to be worth it. And nowadays, perhaps Chapter 3 is a bit late! But I often think of that when I'm writing.

Except for *Chartbreak* all my novels are in the third person – but close to a character's point of view. I always imagine that I'm a particular person looking at the scene. But I don't always keep to the same point of view throughout the book. For example, in most of *The Demon Headmaster* books, it's alternately Dinah and Lloyd. Early on in my career, somebody told me that children don't like books written in the first person, which I now know to be untrue. And I personally have this feeling – which I can't justify – that writing in the first person is self-indulgent. It may be that unless I'm writing in the third person I find it harder to remember that the character is that person and not me, but I'm not sure that's true. Overall, I think I would find it harder in the first person to write on the level I want to write. I can be other people in the first person, but I think it can become slightly jokey, slightly removed from where I need to be, to be able to write something serious. In my new book, *Tightrope*, there are thirty different first person narrative sections by twenty-nine different people! And I did that so I could get a whole neighbourhood into the book. But the main narrative is in the third person.

In one sense I think about my reader as I'm writing. I have in the back of my mind a rather bored twelve- or thirteen-year-old boy that I have to entertain – though I mainly test my work out by my own reaction.

With regards to adaptations of my books, I'd rather leave that to other people like Helen Cresswell. There are many technical things about writing screenplays that I don't know. And I don't want to do it enough to learn. Also, I enjoy working with other people less than working on my own. That's the beauty of novels – you can do it all yourself – you're responsible for all the different elements that go into it, and the book has to work by itself. Whereas if you write a script, you're then dependent upon the special effects, the way the producer produces, the way the director directs and so on. I'm just not a very communal person to do things like that. Having said that, I do love the idea of new techniques and new ways of telling stories. The idea of novels on CD-ROM fascinates me, but it would be completely different from novels as we know them because you could access other media. And then the novels wouldn't have to be linear, and that's the crucial thing.

Why do people read my books? Well, the children who write to me and tell me they like my books say it's because they're exciting. Most of the letters are from junior school children from eight to eleven. I'm not sure that they're old enough to be critical or reflective yet. For if you asked them why they liked such and such, I don't think they would know the answer because they haven't learnt how to do that yet. But I think most people read my books because of the story, because the story moves along fast. And I hope they like reading them without realising that it's because of the texture and the atmosphere the books have – I wouldn't want them to be actively thinking about that all the time. I think they'd perceive that as part of the excitement. But different people read children's books and you can't make generalised statements.

One of the nicest things a child has ever said about one of my books was with regard to *Wolf*. When it won the Carnegie Medal, a nine-year-old girl was being interviewed and she was asked if it was frightening. And she said, 'No it wasn't frightening . . . ' And then she hunted around for a word, and she said, 'it was *thrilling*!' That was so nice!

3 GROWING A BOOK

Before I start a novel – if it's for Oxford University Press – I'll write a synopsis and talk it through with the editor. Usually at that stage I haven't the faintest idea what is going into the book. I often know the beginning scene, and the area it's going to be about, and the feel of it. My editor there is good at understanding that and not hassling me as to what's going to happen on p. 17 or to ask for specific details. I'll sign a contract on the book and then go away and not show anybody anything until I've finished. I won't look at the synopsis again unless I get really stuck – because in a way, the plan interferes with the writing of the book, and I need to start a story with no shape and to find out what it is as I go along. When I finish I often find I've covered everything I wrote in the synopsis, but I'll find that the way the events have unfolded will be different to how I originally planned. Then the editor will read it, having talked it through from the start, but my other editor at OUP will read it cold, knowing nothing about it at all.

The pattern I usually follow is that the first draft – which takes the longest – is where I work out what the story, the incidents and so on are going to be. Thus I've started the novel without much idea of what's going to happen. I make it up, and do the research while I'm doing the first draft. I plan ahead as far as I can, but I usually have to write it to find out. Sometimes I have to go back to the beginning because I get so snarled up! With the second draft I'll go through properly and I'll make sure the story works and I'll make lots of alterations to the plot and to the cast of characters, if necessary. And I'll remove all the bits that aren't doing anything, that aren't pushing the story along. I think of it all quite visually – but I'm not sure I could communicate what it actually looks like!

I tend to concentrate on my language more when I've got the shape of the story right. The hang up I used to have as a child and teenage writer was that you had to get the language right first time. That was something that made it difficult for me. I know some people will correct Chapter 1 until it's right and then go on to Chapter 2, but I'd be on Chapter 1 for ever!

The first draft of a novel – making something out of nothing – is much harder than revising. Some people are good at writing the right thing first time, whereas, because my books rely heavily upon plot, which takes a lot of working out, I'll write much more than I actually need. But when I'm revising, and knowing by then how the plot's working, it's more a question of taking out sentences that don't work, and making sure the connections between chapters are all right. It's all fun to do, but revising is easy fun!

With my story book *The Tree House* I actually made a plot grid. I wanted lots of things, strands running through – and in each chapter there had to be a new present from the father (who was away working in America), a new way of using that present, the letter that the boys wrote that would spark off the next present, the character Sprog progressing as he learned to read and write, the garden progressing through the seasons, food from the garden from each season – like pumpkins and chestnuts. I've only ever done that with *The Tree House*, to make sure I got all the details right.

The Demon Headmaster

First of all, I wrote a book called *Save Our School*, which has a character called Clipper who writes a story about a wicked headmaster. When my daughter Elizabeth read that she said that she liked Clipper's story and that it was much better than the sort of stuff I write! And she said why didn't I write about a wicked headmaster? So I kept putting her off, saying that one day I would. Then also, one of the editors at OUP, who at the time was starting a new range of good story-books for 8- to 12-year-olds, asked me if I had anything to contribute. So I told him about the story that Elizabeth was always on about. But when I sat down and thought about it, I realised it wasn't that simple! I wanted to write about a day school, but at a day school children go home every day, and if they started telling their parents that the headmaster was wicked he wouldn't last long. So, I thought, how can he be wicked and send the children home saying 'The headmaster is a marvellous man and this is the best school I've ever been to'? And of course, the moment I thought that, I realised that he's got to hypnotise them! And when that came to me, it seemed so obvious and I couldn't believe that no one had ever thought of that before! Then I knew it really was the right idea.

Next I got thinking about the school and I realised that because of the way I write in the third person there had to be an outsider coming into the school – and that's why there had to be Dinah. After that, the real problem I had – and I can't understand why I thought it now – was that I thought Lloyd, Harvey, Dinah and their friends needed some special power to combat what was going on in the school. So I made Harvey turn into things, like a teapot and a tape recorder! And that was all very much wound into the plot. And in the very first version, when Dinah takes a tape recorder into assembly to find out what is going on, the tape recorder is in fact Harvey! Because this part of the story was so integral, I think I didn't let myself take it out, I just tried to make it work. But I knew it wasn't right.

I sent it off, and then I got a call from the editor, who said he would come and see me – which isn't the usual response that I get from an editor! I spent the day before we met thinking that I wasn't going to be bullied into re-writing the story! And of course the moment he finally said to me 'What about this book?' I said 'Well, I need to take all that stuff out, don't I?' And I did! But it left huge gaps in the story . One

big scene I put in to fill a gap was where the children are outside clearing up the snow. And I think it's one of the best scenes in the book, and it's one bit that children say they really like.

Sometime later, that editor said to me that he'd always felt rather guilty about *The Demon Headmaster* and making me take out all those bits with Harvey changing into things. And he said that he liked the idea, but just not in that book – and he asked me to write another book with that idea. He thought it would be popular with children. And that's how *Twin and Super-Twin* began.

The Demon Headmaster didn't take very long to write, just four or five months. And I wrote it in longhand first – because I didn't have a computer then – and I would have done two or three drafts in longhand. Then I typed it up. And once David had made his suggestions, I would have gone back and done some more longhand drafts, and re-typed it again from there.

When I wrote the first book I said 'Never again!', but later I thought that I would quite like to write another one. And the idea of writing the first two sequels – *The Prime Minister's Brain* and *The Revenge of the Demon Headmaster* – came not from the publisher but from children writing to me and asking if I was going to write more. However, *The Demon Headmaster Strikes Again* and *The Demon Headmaster Takes Over* happened rather differently. After the first television series – which was adapted by Helen Cresswell from two books, *The Demon Headmaster* and *The Prime Minister's Brain* – the BBC said that they wanted to do another series, but that they didn't want to do *The Revenge of the Demon Headmaster*. So, these next two were written in a *[handwritten insertion at top:]* Did you try + keep 'track of the ? The ~~Jenny nodded~~ " Edward helps us. He

one.'

'That's right!' Paul said ~~eagerly.~~ 'My friend Edward - the

one ~~who signalled about the posse~~ - says his mother's ~~the same.~~

~~She's~~ a journalist and she went to ~~cover~~ the conference. She came

back with a badge *too* and now she won't write about anything except

gardens and cookery.'

'And if Edward asks a question - ' Jenny pulled a face and

chanted. 'Curiosity is the curse of the human brain.'

~~Above them, people were moving off the hill following~~

footpaths in various directions. ~~Dinah turned to watch the Green~~

~~Hand badges spreading into the countryside.~~

'Does your ~~father give out lots of~~ Green Hand badges *like you just*

Paul ~~nodded.~~ 'He came back from the conference with boxes of

them.'

'I'm sure they're the key to the whole thing.' Dinah looked

thoughtful. 'You couldn't get hold of one, could you?'

Paul and Jenny looked at each other. Then Paul stepped back,

looking up the hill. Their father was walking away from them,

towards the stile. Paul waited until he had climbed over, ~~and then~~

~~nodded.~~ *Then he said, 'OK.*

'Hang around here. I'll be back in ten minutes.'

He went flying down the hill towards the Outdoor Pursuits

Centre, and Dinah took a step out of the rhododendrons, to see where

he went.

As she did so, she saw another glint of light from the opposite

hill. Jenny saw it too. Immediately, she pulled the notebook out

of her pocket and started to note down the dots and dashes. Ian

grinned at Dinah.

'It's a great system, isn't it? ~~More reliable than the~~

Internet!'

Manuscript page from *The Demon Headmaster Takes Over*

different way; in a way I don't normally write. For *The Demon Headmaster Strikes Again* I wrote a 25-page outline of a seven-part television serial. Then Helen Cresswell wrote the script while I wrote the novel. And we did the same with *The Demon Headmaster Takes Over*. As a result, the books and the programmes do differ.

Wolf

A long time ago I wanted to write about a rock band. This was long before I wrote *Chartbreak*. It was going to be about a band that had an ocelot as a mascot. I did a lot of research and finally decided it wasn't a good idea. But one of the key images I had for this book was that an ocelot would run away and hide on the roof of Sainsbury's. So I had this juxtaposition of the wild and the urban. And that feeling was quite powerful. Then many years later I was having lunch with my editors from Holiday House, my American publishers. One of them said as a joke, 'Why don't you write a book about a werewolf? If you did, I could sell thousands of copies!'

So, I went off to the library and started reading about werewolves. I could only see two ways of doing this – either something really jokey, with fangs and blood, or else you could try to imagine what it would really be like to be a werewolf. But I decided not to write about werewolves, and I didn't.

In the course of my research I got thinking about the wild and the urban again, and I also related it to the wolf. Although I didn't know what I was getting into when I first thought about wolves, like anybody else I just felt the strength of the wolf thing. I wasn't thinking of it as a book at all then. And then I got the beginning scene – with Cassy waking up in her grandmother's flat, and someone knocking on the door, and this terribly wolfish feeling. I knew that Cassy would be sent away, that she was afraid that she wouldn't come back and that she couldn't ask what it was all about.

When I started *Wolf* I really didn't know what would happen beyond p. 13. I was just inspired to write the book by imagining that opening scene and by the fascination with the wild and the urban. Contrary to what people think, I didn't start by deciding to adapt *Red Riding Hood*. I just started with that idea of Cassy in the flat and with the notion of getting as much 'wolfishness' as possible into the book. I think I knew that her father was chasing her, but I didn't have any idea of the IRA or the bomb at that stage. At one point I thought her father would have something to do with wolves and he might have been a zookeeper. I didn't have the *Red Riding Hood* dream bit.

But I knew what the book felt like, and I knew it would be very dangerous. Then I read Jack Zipes's book *The Trials and Tribulations of Little Red Riding Hood*, and saw how wonderfully the fairy tale fitted all I wanted to do. Getting the wolf in, in as many ways as possible (including the names of the characters), was one of the pleasures of writing the book, and a way of exploring whatever it was that made me want to write it in the first place. All the time I was looking for it to be more and more wolfish. So that was why I included the theatre in schools project, I knew I had to get in all the factual stuff about real wolves, and the tension between mythic wolves and real wolves, and that was the way I did it.

I spent a long time writing the first draft. I think I was some way into that draft when I got the idea of Cassy's dream sequence, and it helped because I couldn't see any other way of exploring the feelings of a practical, non-introspective person like Cassy. Those *Red Riding Hood* dream bits were so easy to write, and such fun! The technically difficult bit was that I wanted to get the climax of the dream sequence, the climax of the theatre-in-schools play and the climax of the encounter with her father all to happen more or less at the same time. It was like holding on to three strands and pulling them all together. Though I think the emotional climax comes for Cassy when she realises her father is at her grandmother's flat and that her grandmother is in danger, not afterwards.

I researched squats by contacting a squatters' association as well as reading Doris Lessing's novel *The Good Terrorist* – in which people do up a squat. I researched Semtex by contacting the Ministry of Defence, who were most helpful. I asked them such things as how squidgy is plastic explosive, how much do you need to make a reasonable size bomb, is it oily and so on.

And I did a great deal of research about wolves, both in literature and in life. This was mostly reading, but I did visit London Zoo. While I was there the headkeeper asked me if I wanted to go into the wolf cage, which was tremendous. I wouldn't have dreamt of asking myself, as I wouldn't have thought it was possible! At first, the wolves ran away to the far end of the enclosure, then they came over and circled us! And there I was, thinking, 'Here I am, standing in a cage with real, live wolves!' But I knew that the keepers wouldn't have let me in if they thought I would have got eaten. And they wouldn't have taken me in on other days, when the wolves were in a different mood. I really enjoyed it. It was a magical moment! In fact, going into the cage is the only thing I've done that I've then directly put into a book, just as I'd experienced it.

4 VISITS TO SCHOOLS

Visiting schools is good for publicity, but mostly I do it because I like it and I enjoy talking to children. And also I enjoy the performing bit of it! I don't do it too often because I don't think it's very good for me, as with doing this interview – communicating as if I know what I'm talking about! You see, it's disastrous for me to think I know what I'm doing when I write a book. When I go into schools, children ask me how I write a book, and I'll tell them – but for my next book I might need to do something completely different. I constantly need to be open about my approach to writing, to take risks. The more you say what you do, the more fixed it becomes.

The first thing I'll say to the children is that the reason I am there is just that I've written lots of books, and that I'm going to tell them what *I* do to write a book. The next thing I say is that the most important thing I have to tell them is that they mustn't expect me to tell them *how* to write books, because I won't! Because nobody can tell you, and that you're not to believe anybody if they tell you that they can! Then, I'll illustrate various different ways that people have of writing. But I will emphasise that what might work for me or for other writers might not work for them.

One way I'll mention is that of writing a book backwards, so you start by inventing the end. And you can write your notes down on little file cards and work backwards to the beginning! Apparently that's an Edwardian way of writing a play – and by doing this, you never get your characters in a situation they can't get out of. And another method I'll talk about is that of drawing story maps for a book. And you don't begin writing until the map is right – and if the map is wrong, the story will go wrong.

I collect these various ways of writing as I think it's useful for children to know that different people do different things, and that ultimately what matters is not the way you do it, but how the story turns out in the end. It's quite important to me that children should understand that if they really want to write, then it must become something that they're in charge of, not something that they do in the way they've been told to. And I think that's hard for children to understand.

On some visits I'll give a talk, and I'll discuss how I wrote *Wolf* or *The Demon Headmaster*. On others, I might do my plot workshop for juniors, where I'll tell them that we're going to invent a monster headmistress, so they come up with this grotesque figure! The children will say that her hair's all spiky, that she's got warts, and we'll do funny voices! Then I tell them that she's going to take over their school, but how will she do it? And the children like that! From there, we make up the story.

There's a writing workshop I do with older children – lower secondary level. It takes quite a long time. We'll all write our own first page of a book – cold, without any preparation – and I'll do it too. And to start, we look at the page I've written. We'll read it, talk about it, and expand it in various directions. Next, we'll make a plan and discuss how we will go about structuring the story, how we can break it up into chapters and what viewpoint we will use. Then I'll ask the class to do the same with their own first pages. Sometimes they'll come up with marvellous things – and all kinds of interlocking narratives.

I usually start the workshop by telling the class that they won't *have* to show their writing to anybody. Some teachers find that hard to take. Before a session I'll explain to the teacher that what we'll be doing is a mock-up of a novel, and that I like to be able to say to the children that they don't have to show their writing, as the main idea is that they understand the process of writing. One of the worst things that has ever happened on a school visit was when after a workshop, a teacher said to me, 'But it's a pity to waste all of these, shall I collect them in?'

When I'm commenting on children's own writing – as children have sent me their stories from time to time – I think it's immensely important not to be discouraging, but also to make them feel that there's room for improvement, that working on it and improving it is a good thing to do. I might point out something that a child has written and say 'I really like this bit here – can we have more of it?' That's my approach. I would think about what editors have done and what has worked with me, such as when they've pointed out various bits but not told me specifically what I should do with them.

One thing I really do prefer with school visits is doing the exercises and using the materials that I have planned. I'm not too keen on teachers telling me what they want me to do and say. Some have asked me to talk about drafting for example, but how do they know that I draft at all? Some writers don't! This way, the teacher assumes it's a process, in the same way that if you had a joiner into school and asked them how to make a staircase. A staircase needs, I believe, to be made in a certain way, but writing fiction isn't like that. If you have somebody in, you have to let them tell what they do and in their own way. My value is not that I fit in with the National Curriculum, it's that I'm a real person doing real things and I've come in to say what I do. I know of one children's writer who goes around to schools saying 'Don't listen to all this stuff about redrafting! I hated it when I was your age!'

5 LIBRARIES

At the Carnegie Medal award ceremony, I was asked if there was anything I would like to say. At that time, our village library was threatened with closure. And during the various visits I was making, I discovered that everybody else's village library was threatened as well, so I was feeling very incensed about it. And I was delighted to have a chance to say something about it.

For anyone who loves books, libraries are delightful treasure troves. Places to find information about existing interests and explore new things. Public libraries are particularly important, because they are a major interface between ordinary people and the riches of all the cultures of the world. One of the good things about living in this country is that each of us is entitled, by law, to a free, comprehensive and efficient library service. Through interlibrary lending we can get almost anything via our local branch library – I'm always surprised we don't boast more about that.

Public libraries are especially vital for children, because, everywhere else, what they meet tends to be controlled by adults: their parents; teachers and educationalists who decide on the school curriculum; big companies who assault them with advertising. Because libraries aim at being comprehensive, they give children a much-needed chance to restore the balance and explore the world on their terms. They can discover things for themselves following their own interests. I think that's worth preserving and fighting for.

SELECTED CURRENT TITLES

Chartbreak (Puffin)
The Dark Behind the Curtain (Point – Scholastic)
The Demon Headmaster (Puffin)
The Demon Headmaster Strikes Again (Puffin)
The Demon Headmaster Takes Over (Puffin)
The Great Elephant Chase (Puffin)
The Iron Way (Oxford)
Map of Nowhere (Mammoth)
New World (Puffin)
On the Edge (Puffin)
Pictures in the Dark (Oxford)
The Prime Minister's Brain (Puffin)
Revenge of the Demon Headmaster (Puffin)
Roscoe's Leap (Puffin)
Tightrope (Oxford)
Wolf (Puffin)

For younger readers

Beware Olga! (Walker)
Gobbo the Great (Mammoth)
The Goose Girl – retelling of the fairy tale (Scholastic)
Mintyglo Kid (Mammoth)
Posh Watson (Walker)
Rent a Genius (Puffin)
Roman Beanfeast (Antelope Books)
Swimathon (Mammoth)
The Tree House (Mammoth)
What Will Emily Do? (Mammoth)

An introduction to . . . Berlie Doherty

WHAT TYPE OF BOOKS DO YOU WRITE? All kinds, from picture books – such as *The Magical Bicycle* and *Paddiwack & Cosy* – through to novels for teenagers – such as *Dear Nobody* and *Daughter of the Sea* – and novels for adults.

WHAT ARE YOUR BOOKS ABOUT? Anything that appeals to me – adventure, family, animals, the past, and now, fantasy.

BORN: Knotty Ash, Liverpool, 1943.

EDUCATION: Honours English degree at Durham University; Certificate in Social Science at Liverpool University; PGCE (English) at Sheffield University.

PREVIOUS OCCUPATIONS: Ten months as a social worker, then I stayed at home with my children until the youngest was five, earning money with a folk group. I became a teacher for a few years, working on local schools radio, and became a full-time writer in 1983.

LIVES: The Peak District.

FAMILY/PETS: I live with my partner, Alan Brown, who is also a writer for children. I have three grown-up children – Janna, Tim and Sally and we have recently been adopted by a black cat, Midnight.

HOBBIES: Reading mostly, fell-walking, travel, music and wildlife conservation.

MOST TREASURED POSSESSION: A little black leather-bound diary that belonged to my grandfather. It tells of the journey he made to Australia in 1896 in search of his wife who had gone ahead of him.

AWARDS: Carnegie Medal for both *Dear Nobody* (1992) and *Granny Was a Buffer Girl* (1987); *Dear Nobody* has also been decorated with the Japanese Sankei Award as well as the Writers' Guild of Great Britain Children's Theatre Award. *Willa and Old Miss Annie* was joint runner-up for the 1995 Carnegie Medal. The New York Film and Television Award was given to *White Peak Farm*, the Writers' Guild Children's Award to *Daughter of the Sea* (1997) and the Nasen Award (1995) to *The Golden Bird*.

LANGUAGES TRANSLATED INTO: Seventeen – mainly European languages but also Japansese and Thai.

BOOKS ADAPTED INTO TV DRAMAS/THEATRE/RADIO PLAYS: The following have all been radio plays as well as books: *How Green You Are!*, *The Making of Fingers Finnigan*, *Tilly Mint Tales*, *White Peak Farm*, *Children of Winter*, *Granny was a Buffer Girl*, *Dear Nobody* and *Spellhorn*. *White Peak Farm*, *Children of Winter* and *Dear Nobody* have been made into television dramas. *Dear Nobody* is also a stage play. I adapt much of my own work, and am currently working on a screenplay of *Spellhorn*.

FAVOURITE CHILDREN'S BOOKS: *Northern Lights* by Philip Pullman and *Tom's Midnight Garden* by Philippa Pearce.

FAVOURITE MUSIC: Classical, opera and jazz.

FAVOURITE FILM: *Great Expectations.*

FAVOURITE POEM: W.B. Yeats – 'He Wishes for the Cloths of Heaven'.

FAVOURITE PLACE: The valley that I live in.

WHICH ONE OF YOUR CHARACTERS WOULD YOU MOST LIKE TO BE? Helen in *Dear Nobody* because she is emotionally strong. But I'd also like to be Tilly Mint – I think I am!

WHAT WERE YOU LIKE AT THE AGE OF 11? Similar to the character Julie in *How Green You Are!* – very shy, lonely and sensitive. I loved my father very much, enjoyed reading and writing poetry and desperately wanted to play the piano.

ENJOYS VISITING SCHOOLS BECAUSE: The nicest thing that can happen to a writer for children is to meet the people she writes the stories for. I think it's a gift that's given to the writer. I don't go into schools nearly as much as I used to, I just don't have time, but meeting children who've actually read your books is a wonderful thing. It reinforces what it's all about.

WHY DO YOU WRITE? Because I have to!

IF YOU WEREN'T A WRITER: I would work in radio or theatre.

AMBITIONS: To have a feature film made of one of my books.

WHAT FOUR WORDS DESCRIBE YOU BEST? Friendly, organised, industrious and imaginative!

WHAT WOULD YOU LIKE TO HAPPEN IN THE TWENTY-FIRST CENTURY? Peace in Ireland.

WHICH OF YOUR BOOKS WOULD YOU LIKE TO BE REMEMBERED FOR? If I'm remembered for anything, it will be *Dear Nobody*. I still get letters every day for *Dear Nobody*. But my choice would be *Daughter of the Sea.*

1 HOW THE READER BECAME A WRITER

The first book I owned was called *Mary Mouse*. I can't remember who it was by. You couldn't join a library until you were nine, and Dad used to go to the library every week and I used to love to go with him. Every now and then he'd buy me a book on the way home – books from the *Mary Mouse* series. When I was older, my favourites were *Little Women* by Louisa M. Alcott and *The Silver Skates* by N.M. Dodge. *The Silver Skates* is set in Holland – and it's about two children who are too poor to have silver skates – and it's very much a family story. I used to think how wonderful to live near canals that used to freeze in the winter and you'd have to skate along them to go to school! That was my very favourite book as a child. As I got a little bit older, the book that really meant something to me as an emerging writer was *Emily Climbs* by L.M. Montgomery. And I loved it so much that I put an inscription on the inside, which I'm very embarrassed about now! I wrote it when I was fourteen:

> One of my most treasured possessions to be read only by those whose intelligence of literature of this kind is profound.

I feel very meek about that! But I felt that I found myself in this book in the character of the girl Emily who wants to be a writer, who is just obsessed by writing.

My mother used to say to her friends, 'She's terrible! She's a terrible reader!' And I used to be really embarrassed because I thought they would think that it meant that I couldn't read, whereas what she meant was that I couldn't *not* read! Oh, she used to threaten to throw my books on the fire and things because if I wasn't writing I was reading! I adored reading.

I began to write from the age of eight. I was very much encouraged by my dad – who was an unpublished writer, but someone who'd always loved writing. He used to type up my first poems for me. I used to have poems published in the *Hoylake News and Advertiser* and the *Liverpool Echo* on their children's pages. I used to get paid the equivalent of 50p – or a box of chocolates or paints or fireworks or something. My first poem was about a gypsy I think – quite a romantic sort of rhyming poem – and there was another about my cat.

So I knew that I wanted to be a writer. I was very firm in that. And I thought that in order to be a writer you had to go to university and read proper books and do an English degree. And at the same time I was being very much encouraged by an English teacher at school who did a wonderful thing for me. When I was about sixteen I complained that there was nothing to read in the school library except *Lives of the Saints*, which was true – it was a convent school. Anyway, this teacher took me to her home and I'd never seen a house like it – every wall was covered with shelves of books but double layered. And she said 'Take what you want – and when you finish those, bring them back and come back for more.' My first batch of books were all American playwrights – Eugene O'Neill, Tennessee Williams, Arthur Miller. And she very much encouraged me to go to university.

And I can remember the day that I went home and turned off the television and said that I wanted to go to university to do an English degree – which was just unheard of in our family. None of my relations had done anything like that. And my mum had this kind of classic feeling that an education was wasted on a girl, which is what she said. And my dad said, if we can afford it, go for it. But I got a grant anyway. But in fact it was the last thing I should have done because it stopped me writing completely. I should have listened to my mum! In those days an English degree meant purely studying literature – not doing any creative writing yourself. It quashed my own creativity. I think it's something to do with (a) there isn't anybody asking you to do any writing – like you have at school, but (b) when you're receiving so much literature, great literature from the world – how on earth can you put yourself into that, you know? That stopped me writing.

I didn't actually start writing again until all my own children started school and I went back to university to do a PGCE teacher training course. Every now and then there would be an afternoon when you could do creative writing. I thought this was a lovely idea. The course lecturer said to us – very sensibly – if you're all going to be English teachers, asking children to write, you should be able to do it yourself. So he asked us all to write a story and he gave us the subject – black and white. My thoughts immediately flew to nuns! – because I'd been taught by them and because of the black and white habits they were dressed in, but also all the associations with good and evil and sin and sacrifice and everything that had been just so much part of my childhood and adolescence. It all tumbled out in that short story that he asked us to write.

I wrote a story which I titled 'Requiem' – about an event at school when a headteacher proposed to me that I should be a nun. It was as if she'd said to me 'you're going to die tomorrow'. I suddenly felt somebody was trying to grab hold of my soul, my being. The lecturer advised me to sell this short story as he said it was good and this gave me a huge fillip. I didn't dare send it off to London or anywhere posh so I took it to Radio Sheffield, where there was a producer named Dave Sheasby who was a wonderful man for encouraging local writing. He's a playwright now. He bought the story for £8 – which I thought was fantastic – and on the strength of it commissioned ten stories to be used in schools. And that was a series of stories for teenagers that he called *Summer of Ladybirds*. And I was off – and I've never stopped writing since. And then he commissioned a second series which was *How Green You Are!* And that eventually became my first book.

2 WRITING: ROUTINES AND REFLECTIONS

I can write anywhere – in fact I prefer to write anywhere – in that I like to be mobile. I write longhand and I sit out on the bench in the garden or sit in a warm chair by the fire, or I can write on the train or in front of the television. When the ideas are just bubbling out, it just doesn't matter where I am. But when it comes to the stage that I know where the story is going, and I've found the ending and I can't read my writing any more and it needs to be put on the computer – then I've got a little writing room at the back, a little barn at the back of the house which looks over the views of sheep and towards the Pennines. It's lovely and quiet there and I haven't got a telephone up there, or any music even. I just need to concentrate at that stage.

I do all my first drafts longhand. I write in these books I call 'Pretty Books' – they're A4 hardback notebooks. Whenever I see one in a shop I buy one, ready for my next novel. They have William Morris prints on the cover.

Some stories go straight onto the computer. The retellings I'm doing at the moment – the fairy stories – I do them straight onto computer because I know the story. What I do is to read *Snow White* or whatever it is and go for a walk and tell it to myself – talk it to myself till I'm starting to get my language into it and then I just go and do it straight onto the computer. I'd find it very irksome, I think, to do it longhand first.

I always have several projects on the go. Now, I'm working on the fifth draft of a film script for *Spellhorn*, and there's the collection of fairy stories – and I'm now up to about number seven or eight. And there's *Man of Passion* – draft three of my third adult novel. And I'm also starting to think about a radio series that I've been asked to do. There are advantages to juggling different writing projects because there are some days or weeks when you're not in the writing mood and it's a waste of time – I can't just sit at a blank page in front of me and think 'oh, I'll see what happens'. But if I'm in a writing mood and it's all bubbling I need to have several things on the go – something in preparation, something simmering and something boiling over!

I write in what I call 'scenes' – which aren't chapters so much as episodes. For instance, if we were talking about *Dear Nobody*, the bit where Helen and her mother come face to face with the fact she's pregnant – I would call that a scene – although it's part of a bigger whole. I would write it as one thing, and it would be totally draining to write it, and I've no idea how long it would take – it might take ten minutes or three hours. I don't know when I come out of it how long it's taken. But that's about as much as I'll be able to do on that book on that day. It's intense concentration and that's why you don't want the phone around at that stage. It's as if you've been somewhere else in that time.

When I was a child, and only writing occasionally, I always knew that I'd got a poem coming on because I used to feel ill, I used to feel sick, a bit faint. Very odd, isn't it? And my mother used to say that she could tell as well. I'd get kind of restless and I didn't quite know what to do with myself. So I'd go and write a poem and I'd be all right again!

Ideas often come when I haven't got room for them and I'm busy working on something else. It can happen at any time – when I'm on holiday, on the bus, at a concert or it's something somebody says to you. When it doesn't happen is when you're looking for an idea. That's when you don't find one. It's hard storing ideas. I'll write something down and lose it usually! My 'pretty books' are full of all kinds of ideas. I used to carry a notebook around with me all the time, and jot things down, and I've got out of the habit of doing that and it's a shame because I always tell other people to do it! I've got a drawer in my filing cupboard called 'Ideas' and it won't open any more – it's jam packed! I think that's rather a nice image!

I prefer writing in the first person, I think. It helps me to get inside a character, and sometimes I change as I'm writing. The adult novel that I'm wrestling with at the moment has jumped from third to first all the time. Every time I think I've lost the characters I start to write it in the first person, because I can feel what they feel. When I feel that I know them well enough, I sometimes decide to write it in the third person.

Editorial involvement varies from one book to another. Sometimes editors are hardly involved at all – they're just a kind of filter, someone to send my work to. Sometimes they play a very big role. Jane Nissen has been my editor from the start. She's not edited all my books, but she's been with me since the first book that I wrote, *How Green You Are!* She has edited all my teenage fiction and I feel she knows my writing better than anyone else does, and so I can talk an idea through in a way that I wouldn't with anyone else. There have been times when she's been very, very wrong – she tried to block *Children of Winter* for instance. I told her I was writing the book and she just sighed and said we can't sell historical fiction. But I was so far into it I couldn't not write it, and she now says it's one of her favourite books. So thank goodness I didn't take in what she said! And *Dear Nobody* she got at an early stage and made a lot of suggestions which made it a much better book. It was her suggestion that I should tell more about the background to the parents. I'd just kind of hinted previously. It turned out to be a very important part of the book.

I try to avoid reading anything that might remotely resemble what I'm writing at the time. If I'm writing something for children I won't read any books by other children's authors till I've finished – and then of course I just gobble them up! All the time I was writing my adult novel *Requiem* I wouldn't read any Irish writers. I was terrified about being influenced by them – or being put off what I was trying to write.

I think a children's writer has a dual responsibility – you must entertain the child, it must be something they enjoy reading, but I think also because we're adult and we have had experiences we need to kind of show a way through what seems to be a hopeless tangle at times. I don't necessarily mean a happy ending, because happy endings aren't always right for a book, more often than not, but the possibility of a solution I think is important. I don't think it's fair to leave a child with a sense of hopelessness at the end, because children do get very, very involved with books. It was a long time before I realised that I was a children's writer because I was just writing. I still do, in a sense, just write. But most of my stuff is published as children's books.

And you make a moral choice in what you choose to write about. I couldn't write about murder, I just couldn't do it as a piece of entertainment. I know very, very good writers who've done it – like Bob Swindells, in *Stone Cold*. But when I've written about teenage pregnancy, abortion – the thought of abortion anyway, with Helen, and adoption too – these are all terribly sensitive issues. I don't think of myself as an issues writer at all, but I realise that I'm treading on very thin ice and people can be very hurt if you don't handle it properly – especially from that vulnerable age of about thirteen or so, if you're adopted or whatever. I've got to get it right. I look on that as being a big moral responsibility or moral strand in my writing.

I was talking earlier about L.M. Montgomery's *Emily Climbs* – and that as a teenager I found myself in that book. I remember the first time I was asked to write for children, which was when *How Green You Are!* was commissioned, I asked myself the serious question – what do children want to find in a book? And I thought they want to find themselves, because that's what I want to find – even in novels for adults that I read now. It's a kind of emotional landscape where the young reader finds that they dare to go into and can find a way out of it again.

I have this label of being a teenage writer. I don't know why! But it's a lovely area to write in – because so much is happening to teenagers, they're physically adults and temperamentally children, emotionally they're in total turmoil and they've got these huge landscapes stretching ahead of them, and behind them is the familiar territory of childhood. Which gives huge potential for drama. A teenager is the centre of her world, she has to be. So everything that happens to a teenager is incredibly important – whether it's falling out with your best friends or falling in love with somebody or being put down in front of your friends. But they're not the only person in their world, they're not an island – they've got all these ripples spreading out and out and out from them. Everything they do affects their family. In my writing I just love to let something happen to a teenager, say, and see what happens to all the people around her because of it. As a teenager myself, I think I was a child a lot longer than most young people are today. I think that was part of having a 1950s childhood. But also, because I'd been brought up in this oppressive but loving Catholic education, where thinking for yourself was not really taken on board and important questions were quashed.

People say to me 'I cried when such-and-such-a-thing happened' and I say, well I did too. When Danny died in *Granny Was a Buffer Girl* I cried – I didn't want him to die, but he did. When I was writing *Requiem*, there's a scene in that which is about a retreat – and it was very much like the retreat at our school, and we were being told to repress our womanhood and how we're prone to evil, and all men are evil. And every time I read that bit I cried because I just thought how awful to inflict that on a child. How could they do it to us? I'm very angry about that.

With some books I use certain things to inspire my writing. When I was working on *White Peak Farm* I was listening to the Elgar Cello Concerto all the time. And I collect postcards that are connected with various stories. *Granny Was a Buffer Girl* came from a painting which is in the Graves Art Gallery in Sheffield. The picture is called *The Sheffield Buffer Girls*.

When I read through the drafts of a novel I pay close attention to dialogue – and whether something should or should not be in dialogue at all, whether a scene would actually move much faster if you take it away. And also, it must be that character talking. You should be able to recognise a character by the things they say and the way they say them. And I think the more we become a film and television watching public, the more dialogue we're seeing in books, and sketchy dialogue at that. So, dialogue moves the narrative forward but also tells you something about the character. It's also got to sound like real people talking, though it hasn't got to have the monotony of real people talking. So I always read what I write out loud to test it out.

You always know when you have finished a book, when it's ready. But you always feel there's another layer you could add but it mightn't help the book. At that stage it's control and craft. And I think there's a sense of destiny, and I think your characters have a kind of destiny and when they've reached that point that's the end of the story and it shouldn't go beyond there. But it's also a kind of instinct, you just know when it's finished and you shouldn't do any more.

3 GROWING A BOOK

Dear Nobody

I don't have a set way of working on a book, it's always instinctive. The evolution of *Dear Nobody* was after I'd had that long ten-month break after writing *Requiem*. My agent said that I should write some short stories again, like in *Granny Was a*

Buffer Girl, and write something about a family – let everyone write their own story. So I went away and thought about it. And I thought about a teenage pregnancy, and a young person becoming pregnant. From the very beginning I thought I want this to be about how it affects the boy, and I thought it would just be about Chris. I started it in the first person as Chris's story, and I thought this isn't going to work because I can't exclude Helen because she's the one who's going to have the baby. Then I started to write it in the third person and that didn't work either because I'd lost Chris then. So I went back inside Chris and then I hit on the idea of letting Helen speak out all her emotions, her anguish and loneliness into the letters she'd write to her unborn child. And so I was away then – I knew what I was doing. This was about thirty or forty pages into the first draft.

Sometimes I don't redraft at all, it's just one draft and that's it – less so now, but certainly at the beginning. I don't think I changed *Granny Was a Buffer Girl* much at all, but *Dear Nobody* was two major drafts. The major changes were developing the other members of the family – drawing the threads between the relationship Helen and Chris had with their own unborn child and with the relationship they had with their parents – going up through the generations as well as downwards. It was a very, very important second draft which was suggested by my editor Jane Nissen.

It had been a long time since I'd been a teenager in love, so I needed to do a bit of research. I went and talked to young people at a local secondary school when I lived in Sheffield. I talked to fourteen-year-olds as they would probably be the readers and I talked to eighteen-year-olds because they were the age of the main characters.

5(1)

hugged between the stiff [illegible] starched sheets

She lay in the bed, curled up with her knees drawn up to the chin, like a child in a womb. She tried to imagine what ~~Nobody~~ a foetus would look like. She was ten weeks pregnant. The baby would be 2 ~~in~~ inches long. It would have little buds of arm and legs, like a tadpole. It was a bud, waiting to open out. She thought of herself on Robin's back, being flung useless up and down, a rag doll. ~~Nobody~~ changing somehow into life [illegible] had clung on inside her, a tiny, pulsing, unthinking, unknowing thing. It ~~had clung on free-diving~~ ~~because that was in its nature~~. It was not an alien thing. It was part of herself, tucked below her ribs. It was her self. She curled herself up in bed. She felt as if she was hanging on to this for something [illegible] [illegible] she didn't understand herself. She was afraid, but [illegible] [illegible] [illegible]. The nurse came back with a trolley. She picked up a syringe and held it to the light. [illegible] as if she had become two people. ~~She wouldn't let go~~ I will not let go, she thought.

'What's that for?' asked Helen, afraid. She was lost and scared. She was panicking just below the surface.

'This will relax you and help you to sleep,' the nurse said. 'You'll be having your operation soon.'

Helen sat up in bed, panicking. She could hardly breathe now. 'I need to talk to someone.'

'Just hold yourself still dear, it won't

Manuscript page from *Dear Nobody*

I talked to boys as well as girls. I found them so incredibly open and interested. It was their interest and enthusiasm that really gave me the courage to write what I knew was going to be quite a difficult book. I asked them what they thought would be the hardest thing for Chris and Helen to face and both boys and girls said telling your parents. In fact we role-played it in the classroom – first of all we role-played telling Helen's mother and then telling Chris's father and it was incredibly useful doing that. The pupils were so immediately involved in the situation I was presenting to them. I did exactly the same thing as when I was writing *Tough Luck* – for the part where Sprat gets a letter from his mother saying she wants to see him again, and I did a role-play then with some schoolchildren to see what they felt the reaction might be.

The language in my books is instinctive. I don't tend to spend that long on individual lines or paragraphs. The language is never the hardest thing for me. The hardest things are giving information, necessary information – whether it be background information or authenticity or the links between two major emotional scenes – and moving things forward. That's where I can spend hours, just puzzling how to do it.

An idea for a book will often stay in my head for maybe months; often I'm writing other things. The idea will actually be developing in my head. And I often find that I'm switched onto this idea – this channel – before I go to sleep, which is desperate because it means I won't get to sleep. And all this time the idea is beginning to grow, beginning to come into place and I feel that there's a thread that's being pulled right through to the end. And when I know what the ending's going to be – when *I think* I know what the ending's going to be – I feel ready to start writing it. I don't need to plan a book formally. I can have all the characters and practically all the language in my head by the time I actually start to write. I then write very fast often, and sometimes it will come out complete. But I didn't know what was going to happen to Chris and Helen in *Dear Nobody* until I got to the end. I just couldn't decide – I let them decide. And I asked some young people in school. I would take in sections of *Dear Nobody* and read them to the class and say 'What do you think might happen?' And the boys would say, 'I'd look after the baby if it was me', and the girls would say that Chris gets killed in a motorbike accident – which finishes him off! So, their solutions weren't any better than mine!

The Snake-stone

This book started when I wrote the stage adaptation of *Dear Nobody*. The actor who was playing the character of Chris said that there was a line in the play that reminded him of a week in his life. I asked what was the line and what was the week and he said, 'You make me say "I'm nothing to my mother now – I'm a speck of dust and I've blown away."' And he told me that he was adopted and that one week during his college career he decided to go and try and find his mother. And this sent prickles up and down my spine; it was really moving. So I said, 'Do you want to tell me about it?' He told me that he was 21, 22 at the time and he described how he and his friend had gone to the adoption society to find out what they could and then had travelled to Bradford and searched around. By the end of the week he hadn't found his mother, but he had found the man he thought was his father. He said he was satisfied with what he found, and that was it as far as he was concerned. It wasn't as far as I was concerned. I thought then that I'd love to write a book about something like that. But I decided to make my central character much younger, obviously because I wanted it to be a children's book. And also that was useful because it meant he couldn't go through the adoption society – because you've got to be eighteen before they will give you background knowledge. So that was my starting point. I decided I wanted the main character to be a boy because I didn't quite like the idea of a girl wandering off on her own at that age. And I decided to set it in the Peak District because I like writing about familiar landscapes. Even if I don't say where it is, I like to know where it is.

So, I started to write the book and about a third into it I got really stuck and thought 'I can't do this'. I rang my editor Jane Nissen up and told her that it was not working. She told me not to worry and said that I should leave it for a bit and I'd be all right. So I did. Then, about four or six weeks later, I thought 'What is it about it that's not working?' And I thought it's James – because I don't know why someone who's fifteen who is quite happy at home should do this crazy thing of going off to seek his mother, chancing everything. And I thought – maybe he's an obsessive sort of kid. I thought back to when I'd been teaching, of children who are obsessed with certain things, who play chess or a musical instrument for hours and hours and hours, or play on the computer or kick a ball around the field, you know for hours. I thought then he was going to be that sort of child because that would give him that sort of drive, and he knows what he wants and he'll go for it. And then I thought he's a sporty child – so what sport? It had to be a lonely sort of sport, not a team thing. But also quite a poetic sport – as what he was doing, seeking his mother, was a poetic kind of quest. Then I thought of high diving. I'd never even dare go on to a diving board myself! I'd known a lad since he was about ten who used to live around here who had been European champion at sixteen, so I went to talk to him. The more he talked to me the more I knew I'd found my character. So I was off then and it just fell into place.

The structure of the book, with two story strands – with the mother and son making the same journey in opposite directions – is unusual. I think it's because of the setting actually. Because it's here. There's a track well known to walkers – called Jacob's Ladder – and it's the start of the Pennine Way. If you just carry on you come to a village called Hayfield. And I thought that I could set it in my valley and also Hayfield. Gradually I got it down to thinking that I could write two stories here – I can write the mother's story as well if she's the same age as he is, or was at the time of her journey. I thought of that before I'd started the book. Hardly a word of the story changed from the first draft to the published book.

I like layering my narratives. I can't do it straight. What I mean is that I like to create three-dimensional characters with a past and a future as well as a present. I don't really like walk-on parts – however insignificant their role, each character should have a personality and should exist in their own right as recognisable people. And, usually unconsciously, I find there's a layering of imagery going on as well. All my early books – *How Green You Are!*, *The Making of Fingers Finnigan*, *Tilly Mint Tales*, *White Peak Farm*, *Children of Winter* and *Granny was a Buffer Girl* – were written for radio originally so they had to be episodic. They had to work as an episode, but for my satisfaction they had to have a unifying whole.

Rollercoaster Sept 17th 199

[illegible] ~~[illegible]~~ [illegible] the tickets [illegible]

[illegible] Up and over, hurtling off the Earth. ~~Hold on Jan.~~

~~Hold me down.~~ Jan screaming, and the world lurching

past us, over us and under us, sky-rocketing us out.

I can't stop. I can't stop. The air's battering me. ~~[illegible] up there~~

on the dizzy top before we were plunged down and down

again, ~~that was when I knew.~~

~~"I'm going to find her." I said to Jan. Her~~ face was

white and her hair was wild. We stood with our arms

around each other, not trusting the ground to keep solid

under our feet. It's important to remember that that was when

I decided to do it. It had nothing to do with what happened

– "Find who?" later. I'd already decided

"What're you thinking?" Jan [illegible] ~~[illegible] Jan said~~ I asked. "How d'you feel?" [illegible]

~~"Jenny." I said~~ "You know," I said. "The [illegible].

didn't I feel sick. I was [illegible] the world [illegible] going up again. I

She knew what I meant, though she pretended not

wouldn't let [illegible] go up in the air

She screwed up her face as though her memory

was I ~~[illegible]~~ to kissed her, but my mind was

Manuscript page from 'Rollercoaster' (published as *The Snake-stone*)

The idea of the snake-stone came from a trip to Lyme Regis. And this is where the obsessive child came in as well. We'd been looking for fossils. We were staying in a bed and breakfast place, and I happened to say to this little boy next to me 'Have you seen *Jurassic Park*?' And he went on and on about it and about his fossils and he talked and talked. And he talked about ammonites. But this image of this tight structure – which had been a living thing which breathed and moved – was very strong in me and that became the central image of the book. And obviously it's the description too of the dive that's so important to James – the double reverse somersault, which has a rolling and opening out visual image. I don't look for these symbolic images, they just come. People often find metaphors in my books that I'm not even aware of.

4 WRITING BOOKS IN SCHOOL

Tough Luck came about when I was doing a writing residency in a school in Doncaster. I was asked to make eleven visits to the school in a term, and I was working with different age groups. I was working with sixth formers writing poetry, a Year 10 group writing plays and a Year 8 group doing story writing. As soon as I met the Year 8 group I thought: I want to do something sustained with them rather than doing eleven different writing exercises every Wednesday morning. So I said 'Do you fancy writing a book with me?' And they all said 'Yeah!' I was really pleased and said that they could choose what the book would be about. Then I crossed my fingers, in case they chose horror!

I gave them all a piece of paper. There were twenty-eight of them in the class. I asked them to write down what they wanted our book to be about and I told them not to let anyone else read what they had put. Sixteen out of the twenty-eight wrote that they wanted it to be a book about ourselves – or words to that effect. That gave me a wonderful starting point, because there was the raw material for a book about thirteen- and fourteen-year-olds. We talked about that age group and friends and money and clothes and music and boyfriends and teachers, whatever they wanted to talk about.

We decided the story would be set in a comprehensive school like theirs, a class just like theirs, with children just like themselves, but not about them – and that was the most important thing for me to say. We were going to invent characters who could be in the school. Having thought about the class as a nucleus, I wanted an outsider to set against that nucleus. I asked them 'Who or why or what could this outsider be?' And they said that he could be a twagger! I'd never heard of a twagger so I was bought straight away! So this child who doesn't go to school, who plays truant became Twagger, one of the main characters. I told them that we couldn't have twenty-eight other characters, so I asked them to find three – another boy, and a girl – and the group of Asian girls in the class said that another main character should be black. They decided it would be a girl, who became Naseem.

I split the class into groups and each group had responsibility for a character. We had groups working on all the characters: Twagger, Sprat, Naseem, Caroline, Mr Bead, Miss Peters and so on. We drew up character descriptions. I fired questions at each group – such as 'What does he like to eat?', 'What did he dream about last night?', 'What does he wear when he's not wearing school uniform?' Next I gave them scenes to think about. So the 'Twagger' group would write a scene taking place in his house – and I would write the same scene or chapter or whatever and then the next week we'd read them out to everyone and talk about them. We'd discuss what worked and what didn't and why. Therefore there were two books growing at the same time – the one I was writing at home and the school one. By the time I'd finished – which was after the eleven hours of seeing them – there were sixty pages of their book, which they called *Twagger*. We had it reproduced and everyone in the class had a copy.

Initially it was meant to be a prolonged exercise in character, and how you can weave characters in and out. I told my editor Jane Nissen about it and she thought that it was a lovely idea for a new book. And there I was, with a new book to write. So I did a huge amount of research with the ethnic minorities adviser in Sheffield, and going to the Mosque and talking to the Imam at the Mosque. I needed to know more about the character Naseem, as her background was so different from my own. I kept popping back into the school to tell the children how things were developing, to read drafts to them and then we had the launch at the school, which was brilliant.

Spellhorn came immediately after *Tough Luck*. I got a commission from the BBC to do a drama series about unicorns. I instantly thought that as I enjoyed writing *Tough Luck* so much with that class, that it would be great to try and build up a radio play with a class of children. Then I thought – because it's radio, it would be really interesting to talk to children for whom sound is really important. There was a school for the blind in Sheffield – and I rang them and asked if I could work with a few children, so they gave me four. Again, I liked the children immediately, and really wanted to get to know them all. I got into the habit of just popping in once a week or so, and just doing anything with them really – reading a story to them or going for a walk with them or getting them to write poetry. It wasn't a research project at all, but it became that eventually.

From there I started to work on the radio play of *Spellhorn*. And because I wanted to share it so much with the children – and it was difficult reading the characters from a radio play script to them – that's when I thought of writing it as a novel at the same time. And only then did I decide that the central character was going to be blind. I wanted it to be a book for them. It would never have entered my head otherwise. Then I was a bit nervous about it. I read the first chapter to the children and didn't mention that Laura was blind. It doesn't actually say so in the book. It was deliberate.

At the end of the chapter I asked the children what they thought of it. And there were lots of positive comments. But I asked them what they thought about Laura, what they noticed about her. They said she was nice, and kind to her mum and things. And I gave up eventually, and said 'She's blind.' 'Well of course she is!' they said.

It was a different working experience from working with a whole class, of course. This was very much more a case of reading it to them to see what they thought of it. But they were so attentive and also retentive – I would go in the next week and they could repeat the chapter I'd read before almost word for word. It was a joy to read to them.

Ideas started coming from them. Thoughts were flying all the time. It was brilliant. I got them all to write a song, to help me invent the Wild Ones' language and words. We had a lovely time doing this. Something that they did which impressed me very much was when we all wrote the battle scene together. The children did it on a Perkins typewriter. When I came in and read my bit about Spellhorn fighting with the hornless ones and the moonbats and everything, and they read me theirs, theirs were full of ripping flesh and dripping blood and screeches and screams! I said to them 'How bloodthirsty!' And they said 'Yours is so tame!' I told them that I find it really hard to write about violence, to be honest. And they said fair enough, but a battle is a battle! So I tempered mine – there's a lot more gore in it now than there was, but it's still not as bloodthirsty as theirs was! I learnt a lot from them because of that.

We also had discussions about how the book would end. I wanted very much for Laura to come home to her parents; they very much wanted Laura to stay in the wilderness. So there's a kind of compromise at the end. It's funny that – they weren't bothered about her going back! A lot of people have since said to me that surely what the children would want for Laura is for her to see at the end, but that never arose, they never once questioned the fact that she became blind again at the end of the book.

I'm having the same discussion now with the man who wants to make *Spellhorn* into a feature film. He's feeling that maybe the strong ending would be if Laura gets her sight back, and I'm saying no, really it's about the imagination actually being more powerful than anything else. We haven't decided yet, and the project is only in the early stages. Of all my books, it's very strange that it's the one about a blind child that has attracted the most interest from film people. But film is a totally different animal. I'm making a lot of changes to make it much more of an adventure. More of a real adventure than an emotional adventure.

SELECTED CURRENT TITLES

Children of Winter (Mammoth)
Daughter of the Sea (Hamish Hamilton)
Dear Nobody (Lions Tracks)
Granny was a Buffer Girl (Mammoth)
How Green You Are! (Mammoth)
The Making of Fingers Finnigan (Mammoth)
Midnight Man (Walker)
The Sailing Ship Tree (Hamish Hamilton)
The Snake-stone (Collins Tracks)
Spellhorn (Collins)
Street Child (Heinemann)
White Peak Farm (Mammoth)

Poetry

Walking on Air (Lions)

Short stories

Running on Ice (Mammoth)

For younger readers

Bella's Den (Yellow Bananas – Mammoth)
The Golden Bird (Heinemann Young)
Tilly Mint Tales / Tilly Mint and the Dodo (Mammoth)
Willa and Old Miss Annie (Walker)

Picture books

The Magical Bicycle – with illustrator Christian Birmingham (Picture Lions)
Paddiwack & Cosy (Hodder & Stoughton)

Collections

The Forsaken Merman and other story poems – selected by Berlie Doherty (Hodder & Stoughton)
Tales of Wonder and Magic – collected by Berlie Doherty (Walker)
Trickster Tales (Walker)

An introduction to . . . Alan Durant

WHAT SORT OF BOOKS DO YOU WRITE? I write a wide range of books – from picture books such as *Angus Rides the Goods Train* and *Mouse Party* to young fiction such as *Jake's Magic* and the *Spider McDrew* stories and teenage novels such as *Blood* and *A Short Stay in Purgatory*.

WHAT ARE YOUR BOOKS ABOUT? Anything and everything. I write funny stories, football stories, thrillers . . . I don't think there's any common thread that links them all – except me, of course.

BORN: Surrey – 6 September 1958.

EDUCATION: Trinity School, Croydon. Keble College, Oxford University – studied English Language and Literature.

LIVES: South of London.

FAMILY/PETS: I have a wife, Jinny, three children: Amy (10), Kit (8) and Josie (6), and a cat called Puddy.

HOBBIES: Manchester United, football generally, reading and playing badminton.

HAS ALSO WORKED AS: Animateur at The Centre for Spontaneous Expression in Paris and copywriter for the charity SCOPE. I currently work for Walker Books as their Senior Copywriter.

MOST TREASURED POSSESSION: My 1969 Manchester United Football Year Book. It's signed by my idol, George Best.

LANGUAGES TRANSLATED INTO: Italian, Spanish, Dutch, Danish, Norwegian and Japanese.

FAVOURITE BOOKS: *The King of the Castle* by Meriol Trevor and *The Catcher in the Rye* by J.D. Salinger. I also particularly enjoy Raymond Chandler, Ross MacDonald, Graham Greene and the short stories of William Trevor.

FAVOURITE LINES OF POETRY: Samuel Taylor Coleridge, *Kubla Khan*:

In Xanadu did Kubla Khan
A stately pleasure-dome decree:
Where Alph, the sacred river, ran
Through caverns measureless to man
Down to a sunless sea.

FAVOURITE QUOTE: Taken from Isaiah, the Old Testament: 'The people who walked in darkness have seen a great light.'

FAVOURITE MUSIC: Samuel Barton's *Agnus Dei* and Leonard Cohen's *Famous Blue Raincoat*.

FAVOURITE FILM: Woody Allen's *Sleeper*.

WHICH ONE OF YOUR CHARACTERS WOULD YOU MOST LIKE TO BE? Oliver in *Creepe Hall*, probably.

WHAT WERE YOU LIKE AT THE AGE OF 11? Utterly football obsessed!

ENJOYS VISITING SCHOOLS BECAUSE: I enjoy being with kids. I also like performing my work.

IF YOU WEREN'T A WRITER: I couldn't imagine myself doing anything else – I feel it's the only thing I'm any good at!

WHY DO YOU WRITE? When I started writing at fourteen it wasn't really to tell stories, it was much more to do with the power that it gave me to express myself – a power which I didn't have in everyday speech.

AMBITIONS: To meet George Best and/or Leonard Cohen.

WHAT WORDS DESCRIBE YOU BEST? According to my wife, Jinny : 'Humorous, sensitive, positive and kind.'

WHAT WOULD YOU LIKE TO HAPPEN IN THE TWENTY-FIRST CENTURY? I'm quite pessimistic about the future of mankind. I'd like the world to survive, but with all the mass-destructive weapons around, I fear it won't.

WHICH OF YOUR BOOKS WOULD YOU LIKE TO BE REMEMBERED FOR? One I haven't written yet! It's something that I'll write within the next ten years.

1 HOW THE READER BECAME A WRITER

The first books I remember loving were the C.S. Lewis *Narnia* books when I was nine. I wasn't a particularly advanced reader, but once I got going I read a lot and I became a real bookworm. I used to read, read, read all the time. At that age I also read *The King of the Castle* by Meriol Trevor, *Little Grey Men* by BB and *The Children of Green Knowe* by Lucy Boston – which I'm now reading to my elder daughter. It's great to go back to all those books with my own children. *The King of the Castle* meant so much to me as a child, and it had a very big effect on me. I'll never forget the opening scene, when this young boy is ill in bed, and his mother is looking after him. It's winter outside, and it's a very cosy image. His mum brings him this picture which she puts on the wall. The boy keeps looking at it, wondering what the landscape is like beyond the picture. Then suddenly, he's there, in the landscape himself. I can remember looking at pictures like that myself as a child.

Enid Blyton's *Famous Five* books were also very important to me. I got about to the end of the whole series – number 21 or something – when I ran out of interest, and I failed to finish the last one. I loved all those books – with the children, the smugglers, the kidnaps and everything. I think those books are what developed my interest in mystery stories, I can definitely trace it back to them, because really, *The Famous Five* are classic crime books – in every book the 'gang' have to solve a mystery of some kind.

My mother was very keen on the arts. She used to give my older brother and me a lot of encouragement. There was a rivalry between me and my brother – well I saw it that way, in any case. He's about two and a half years older than me. I idolised him. I wanted to copy him in everything. He used to write a great deal as a teenager, and that inspired me to write. He wrote, so I wrote.

In one of the exercise books I've kept from my early teens is a list of the books I was reading at that time. There's quite a wide range: *Snowfell* by Malcolm Saville, *The Pied Piper* by Nevil Shute, *The Last Battle* by C.S. Lewis, *Mike at Wrykyn* by P.G. Wodehouse, *As I Walked Out One Midsummer Morning* by Laurie Lee, a couple of plays by Harold Pinter and *The First Circle* by Solzhenitsyn, *Goals in the Air* by Michael Hardcastle, *The Coming of the Kings* by Ted Hughes, the Sherlock Holmes stories by Arthur Conan Doyle and many books by Agatha Christie. There weren't such things as 'teenage' books when I was that age, and everyone read a mix of children's literature and adult books.

The stories that I wrote then were nothing like the books I was reading. Although I was into detective fiction like Agatha Christie and Sherlock Holmes I wasn't interested in writing that stuff. Then, I wasn't writing to tell a story, I was writing more to express my emotions – it was more of a catharsis. I wrote almost exclusively about the crucifixion. Whatever the title or theme of the essay I was given by my teacher, I'd end up working it round so that I'd write about the crucifixion – over and over again. My teachers found it slightly bewildering. They appreciated the creativity of the writing, but they were bemused by it. I remember one English teacher who published a poem I was particularly pleased with in the school magazine. When I read it in the magazine I saw that he'd hacked it – he'd radically changed it without even speaking to me about it. I was incensed. He said he did it to make the poem better, but in my eyes it was much worse.

It was when I was fourteen that I decided I wanted to be a writer. I wrote quite a lot of horror. Many of the stories involved cannibalism, torture and death – it was quite lurid stuff! I don't write about horror at all now, and I look at a story such as 'Judas Iscariot' – which I've included here – and I've never written anything as horrible since. I think all this was a reaction to the changes that were happening to me and of me trying to cope with being a teenager. I wasn't happy at that time, I wasn't comfortable with myself, I was very shy and awkward. I wasn't very good at being a teenager, and the only way I could assert myself was by writing. I found writing quite empowering. It wasn't until I was about seventeen or eighteen that I started enjoying being a teenager. I had more friends then, especially girls.

From the ages of 14–19 I wrote a lot of poetry. I used to write it all the time – in lessons, on the bus, everywhere. I was very influenced then by Roger McGough, who was an absolute favourite of mine. I went to many of his poetry readings when I was still at school. And the singer and lyricist Leonard Cohen was a big influence

Judas Escariot.

The hot dog that Marlo was sucking burn his mouth. He squealed. The burger though a tasty mixture of herbs and roasted flesh, lacked enough bite. He reached for the salt. 'Toady' Harris had contributed generously too this meal. He had given his hand. The delicious smell of burning dogs, cats and humans wafted delicately down the street. Marlo couldn't underst why people hadn't thought of the idea in the past. They had always seemed to bury and forget people 'The bible had only said 'thou shalt not kill'; not thou shalt not eat the dead'? There was no other form of real meat, except dogs and cats, all other animals were dead.

. . . . He sat down hard on the passenger's seat. The car drove him to the small house on the hill. He thanked his chauffeur. The car door slammed and he walked towards the front door. He opened it with the key he possessed. He went into the living room. She was waiting for him. The sight of her naked body made his blood boil. His thoughts first centred on her as a tender meal, not as his love. He looked at her breasts thinking of what a delicious meal they would make. He was a cannibal. He could see nothing but meat, raw and beautiful, and he wanted

Short story written by Alan Durant as a teenager

nothing more than to eat the food he saw in front of him. His eyes gleamed with evil intent. He had eaten no meat since last month when he had tasted a flesh-burger. He could see nothing but food, glorious, plentiful food, a complete meal. He drew a knife from his pocket. She gasped as he moved towards her, his eyes glazed with madness. He had to go on. He reached her and tore from her body the first piece of meat he saw; blood streamed from her dead arm. He tore and tore, the knife acting as a fang, ripping her skin, and then all of a sudden... he stopped. He remembered who he was. He already knew what he was. He felt, and, when he touched the clerical collar, he burst out crying.

    "Oh Christ!"

    <u>Macabre but effective.</u>

5/10

on me. I started to write songs as well at that age too. And even in my early twenties, when I was at university, I still wasn't writing as a storyteller; I don't think I was interested in telling stories. I was still only expressing my emotions – most of the songs and poetry were about unrequited love, about which I guess I was something of an expert! The storytelling came later, when I began working in children's book publishing.

When I left university and went to work in Paris I continued to write songs. But at that point I also started writing a few short stories – based upon my own experiences as a teenager. Some of these stories, such as 'The Star', resurfaced much later, when I reworked them for my collection *A Short Stay in Purgatory*. My interest in writing for young people revealed itself when I began working for Walker Books, who started publishing teenage fiction soon after I joined. As soon I read those books, I suddenly felt *this is it* – this is the age I want to write about. Soon after I wrote my first two books – both novels for teenagers – *Hamlet, Bananas and all that Jazz* and *Blood*. At that stage I was simply writing for myself, not really for a specific audience at all. I was writing *about* teenagers and being published *for* teenagers.

2 WRITING: ROUTINES AND REFLECTIONS

I write in my garden shed. It's a small shed with just enough room for a few shelves and bookcases and my computer. I do like to work in an enclosed space. If I have too much space I tend to get up and wander about, and I can't get myself focused.

I organise my work with great difficulty. I have one day a week to write – Wednesday – but that's also the day on which I have to arrange my school visits. I'll also write for a couple hours on a Saturday and Sunday. And I try to do an hour in the shed before I go to work every morning. Bernard Ashley once said to me that a writer should write something – even if it's only to change a line – every single day. And that's what I try to do. In general, I work very quickly and I write in very concentrated bursts.

Computers are very important to me. I don't think I'd be writing now if I didn't have one. Even my first novel was written directly onto the computer. I just don't like writing by hand. My handwriting is pretty illegible, anyway. Computers are so liberating for a writer, and for me they're essential. But I do make some notes by hand. I have a notebook in which I write various bits and pieces – ideas for titles, jokes, interesting names, descriptions of interesting faces – all kinds of things. For example, I came across the name Calico – my main character in *Publish or Die!* – during one of my school visits, and I made a note of it in my notebook, and it resurfaced later. Every now and then I go through my notebooks to see if there's any material I can use. The books have to be hardback pocket books with lined paper. And I only ever write with a blue Artline 200 pen. It has to be blue.

I find editors very useful. I look to my editors to give a lot of feedback. They pull no punches in their criticism, but not in a nasty way, because we've got a decent relationship – and because I respect their criticisms I usually take on board their ideas. Which is good, because my own personal feeling is that I'm never going to improve as a writer unless I get that kind of input from somebody I respect. One editor who has been very helpful to me is Anne-Janine Murtagh, who is now the publisher at Kingfisher. She's a phenomenally good editor. I fully respect her judgements, but I usually give her a hard time before accepting them! She was the editor that accepted my very first novel. I also have an excellent rapport with my agent, Hilary Delamare. She's been my agent for about seven years now. I trust her so much that I'll show her very early drafts and ideas. Hilary is good at highlighting any problems or things that need working on.

Research is something that I don't tend to do that much of. I do a lot of reading, and often the ideas for my books will stem from my own interests. For *Blood*, I researched forensic science a little. For *The Good Book*, I read a great deal of the Old Testament. And in the football series I'm writing at the moment, I read up on Herbert Chapman, the Arsenal manager from the 1930s. Generally, though, I don't have to do that much research for my books.

Ideas come in all shapes and sizes. Sometimes I know where to put an idea – if it's a novel or a short story or picture book. But ideas can change at times. One of my new books, *Little Troll*, for example, started out as two different picture books. However, something wasn't quite right about them, and I re-wrote them as one story-book text for younger readers. Most of my ideas now come through my school visits or conversations with my children. My children have become the primary audience I write for now, and I will often write according to their tastes and interests.

It's quite common for me to have an idea in my head a long time before I actually write it down. Particularly with my fiction for older readers, the stories have been with me for a long time before I really start working on them. With novels, I'll often have been mulling over the ideas for a number of years before I start. I won't have the whole book worked out, but I'll have worked out the basic plot, specific lines, specific moments and whether it's going to be first, second or third person. This new novel I'm hoping to do, called *Flesh and Bones*, has been running in my head for about five years now. It's going to be – wait for it! – a realistic, supernatural, historical murder mystery!

With plot-driven stories, like my crime novel, *Publish or Die!*, I structure the book quite carefully. I work out the events chapter by chapter – what will be revealed and when and what the clues will be. In crime books the plot is so important and you really have to have a very clear idea of what's going to happen beforehand and how it's going to happen. With all the twists and turns, it's like a puzzle, and if you don't plan it properly the whole thing will go haywire. But I do deviate from my original plan to some degree.

I will try out my stories for younger readers, when they're in manuscript form, on my children. They love it! I think they're quite proud of me. I know when I ask them if they've liked a story or not, they're always going to say yes. So, I gauge their response more by which parts of the stories went over their heads, or they found funny, and the questions they ask.

3 GROWING A BOOK

Mouse Party

The original seed for this picture book came when my elder daughter was very young. I was thinking about word sounds, and the coupling *mouse–house* came to me, and I thought of a first line – *A mouse moved into a house*. Then I thought of a few other rhymes – such as a cat with a mat, a cow with a plough and a fox with a box – and started jotting them down, and from there I started the text.

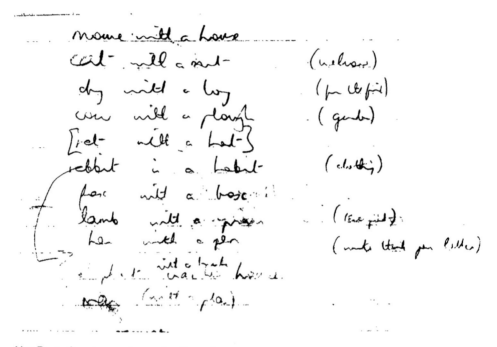

Alan Durant's notes on rhymes for *Mouse Party*

Altogether, the book must have gone through about thirty or forty different drafts. And all in all, it took five years from those initial couplings to the book appearing in the bookshops. The thing about picture books is that even though there are often very few words, they can take a long time to write and even longer to illustrate and publish. It's quite a complicated process – getting the illustrations done as well as the book printed. You see, most picture books are reproduced and printed in Hong Kong because that's where the technology is, and it's cheaper to get them done there. So the whole thing of sending the artwork out there, waiting for proofs and so on, can take quite a while.

It may seem very easy to write a picture book, but getting the text right, choosing the right words, is difficult. All the words you use have to carry weight, they have to serve a purpose. Every word counts. In the first place, you have to take your idea for the story and then you have to put it over as simply as you can. One practical concern is that you can only get so many words onto a page – and it isn't that many

– without it looking too dense. You've got to be very disciplined. I found that with *Mouse Party* particularly; I had to scrap a lot of words I liked. The original story was like a poem, and I liked the cumulative parts and all the repetitions, listing the party guests, but it was getting too much – and I had to cut out a great deal. There were just too many words on the page. The original had about a thousand words, and I must have pared it down to about three hundred words.

Mouse Party works well when I read it during school visits. I often read out the original version in class as the children really like the extra cumulative bits. I try all my stories out on my children first, so I put a lot of emphasis on how they're going to read aloud.

When Sue Heap, the illustrator, started doing the artwork I made further changes to the text. I love her illustrations. I think they're great – very colourful and wild. Sue and I met perhaps once whilst she was doing the pictures. Most of our contact was via the post. She would send me various sketches and roughs and I would return them with my responses.

It fascinates me how much Sue put into the book, with all the details in the pictures – and little stories going on in the background of the illustrations. That's one of the things I really love about picture books – the layers that you can have. You have the words as a base, and then the illustrator can add their own stories on top – stories that are not even mentioned in the text. So it's very much a collaboration – and that excites me a lot. Sometimes I get frustrated that I can't do pictures. Describing things to illustrators is really difficult if you can't draw. But other times I'm almost grateful I can't draw as I love that collaboration with an illustrator. I love it when I send stuff off and it comes back – and often it's not at all as I've imagined it! It's great when it takes your text into another medium, a different dimension. I've been lucky to work with some very good artists.

At times I'll change my text slightly according to an illustrator's needs. Sometimes an illustrator will say 'I've done something here, and it doesn't quite work with your text', and if I agree then I'll make the necessary changes. I'm not precious about my text. When I did *Angus Rides the Goods Train* with the illustrator Chris Riddell, there were many clever devices that Chris included of his own – such as the train changing gradually from grey to gold throughout the book, and representing the carriages of the train as a milk bottle and a honey pot, etc. – none of which were specified in my original text. The things that illustrators bring to a book are just fabulous. I'm never specific about what I want in the way of artwork. I know a lot of writers can be, but I'm not. I once heard Martin Waddell say that you have to give an artist space, you have to allow them to express themselves, and if you're too prescriptive about what it should look like, they can't do it. You have to trust the illustrator and let them get on with it. I'll only intervene if there is something glaringly wrong – which is rare.

4 SCHOOL VISITS

I like performing my work. There's one story I read a lot when I go into junior classes. It's a football fantasy story called 'The Dream Team'. It's about a boy who's collecting these football figures that are free with a breakfast cereal. And there's one

From *Mouse Party* by Alan Durant and Sue Heap

Dog with a log.

player that he needs to complete his dream team. This is a good one to perform because it has a lot of slapstick humour. The story's good for getting the whole class involved – especially those boys who are not particularly interested in books. It seems to appeal widely. I also read my *Spider McDrew* stories a lot.

Most of my visits are to primary schools. And the nature of my visits varies. But more often than not, my preference is to start with a reading, then talk about my writing in general, and then answer the children's questions.

Other times, I will talk about how books are made, and I'll go through the creative process – getting ideas, noting them down, mulling them over, getting them down on the page and the continuous redrafting – and also the process of how books are physically produced. I always get a good response to that. Kids have no idea how long it takes to write and make a book. Sometimes I test out new material during my visits, but only if I'm confident that the material works.

I've still got an exercise book from when I was thirteen or fourteen, as I've already mentioned, and when I go into secondary schools I find that it's a really useful tool. I hope that it helps to put me in a real context. Okay, I'm now an adult, but I was once a teenager and this is what I wrote then. It shows me in the very early stages of becoming a writer.

My writing workshops for primary are similar to those for secondary schools, I just adapt the material. In the main, my secondary school workshops are based on genre writing. I'll ask the children to consider different styles of writing. I'll begin by reading an extract from my Point Crime novel, *Publish or Die!*, and then get the class to think about something that they do every day – something mundane such as getting out of bed or brushing their teeth or walking to school. Then I'll ask them to write it up in a genre style – horror, mystery, romance, adventure, sci-fi. The horror one is the most popular. I give them licence to make it as graphic as they want – with blood spurting everywhere or alternatively subtle and chilling. And even the most reluctant, least literate twelve-year-olds will produce something because it's horror, which has got a street cred that other genres don't have.

With larger classes I get the children to work in groups – with each writing a sentence or two. They'll brainstorm together initially, then they'll start by one writing the first sentence, and another continuing and so on. It doesn't matter if a child writes three lines or three words, just so long as everyone does a bit. They won't have time to complete a whole story, and maybe the teacher will get them to finish it off at another time. In the longer workshops I'll do some work on character as well.

One thing I always talk about during my visits is the relationship between reading and writing, which I think is completely fundamental. I always say, 'To be a writer, you've got to be a reader. You write first for yourself as a reader.' Invariably I'll be asked where I get my ideas from. And that's really what my workshops are all about – showing that everyday, mundane events can be made interesting or dramatic. I tell the class that if they're stuck for ideas to look into their own lives, what they do or what members of their family do – and there they'll find ideas.

I advise children to do some preparation. I do think this is useful – just spending a few minutes to think about where your story is going to go. So many children start and they'll be writing away and then get stuck. I don't encourage anything as formal as a detailed plan, but I'll get them to think how the story will start, roughly what will happen and how it will end. Endings are often where children get stuck. Too often you get 'I woke up and it was a dream' because there hasn't been enough planning beforehand. I don't tell them to stick rigidly to their initial ideas – all I'll say is that they should know roughly where they're going with the story. You can know what the ending is going to be, but it can be left open as to how you will get there and how it will be presented.

Often I'll ask the children to read out what they've written. I like it when they come up with unusual descriptions, and unusual ways of looking at things. I try to encourage that. I've actually used some ideas I've come across in class. At one workshop a boy described a character as having skinny lips – which I thought was brilliant. And there was a girl I met recently in one secondary school who described a character as having warm blue eyes. That struck me as very interesting as you usually think of blue as cold and icy. Putting the two together – warm and blue – I found very striking. I try to encourage metaphor and simile and for the children to put colour into their language.

I do feel that it adds a lot to the sessions if the children have read my books before I go in. It's not essential, but it helps start things on a good footing – the children are already enthused, they've got questions they want to ask you, and you're someone that they already half-know. It makes a big difference if you've got an enthusiastic teacher who's already read your work with the class. And it's nice also if the teacher shows some interest when you're there – and doesn't sit at the back marking books!

I have recently been 'virtual' writer in residence for Gors Junior School in Swansea. The children sent me their stories by e-mail, and I responded to them. As far as I'm aware, it was the first 'virtual' residency to have been set up.

5 WRITING FOR DIFFERENT AGES

At any one point I have a number of projects on the go, from a picture book to a chapter book to a teenage novel. I never find it difficult to change from one to another. With the teenage stuff I'm writing from my own experience. I think most people have times in their lives that are particularly vivid – for me the teenage years is the time I tend to go back to a lot. Whereas the other books – picture and chapter books – I write because of the contact with my children. And I read so many picture books with them anyway that I get into writing that style of book quite naturally. The only area that I don't write for and I haven't cracked yet is the 9–11 age range, which I may do as my children get older. The age I write for to entertain myself are the teenage books. But I do enjoy writing for all ages. If I'm writing a novel and it's getting a bit heavy or I'm stuck it's quite nice to flip out from it and work on a picture book or chapter book as relief. Then, I'll come back to the longer, weightier text refreshed. But I couldn't write two of the same type of book at the same time.

I'm fairly prolific, and that's partly because I'm pretty versatile as a writer. As a copywriter I'm used to writing copy on many subjects and it doesn't really phase me. I like a challenge. I quite enjoy writing about anything at all. I also have this mentality that when I see a different style of book I'll think, 'I'd like to have a go at that.'

My own children are a great help with my writing. I've written one book specifically with my own children in mind. It's a sort of junior *Star Trek* – called *Star Quest: The Voyage to the Greylon Galaxy*. I'm hoping it will be the first in a long series. I wrote it for my son Kit because he was interested in *Star Trek* and *Star Wars* and there aren't many serious science fiction books for the lower junior age group – they're usually humorous. Kit wanted real sci-fi adventure – so I wrote one for him! My daughters Amy and Josie are in the book too. It's the only time I've used my children's real names in one of my books.

Pitching the level of a book – in terms of vocabulary, sentence length and sophistication – is quite difficult. With the *Leggs United* series, for example, I had to do a lot of work to get the level right. Initially it was too complicated and the language was too sophisticated and it was not quite snappy enough for a younger reader. The paragraphs and sentences were too long. It wasn't so much the story itself as the way I was writing it. I was pitching it slightly too high. It took me a while to get it right with that one – but hopefully, I succeeded.

With my teenage books, the only constraint I have is what a teenager will have experienced. So, if you have a teenage narrator you can't write out of their experience – that's the only ceiling. Language-wise I've never made any concessions at all, I just write. With all my books that are published for this age, I don't feel that I'm actually writing them *for* teenagers, I'm just writing fiction. But that's the market they're going into. And I don't believe there should be any taboos in teenage books, no constraints in subject matter. The thing is, you just have to write about the way you see things, you have to be true to your vision, you can't falsify.

I'd like to write more picture books, but whether I'll carry on writing them indefinitely when my children are older, I don't know. I think the teenage end of my writing is nearly finished – I'll write maybe just one more teenage novel. Next, I think I might write an adult novel and carry on with the younger books as well. Whatever the readership, I'll always write. I've always had this thing about writing – it's a kind of showing off. 'Look what I can do!' you say. 'Aren't I clever – funny or whatever.'

I think I'm still learning a lot about writing. I've been published for about eight years now, and although I've done a lot of books, and a lot of different kinds of books, there are still many areas I haven't covered yet. I feel strongly that my best is yet to come.

SELECTED CURRENT TITLES

Creepe Hall / Return to Creepe Hall (Walker)
Jake's Magic (Walker)
Leggs United – football series of eight books (Macmillan)
Little Troll (Collins)
Spider McDrew / Happy Birthday Spider McDrew (Collins)
Star Quest: The Voyage to the Greylon Galaxy – to be published 1999 (Walker)

Picture books

Angus Rides the Goods Train (Viking)
Mouse Party (Walker)
Snake Supper (Picture Lions)

For older readers

Blood (Bodley Head)
The Good Book (Bodley Head)
Publish or Die! – a Point Crime novel (Scholastic)
A Short Stay in Purgatory – short stories (Bodley Head)

Anthologies

Short story in *Same Difference* (Mammoth).
Short story in *Gary Lineker's Favourite Football Stories* (Macmillan)
Vampire and Werewolf Stories – edited by Alan Durant (Kingfisher)

An introduction to . . . Philip Pullman

WHAT TYPE OF BOOKS DO YOU WRITE? Novels, such as *Northern Lights*, *The Subtle Knife* and the Sally Lockhart books as well as (longish) fairy tales, such as *Clockwork or All Wound Up* and *The Firework Maker's Daughter*.

WHAT ARE THEY ABOUT? Impossible to answer except with the words 'anything and everything'.

BORN: 19 October 1946, in Norwich.

EDUCATION: I went to all sorts of different primary schools in all different parts of the world because my father was in the RAF and was posted to Zimbabwe and Australia. My secondary school was in Harlech, North Wales. I went to Exeter College, Oxford to read English in 1965 and later I did a postgraduate teaching course at Weymouth.

LIVES: Oxford.

PREVIOUS OCCUPATIONS: I have worked at Moss Bros and in a library, and I have also been a teacher and lecturer.

FAMILY/PETS: I am married to Jude and have two sons – James (27), a professional viola player, and Tom (17), who is studying for his 'A' levels. We have a Lurcher called Daisy and two young pugs called Hogarth and Nell.

HOBBIES: I do a lot of drawing and I make little notebooks to draw in. I go to life-drawing classes. I love working with my hands. Currently I'm building a clavichord (an old keyboard instrument) with my son Tom.

MOST TREASURED POSSESSION: A Byzantine ring. The man in the shop claimed that it's 1,200 years old. It was a 'Good Lord, we've been married twenty-four years and three-quarters' present from Jude.

AWARDS: The Carnegie Medal, The Guardian Children's Fiction Award and the Children's Book of the Year at the The British Book Awards for *Northern Lights*, The Smarties Award (Silver) for *The Firework Maker's Daughter*, The Smarties Award (Gold) for *Clockwork*, The American Bookseller's Award for *The Golden Compass* (USA title for *Northern Lights*), The International Reading Association Book of the Year for *Ruby in the Smoke*, amongst others.

LANGUAGES TRANSLATED INTO: Eighteen – mostly European languages as well as Hebrew and Japanese.

TELEVISION: *How To Be Cool* (Granada TV). I have sold the film rights for *His Dark Materials* to Scholastic Films in America and *Clockwork* to the BBC.

FAVOURITE BOOKS: *The Magic Pudding* by Norman Lindsay, Tove Jansson's *Moomin* books, and TinTin books, including *The Castafiore Emerald* and *The Secret of the Unicorn.* Also, George Eliot's *Middlemarch* and Flann O'Brien's *At Swim-Two-Birds.*

FAVOURITE LINES OF POETRY: The passage from Milton's *Paradise Lost,* that describes Satan as he's flying:

> As when far off at sea a fleet descried
> Hangs in the clouds, by equinoctial winds
> Close sailing from Bengala, or the Isles
> Of Ternate and Tidore, whence merchants bring
> Their spicy drugs, they on the trading flood
> Through the wide Ethiopian to the Cape
> Ply stemming nightly to the Pole; so seemed
> Far off the flying fiend.

FAVOURITE MUSIC: Twentieth-century classical – Prokofiev's 'Second Piano Concerto'; nineteenth century – Weber's opera *Der Freischütz*; eighteenth century – Bach's *Goldberg Variations*; jazz – Miles Davis's *Milestones*; pop song – 'Save the Last Dance for Me' by The Drifters.

FAVOURITE FILMS: *Celine et Julie Vont en Bateau* and *Ask a Policeman.*

FAVOURITE PLACE: My bed.

WHAT WERE YOU LIKE AT THE AGE OF 11? I was furtive, devious, ingratiating, nervous, pious, and a proper little goody-goody.

WHICH ONE OF YOUR CHARACTERS WOULD YOU MOST LIKE TO BE? Dr Cadaverezzi from *Count Karlstein,* because he's a showman, a magician and a conjurer.

WHAT WOULD YOUR DAEMON BE? As I explain in *Northern Lights,* one can't choose one's daemon, one has to put up with it. But I would like to think that my daemon would be a raven because that's the bird in North American mythology that stands for the trickster, the storyteller, the creator.

WHAT QUESTION WOULD YOU ASK OF AN ALETHIOMETER? I wouldn't, because I would be afraid of finding out what the answer would be. What I would like to know are the things we'd all like to know, but they all have a sting in the tail.

IF YOU WEREN'T A WRITER: I'd be a *commedia dell'arte* actor.

AMBITIONS: To keep living and writing as long as I can, and keep a grip on my own marbles!

WHICH FOUR WORDS DESCRIBE YOU BEST? According to Jude – inventive, funny, erudite and a workaholic.

WHAT WOULD YOU LIKE TO HAPPEN IN THE TWENTY-FIRST CENTURY? I want my family to live long, happy, prosperous and useful lives.

WHICH OF YOUR BOOKS WOULD YOU LIKE TO BE REMEMBERED FOR? *Clockwork* and *His Dark Materials*.

WEBSITE: This is the address of Random House, my American publishers. At this site is a piece I wrote on the alethiometer from *His Dark Materials*: http://www.randomhouse.com/features/goldencompass/aleth.html.

I HOW THE READER BECAME A WRITER

I learnt to read with *Noddy*. This was when I was living in Southern Rhodesia, as it was known then. I remember being given the first *Noddy* book. I was just able to make out the sense of the words, and enjoying it very much because Noddy and Big Ears were building a house, and it started raining. And Noddy said, 'I know, let's put the roof up first, and we can keep dry while we're building the walls!' And I thought that was pretty funny!

About the same time I'd been given a copy of *The Just So Stories* by Rudyard Kipling. My mother read some of the stories to me, and I loved the sound of the words, like 'the great, grey-green greasy Limpopo river all set about the fever trees'. And because we were in Africa, where 'the great, grey-green greasy Limpopo river' is, it was a world I was familiar with. A little later on I met the *Moomin* books and *The Magic Pudding* by Norman Lindsay. All the books I liked initially had important pictures, including *Emil and the Detectives* by Erich Kästner, with very distinctive and evocative illustrations by Walter Trier. And I loved comics too – *Batman* and *Superman*, in particular.

My grandfather was very influential. He was a clergyman and a wonderful storyteller. When we were living in Norwich he brought the places around us alive by telling us stories about them. But my parents' – and indeed my whole family's – attitude to the arts was one of benign indifference. I was seen as a silly dreamer that read books and would never come to anything.

My stepfather's parents gave me all the P.G. Wodehouse *Jeeves* books, as well as Leslie Charteris's *The Saint* books. The first adult book that knocked me sideways was Lawrence Durrell's *Alexandria Quartet*. I got it out of the travelling library in Llanbedr, North Wales. I must have been fifteen, sixteen. Those books are just the thing for an overheated teenager. And it was around that time I became interested in the visual arts and painting. We were a long way from any museums and art galleries and we never went to London. But I came across a book by Ruskin and that taught me a great deal on how to look at pictures.

I wrote a lot of poetry then. I was very influenced by Dylan Thomas and by the metaphysical poets – people I'd come across at school and by myself in various anthologies. My poems were imitations, of course. But from that I learnt how to write iambic pentameters, I learnt what a sonnet was, what a rondeau and a villanelle was. I used to practise these, getting them technically right. And doing proper rhymes rather than half-rhymes. I don't write poetry now because I know what I'm best at, which is probably prose, though the experience of writing verse underlines my command of prose. Rhythm is profoundly important. When you write a sentence in prose, you have to be aware of the rhythm. It's having a vocabulary for it – if you've written an iambic pentameter you just feel when something's right and when it's not.

When I was studying at Oxford I carried on writing poetry, and I also wrote songs. This was the mid-60s. Everybody had a guitar and wanted to be Bob Dylan. I bored my friends to death with the songs I wrote. I busked a bit too. And I also wrote some short stories, without any thought of publication, except in the college magazines.

I did several things after I left university, mostly menial jobs whilst I was beginning to write. I worked at Moss Bros in Covent Garden and I worked in a library. And then I thought that I'd better find a better job to work at while I write my books, so I did a postgraduate teaching course at Weymouth.

I'd had an adult book published by then. This was a book which I now disown – it's a terrible piece of rubbish. But the New English Library publishers had a competition, offering a prize of £2,500 – which, in 1971, was enough for a substantial deposit on a house. I'd written one book which I'd put aside, and I entered my second book for the competition. And I shared the first prize with Cynthia Harrod-Eagles. I thought winning would change my life, but of course it didn't. Nothing happened. The book came out and it was completely ignored because it was terrible. I've kept quiet about it ever since. But it did give me a bit of money – I got half of £2,500. We lived on that while I did my teaching diploma at Weymouth. I was 25 then and married with a small child. Then I got a job teaching on Blackbird Leys in Oxford in a middle school for three years. From there I moved to another school in a very different part of Oxford, where I taught for another three years.

I wrote a second adult book called *Galatea*, which was a science fiction–science fantasy–magic realism sort of thing. It came out in 1977. And I was enjoying the teaching I was doing. We weren't bound by the National Curriculum then. And the kids I was teaching were very bright and motivated, and came from academic homes that were well furnished with books. In every way, teaching there was a pleasure. I used to write plays to put on, because I couldn't find any to do. I used to love this. I did a number of these – *The Ruby in the Smoke*, *Count Karlstein*, *The Firework Maker's Daughter* and *The Gas-Fitter's Ball* – these were all originally written as plays at this time. What I was trying to do in those plays was to entertain two audiences – the children and the parents. So I thought, I can probably do this, I can do something that would amuse the kids and the parents, possibly in different ways. So I learnt to do that and I enjoyed myself enormously. Having written these plays, I thought I'd turn one of them into a book, so I did it with *Count Karlstein* and Chatto published that. Then I also did it with the play I'd called 'The Curse of the Indian Rubies', which became *The Ruby in the Smoke*. That was the book in which I first found the voice that I now tell stories in.

Another thing I was doing was telling Greek myths to the children. I would tell them *The Iliad* and *The Odyssey*, all the way through. Whatever the children were getting out of it, I was getting several valuable things. Not least the thing that writers don't always have in a technical sense, which is a set of exercises –

like a musical exercise. Musicians will play scales and studies and arpeggios to focus on technical things. Similarly, a visual artist will do the same – they will study perspective. They will draw the figure over and over again. Writers don't do this. There's no real equivalent in the literary arts. But I found one, and it's telling stories – the same stories, over and over, but not from the same words, always fresh, always speaking them – without a book or any props. I was very lucky to be in a situation where I could do that. If you're not a teacher you can't do that, you haven't got an audience. If you're a teacher these days you can't do it because you've got the National Curriculum telling you not to. So it was at a time and in a situation when I could.

With storytelling you can learn so much about timing and also the kind of writer that you are. You can find out what you're good at and what you're not. I'm not good, as I've discovered, painfully, at telling funny stories that make people laugh – not aloud, that is. What I can do is evoke an atmosphere, I can paint a picture in the mind's eye. I can make it exciting, so that people will want to know what happened next. So you learn your strengths and weaknesses, and what to improve upon. So I sort of stumbled on this wonderful training. And if you think about it, it goes back to the very dawn of storytelling, because Homer and the bards would have done this sort of thing. They would have learned the stories and they would have told them, orally, again and again – refining their skills, finding a little bit that works, using it next time and embellishing it. That was the most valuable thing I ever got out of my years of teaching.

Next I moved to Marston Middle School, where I was for three or four years, until I was seconded to Westminster College. Initially I went there to establish a language centre, somewhere to co-ordinate language teaching in Oxfordshire. I had a small budget and I set the place up. I did this for two years. And when Westminster eventually offered me a part-time lectureship I jumped at it. I was there for about eight years in the English department, lecturing in adult and children's literature. My books were still coming out, and getting a little bit more notice, and were getting on shortlists for prizes. And then came *Northern Lights*, which changed my finances and my life, really. You can never predict what sort of effect or success a book is going to have. It was an important book for me because I knew that in it I was going to say everything I knew.

2 WRITING: ROUTINES AND REFLECTIONS

I write in my shed down the garden. I have to have silence when I'm writing, and it's very quiet down there. It's a twelve feet by eight wooden shed and it's been up for ten years. It's insulated and heated. The chaos and filth and mess in there are indescribable and it's crammed with books and manuscripts; I can never find anything in there – I'm ashamed of it. I go down there every morning and generally write three pages by lunchtime, always by hand.

I write with a Mont Blanc ballpoint pen and I always write on the same paper – which is narrow feint A4. I can't write on recycled paper as it's too gritty and full of bits of twig and stuff! I'm sure I'm not using up too many forests, and I think on the whole I'm doing good things with paper, so I think I'm entitled to proper paper. When I use paper for a particular book, it's got to be only used for that book and nothing else. So when I tear a wad of paper out of the pad I colour the top right-hand corner of each manuscript page, so the paper I'm going to use for that book has that colour on it and no other. The third part of the trilogy is coloured gold. *The Subtle Knife* is yellow and blue. *Northern Lights* was indigo.

And I also use those Post-it notes – the smallest yellow ones. I use them for planning the shape of a story. I'll write a brief sentence summarising a scene on one of them, and then I'll get a very big piece of paper and fill it up with sixty or more different scenes, and move them around to get them in the best order. However, I don't like to plan a story too much – some of it has to remain unknown – or else I lose interest.

I don't agree with the emphasis that teachers lay on drafting. I never write drafts; I write final versions. I might write a dozen final versions of the same story, but, as I set out to write, each one is a final version not a draft. If you set out to write a draft you'll take it less seriously than you should.

I find the omniscient narrator a very interesting character. When you're telling in the first person you're limited to what that person knows, one sensibility. I like the third person voice because I like swooping in and drawing back, and giving a panoramic view – in the same way a film camera does. I like directing the story, and organising the *mise-en-scène* as one would direct a film.

Jude, my wife, is the first person to read a new piece when it's finished and when I'm ready for it to be shown. With *The Subtle Knife* she read the manuscript in one sitting – from four o'clock one afternoon right through to one o'clock in the morning. Meanwhile, I was pacing around downstairs awaiting her response.

For me, prose should be a plain glass window and not a fanciful mirror – not that you need make it so workmanlike that it's drab. There are some writers whose prose is like that. Jeffrey Archer is a case in point. He's not concerned with the surface of the prose, he's concerned with what you see through it. At the opposite end of the scale you have someone like Nabokov, where the surface in some of his books is all-important, and what you see through it is only the excuse for the surface. Occasionally I'll want to do more than have a plain glass window, when the precise way of describing something is to use a word which is not common or a phrase which is slightly unusually put together. I don't do that to say 'Look how clever I am' – I'm doing it because it gives the clearest possible view of the subject matter.

As a writer, you have to write whether you've got ideas or not, whether or not you're feeling inspired. People who don't write talk as if it all depended on inspiration, and if they had this mysterious inspiration they'd be able to write as well. The trick is to write just as well when you're not feeling inspired as when you are. Ideas come to me all the time – when I'm writing and when I'm not writing. Often, when something catches my attention I'll think how I could make it into a story. Pretty much everything is tested automatically in that way by my mind. I store all my ideas on a shelf at the back of my head. If they're any good, they'll grow in the dark and put out long tendrils and kind of pluck at me. Though if an idea's no good, it will just die. I've never kept a notebook.

Often, as I sit down to write I'll think, 'Oh that's interesting, let's see what happens if I try . . .'. And you try a paragraph of that, and then you can see other possibilities inherent in this, so you go with that, and develop it more. So, before you know it, you've written six or nine pages and something quite unexpected but potentially very good has occurred. But you still won't know if it's going to work yet. You won't know until you've got the whole thing together. And that's happened several times.

I believe that success in writing, as with any other enterprise, is due to three things: talent, hard work and luck. Of those, the only one you have any control over is the hard work. You can't decide to be talented; nor can you say 'I'm going to my room to be lucky for two hours.' But you can say: 'I'm going to write a page every day', and you can go on doing it. It soon mounts up. After a few months, you'll have written the equivalent of a book. You might want to change most of it, but at least it'll be there to work on, which it won't be if you waste your time wishing you were talented or waiting for your luck to change.

What are my strengths as a writer? I do know how to time and structure a story, to find the right place to start, and to make it take the right course. That's probably what I'm most pleased with. I think I have a flexible style – I'm not a prisoner of one way of telling a story. I think my dialogue is quite good too. But dialogue is a lot easier to write than narrative. In the context of children's own writing, children are very good at writing dialogue, and very poor at narrative because most of their experience of story comes from the screen, and the only language we get in drama from the screen is dialogue. For a similar reason, if you've got characters speaking to each other in your head, you can write down what they say, because they say it in words. Yet if you write down what they do, you've got to find the words yourself and choose between alternatives, and so it's harder. It's easy to fill space with dialogue.

There are many reasons why I write. I write for money and because I would go mad if I didn't. And because I have the not-dishonourable ambition to be famous. And I don't mean famous in the sense of slightly celebrated now, but I mean known in two to three hundred years' time. If you're doing something really well, you should want the results to last that long. Also, there's the pleasure of writing – it's the pleasure of the making, the craftsmanship. You have a particular set of materials, a particular structure in your head – how can you best use the materials to make this structure? Or, given these materials, what sort of structure could you make with them? They seem to fit together in this kind of way, but not in that. So, let's see what we can make of it. That's the way I sense it in my mind. My apprehension is fitting things together in a way that makes them work mechanically and stand firmly on the ground and not fall over and be pleasing to the eye. It's all these things. I can't rank those various reasons in order, but they're all true and they're all valid.

3 GROWING A BOOK

Clockwork or All Wound Up

The first idea for this book was something that worked like clockwork, something that fitted together in that very tight, mechanical way, where everything was connected, so that if you moved one bit something else would also move. And

Unused artwork by Peter Bailey for *Clockwork*

everything was logical and everything fitted. I came to that because I like machines and machinery, and because somewhere in this house I've got the plans for a clock made of wood which I'm going to make one day. As I've always liked that kind of notion, I thought wouldn't it be fun to have a story that fitted together like that. And the title came to me at about the same time – *All Wound Up* – that can mean all sorts of things. So that was the starting point. And I had the title long before it was ever a book, which was also the case with *The Firework Maker's Daughter*.

I had a number of mental pictures which came with this original idea. One was a big, old clock in a German town square somewhere, with these little figures that come out and wave their swords about. Another picture was the whole atmosphere of German Romanticism, and the atmosphere I get when I listen to the music of Weber, or to Schubert's extraordinary song 'Erlkönig'. It's a poem in which a father and child are riding through a wood. The child cries out 'Father, father! It's the Erlkönig! He's coming for me!' And the father says, 'Don't listen!' The Erlkönig, the evil spirit, whispers to the child all the enchantments and the wonders and the delights in the world. And when they get home, the child is dead. This wonderful atmosphere of creepiness and darkness and the forest was just what I wanted.

I began by putting a number of these elements together. I had a couple of fragments from stories that I'd started and got nowhere with from a long, long time ago. One of these was the odd scene of the prince arriving at the castle and his subjects find out that he's dead and that his heart has been replaced by clockwork. I also had the idea of the terrible embarrassment of a storyteller who begins to tell a story and then the door opens and a character that he has just described walks in. It's a hideous moment – what's he going to do now? – especially when the character says 'Don't mind me, please carry on as if I wasn't here at all.' How can he? So that comes from my experience of storytelling and both the exhilaration of telling a story and the sense that every step you take is actually on the edge of a yawning pit that you might suddenly fall into by getting the story wrong or by failing to find something. It's that vertiginous delight of storytelling. That part comes from a play I wrote about fifteen years ago, though it was in a very different context overall. So I removed that bit from the play and I connected it up with the other ideas I had of the prince and the clockwork. So really, I was cannibalising lots of other fragments.

And as I put all these bits together, some bits didn't work. What I was doing, in effect, was trying to make a clock by putting all the gears and wheels and cogs in a box and shaking them and opening the lid and looking to see if they'd formed a clock yet. So I'd shake it again, try again. I was seeing that some bits were connected, and then I could move other bits together. I was trying to put them together without any clear idea of where it was going. Once I'd joined the dead prince with the clockwork inside him with another bit I then began to see how I could make the connections. Little by little, I got a sense of the shape the story could be, and how one bit could work another and so on.

The boxes in the book, my comments, came in when I'd finished writing the story. I wanted to do something slightly different with the illustrations, and to use them to comment upon the story. The publisher, designer, artist and I tried doing it in different ways. At one stage we had a running header, but that didn't work, it was too obtrusive. There are now far fewer boxes and far shorter comments than there were when I started.

I did quite a lot of drafts. The first draft was chaotic because I'd leave a bit and go to another bit. It began to cohere once I'd put it onto the word processor and I could then move bits about more easily. It's difficult to know exactly how many drafts I did for this – because when is a draft a bit of a draft or a re-editing of the first? And as a rule, I always do a first draft by hand, and later transfer to the word processor, where a lot of editing will take place.

Northern Lights
(first book of *His Dark Materials*)

I did *Paradise Lost* at 'A' level, and it's stayed with me all the way through until I was beginning to think about *Northern Lights*. But my writing of the book came as a result of a meeting with David Fickling of Scholastic Books. David said he wanted me to do a book for him. I said that what I really wanted to do was *Paradise Lost* for teenagers. So he asked me to develop the idea. Off the top of my head I improvised a kind of fantasia on themes from Book 2 of *Paradise Lost*. And he got quite excited by that, because he loves *Paradise Lost* as well. By this time I knew the kind of thing I wanted to do – I knew the length, I knew it was going to be in three volumes and

I knew it was going to be big and ambitious and enable me to say things I'd never been able to say in any other form.

So I sent David a synopsis which bears little relation to what the book turned out to be. On the strength of that, he gave me a very generous contract to write all three books. With the confidence of that behind me, I started to write. I didn't map out the narratives for all three books when I began *Northern Lights*. I had a vague idea of what would be the central theme for each one, that's all.

One problem I had with the trilogy that I never had before was that each volume would be published separately, so I couldn't go back and alter them. So, rather than write the whole thing through as I would with a story and then do the editing and make sure everything fitted, I had to think ahead and leave enough loose ends after the first and second books to be tied up later. So I had to do a bit more planning than I normally like to do. And throughout the writing of it I worked hard at keeping all the various narrative threads going. This issue of the keeping the threads going is what Evelyn Waugh said somewhere was the most important attribute for a writer of novels: namely, a sort of architectural sense – an apprehension of the shape of the whole before it's completed. That's why some very fine writers, people who can turn an exquisite sentence or paragraph, fall down when they try to write at length – no sense of architecture or structure.

When I started *Northern Lights* I soon realised it was a different universe I was writing about. But I didn't want to get too far away from this one because I like making references to things which are half-familiar, half-not. I wanted to show people more clearly than you can show them in this world, as well as explore ideas about good and evil and fate. As with Milton, what I'm writing about may be philosophical abstractions, but by personifying them as Gobblers or Mrs Coulter or Lord Asriel or whoever, I can use them in my story.

I had the character of Lyra at this point and I had her name. There are two sources – one is a couple of poems from Blake's *Songs of Experience*. William Blake was hovering just as Milton was hovering behind this. In Blake's *Songs of Experience* there are a couple of poems about a little girl called Lyra, a little girl lost and a little girl found. The other source is an Easter hymn that I used to sing in my grandfather's church. It came from a collection called *Lyra Davidica*, which of course means the harp of David. And when I was young I thought the writer of the hymns was someone called Lyra Davidica! But the name doesn't mean that she's musical, or she's a harp or anything like that at all, as some people have suggested.

So I had the idea of Lyra, and I had the idea of the North and polar exploration. I knew there'd be a balloon in the story somewhere, but I didn't know why or how. I started to write the first chapter and I didn't really get anywhere with it. I started that chapter at least five or six times. Then things slowly began to gel. There was a college, there was an Oxford, like this one but different – full of grandeur and ritual and crabby old men. It was shabby but also immensely luxurious. And there was an air of tension, religious, political tension. Something was going on in the background that they didn't quite know about. It was making everybody anxious. These things were on the go, as well as the sort of machinery you get at the end of the nineteenth century – polished rosewood and brass magic lanterns, slide shows – an air of that sort of machinery. And Lyra was hiding and overhearing something she wasn't meant to hear. I got all that.

(96)

After Norlam Gardens:

Lyra to DM (at lab?)
~~They drive to~~ Headington
Confrontation - passing
 policeman - they leave
 for lab, but police
 note 2 follow (to flat)
Lyra desperate to
question the cave

MC in this world   Will
 finds her way
 to Headington,
 arrives after
 they leave,
 beguiles (or
 starts to
 beguile) Collector

- Lyra to DM at lab
- They drive to Headington
- confrontation
- policeman - they leave for lab
- tartan skirt - radio -
- police go to her flat

How does he get to
Headington? Why not a bus
Why not with others? The

Will goes with them to Head -
~~Steps in one~~ sees where he
 keeps the a/m.
 - when he sees policeman, goes
 through window - Lyra & DM
 don't know where he's gone -
 - Lyra so distraught she forgets h
 - he cuts back through, is
 about to steal the a/m when
 he hears MC's voice & her
 conversation with the Collector.
 learns what she's up to -

tricks his
way out

 - takes the a/m himself but is
 seen and very nearly trapped
 ~~but by~~ ~~...~~
 - MC & police set off on foot
 for Lyra

How does Will get there?

Lyra in lab interrogating the Cave
learns about Dust & angels and that
she must help Will
Learns police coming, MC
DM goes to hold them off,
Will appears - he & Lyra escape just in time
[Darkness falling] MC frustrated, turns to DM - snake?

     ↓ Will & Lyra — witches appear

Yet it still wasn't working and I was getting more anxious. Then one day I found myself writing the words 'Lyra and her daemon' and that was the key. I had to write the rest of the page and the rest of the chapter to find out what daemons were. In my first draft they were a sort of animal companion which changed shape according to your mood, and adults' daemons changed as well as children's. I thought this daemon concept was very intriguing, but one of the things I now know about storytelling is that if you put something in that doesn't add to the story it makes it weaker. This wasn't adding anything to the story, it was just picturesque. The main theme I had now discovered – from all my thinking and my fretting and my writing – was Adam and Eve and the Fall: the story of innocence and experience, and innocence becoming experience. The whole business about being a child and being a grown up was becoming a very big theme.

So then I thought, how can I use this daemon thing to strengthen the theme? If I don't, it will just be a picturesque detail. So by allowing children's daemons to change form and having adults' daemons as set, I realised that I could use the idea to symbolise the difference between the infinite plasticity, the infinite potentiality and mutability of childhood and the fixed nature of adulthood. And when I'd seen that and I realised what I could do with this very picturesque idea, I realised I'd got something very valuable and very rare. I felt profoundly grateful, grateful for all the years of work and craft that had enabled me to see what it was that I'd got when I'd got it and to make it work in the way it needed to work. That's the most exciting moment I've ever had as a writer. It even beat the first letter which said 'We like your book. We want to publish it and we'll give you some money.' So what a daemon eventually became was the human spirit in animal form – integral but separate.

The alethiometer came along quite early. It's this picture and word thing again. I was interested at one stage in Renaissance emblem books – a means of making a moral point, telling a story by means of an illustration, and what does such-and-such symbolise. I thought it would be interesting to use that concept somehow in a story. So I concocted the alethiometer, a truth-telling instrument. It serves a purpose as well, for Lyra needs a companion who can tell her things. She has a confidante in her daemon, but she needs a guide as well. I'm going to do something else with the alethiometer in the third book, which will take the idea further still.

I knew there was going to be a talking, armoured bear in the story early on. But I didn't know Iorek Byrnison was the king of the bears in exile, or that Lyra was going to help him. Again, it's that what doesn't add subtracts thing. Having met the bear, and heard his voice, and seeing how powerful and impressive he was, it was natural Lyra would fall in love with him, in her girlish way. Then, given this powerful, emotional bond, I thought, how can I use this and how could that advance the story? So I introduced the notion of him being in exile and that she would help him to regain his throne.

Lord Asriel and Mrs Coulter are Satan and the Ice Queen, if you like. They're very powerful, glamorous figures. 'Glamour' is a word I use a lot – to myself. Partly because of the association with its original meaning, magic. Mrs Coulter's young and beautiful. She wears expensive clothes and lives in luxury. Lord Asriel is powerful and Byronic. He sets everything in motion. We don't see very much of him: we see him at the beginning and the end of Book One; we don't see him at all in Book Two – but everything in that book happens because of him. He's a figure of enormous authority and power and we'll see more of both of them in the third book, of course.

One of the notions behind the book is that of dark matter – or 'dust' as it's known in Lyra's world. It's a cosmological phenomenon which astronomers tell us has to exist in order to keep the universe as it is, because otherwise it will fall apart. There must be a lot more stuff out there than we can see. But the beauty of it is that they don't know what it is yet. I trawl the Internet for anything on dark matter. It's a wonderful phrase – 'dark matter'. When I came across the passage that I quote from the beginning of the book from *Paradise Lost* – 'Unless the almighty maker them ordain his dark materials to create more worlds . . .' – it leapt out of the page at me that this would be the title for the trilogy.

I'd been thinking about the notion of religion, evil, sin and the business of philosophical dualism and Platonism – all this sort of stuff – for a long time before writing *His Dark Materials*. I'd come to some conclusions about it, which I don't think are necessarily unshakeable and eternal truths. I'm not trying to found a church! But I have thought it through quite coherently and rigorously and I do now know that I know what I want to say. And so this was a time when I had the skill and the craft also, I had the tools to do the job, and still enough energy to see it through.

I'll read a passage from the book. It's where Lyra has induced Iofur Raknison, the usurper, to fight the exiled Iorek Byrnison. Having built up to this event, it had to be a big, powerful fight.

> Then with a blur and roar of snow both bears moved at the same moment. Like two great masses of rock balanced on adjoining peaks and shaken loose by an earthquake, that bound down the mountainsides gathering speed, leaping over crevasses and knocking trees into splinters, until they crash into each other so hard that both are smashed to powder and flying chips of stone: that was how the two bears came together.

In LitCrit terms, that's an epic simile – a simile which goes on and gets bigger and more detailed. The one I quoted in the introduction from Milton – that's an epic simile too. Knowing that this was a big combat, a big important part of the book, I wanted to give it big language and I couldn't find anything bigger and more appropriate than an epic simile. And I end the section with another one:

> Like a wave that has been building its strength over a thousand miles of ocean, and which makes little stir in the deep water, but which when it reaches the shallows rears itself up high into the sky, terrifying the shore-dwellers, before crashing down on the land with irresistible power – so Iorek Byrnison rose up against Iofur . . .

It's not just an ordinary simile, 'he was like a great wave' or 'he moved with the power of a thunderstorm'. This is much bigger than that. I add to it, I add detail, I make the picture clearer. That's why I do it.

1
The Decanter of Tokay

*L*yra and her dæmon moved through the darkening Hall, taking care to keep to one side, out of sight of the kitchen. The three great tables that ran the length of the Hall were laid already, the silver and the glass catching what little light there was, and the long benches were pulled out ready for the guests. Portraits of former Masters hung high up in the gloom along the walls. Lyra reached the dais and looked back at the open kitchen door and, seeing no one, stepped up beside the high table. The places here were laid with gold, not silver, and the fourteen seats were not oak benches but mahogany chairs with velvet cushions.

Page one from *Northern Lights*

At the chapter-openings of *Northern Lights* and *The Subtle Knife* are the vignettes. I drew these myself. I chose what to draw on the simple and pragmatic basis of what I *could* draw.

I finished the book where I did as I felt it was a good place to stop. It was about a third of the way through the entire narrative, and it made a book, a substantial book in its own right. It finished the first part of the story satisfactorily, and ended on a cliff – literally. I can't remember how long it took to write this book, but it was many, many months.

It's a mistake really to call it a trilogy as it's one story, one book in three volumes. It had to published in three volumes for various financial, physical and marketing reasons. Which raises another slightly different point – why did they give me the Carnegie Medal for only part of it?

I've been asked if *Northern Lights* will be my best work. If I thought that I'd never do any better than this, I might as well give up now. You always hope that every-thing you write is the best thing that not only you've written, but the best thing that anybody's ever written. You should start every book with this view. If you think that you're just going to do a modest little thing – then why bother? So I hope that there will be bigger and better and more accomplished books to come. In terms of scope, it's probably the biggest thing I've ever done. In terms of perfection of structure, we'll have to see, as it's not finished yet. It will be hard to be better than

Clockwork. I would say that *His Dark Materials* is the best long book I've done and *Clockwork* is the best short book I've done.

4 WORKING WITH ILLUSTRATORS

As I said earlier, as a child I loved illustrated books and comics but as an adult I became interested in the interplay between text and pictures when I was running the language centre in Oxford. We had a conference there and we needed somebody to talk about media studies – which was a hot thing at the time. It sounded interesting, so I said that I'd research that area. I discovered that the interplay with word and picture operates at so many levels and in so many different places – I found it absolutely fascinating. I've written articles on this area for the journal *Signal* and the book *Graphic Account*.

The illustrators I have worked with have all been very good in very different ways. The two I probably respond to with most enjoyment are Peter Bailey and Ian Beck. Peter Bailey works in black and white, and does wonderful drawings. It's nice to find an illustrator with intelligence, who appreciates what you're doing in the story and sees a way of enhancing the atmosphere that you're building up. And it's important for me to actually meet the illustrators and talk through the story before they begin work.

I like Eric Rohmann very much too – he's done the covers for the American editions of *Northern Lights* and *The Subtle Knife*. He actually based his pictures of Lyra on Vermeer's painting *Girl with a Pearl Earring*. Eric's a very careful painter.

With the semi-graphic novels *Count Karlstein* and *Spring-Heeled Jack*, I was just trying to be a film director in a way, and telling stories in pictures and words. We would use pictures to suggest atmospheres, and also some dialogue is better done in pictures because you can see immediately who is saying what and it's quicker.

At times I'm very specific about what I want from illustrations. With *Spring-Heeled Jack* and *Count Karlstein* I was, because the pictures had to tell some of the story, so the illustrators had to do what I had described for them in the working pictures I'd prepared. It must be very frustrating for the artist, as there was an awful lot of work in those books. But, with Peter Bailey – who did *Clockwork* – I try not to be too specific. I let him find the bits he wants to illustrate. Though with *Clockwork* I drafted some of the pictures for him. Peter is doing the illustrations for my new book, *I Was a Rat*, at the moment. With that book he's had complete freedom as to the bits he wanted to illustrate.

Usually it's the publishers that suggest an illustrator to me. Transworld are very good at finding them. They take a lot of time and trouble to find an illustrator to suit my work. It was Transworld that found Peter Bailey for me.

Eventually, the ideal thing for me will be to illustrate them myself, which I will. And when I do, I'll go back to a more comic book, comic-strip style, I think. I'm wary of doing that with the stuff I do with Peter as I know how long the process takes, and I don't want to occupy either of us with something that might be tedious for him.

The writing process for a graphic novel is similar to any other text I write. Ultimately, it's still you and the page, and I still sit with my ballpoint and my A4 paper. And if there's a picture, I describe it in the same way one would do stage directions for a play.

Some narratives work very well in graphic or comic-strip form. Henry James wouldn't be very good, as a lot of his narratives are interior, and you'd have a lot of people looking around moodily at each other. So, if there's a fair amount of action, that's good because then you can see things being done. Though if you had a very skilful artist you could do quite an interesting Henry James comic. You could do it rather like an Ingmar Bergman film, because you'd be finding the pictorial or visual equivalents for these subtle states of mind which would need subtle pictures. You couldn't have the artists for *Superman* or *Batman*; you'd need a different sort of picture.

Peter Bailey's response – on illustrating *Clockwork*

My involvement with *Clockwork* came about as a result of a 'phone call from Ian Butterworth, the book's designer. Ian told me that he had a text by Philip Pullman which he felt suited my approach to illustration and that he thought the story was 'something very special'. When I read the manuscript I knew that Ian was right and that it was a modern classic.

Ian established the strong typographic identity for the book and Philip – who is a talented illustrator himself – made positive and helpful suggestions about the kind of 'feel' he wanted the illustrations to have. Collaboration between author and illustrator is actually quite rare but can lead to a well-resolved relationship between textual content and illustration. My main concern was to establish a visual tonality for the story which leads, as it were, from dark to light, and to try and make illustrations which were sufficiently oblique to complement a very subtle text, whilst giving characters and settings a convincing appearance.

I like Philip's use of captions with the illustrations. Whilst on the one hand they are a nice tribute to the traditions of the nineteenth-century illustrated book, on the other hand they are a clever device to lift one temporarily out of the narrative and introduce the authorial voice to remind the reader of the artifice and illusion involved in the making of a story and a book.

When Philip and I met to discuss the project, we found that we were kindred spirits. We felt that the feeling of Caspar Friedrich's work should be reflected in *Clockwork*. Friedrich was a German Romantic painter of the late eighteenth and early nineteenth century. I didn't need to research his work whilst doing the illustrations, but I did have his style very much in mind throughout. Overall, the book took about two to three weeks to illustrate.

SELECTED CURRENT TITLES

His Dark Materials trilogy (Point-Scholastic)

Northern Lights
The Subtle Knife
Third part scheduled for September 1999

Sally Lockhart novels (Point-Scholastic)

The Ruby in the Smoke
The Shadow in the North
The Tiger in the Well
The Tin Princess

Clockwork or All Wound Up (Corgi Yearling)
Count Karlstein (Corgi Yearling)
The Firework Maker's Daughter (Corgi Yearling)
I Was a Rat (Doubleday)
Spring-Heeled Jack (Transworld)
The New Cut Gang: Thunderbolt's Waxwork (Puffin)
The New Cut Gang: The Gas-Fitter's Ball (Puffin)

Fairy tale retellings

Mossycoat – illustrations by Peter Bailey (Scholastic)
The Wonderful World of Aladdin and the Enchanted Lamp (Scholastic)

For teenage readers

The Broken Bridge (Macmillan)
The Butterfly Tattoo – previously *The White Mercedes* (Macmillan)

By Peter Bailey – picture book *A Scary Story* (André Deutsch-Scholastic)

An introduction to . . . Celia Rees

WHAT TYPE OF BOOKS DO YOU WRITE? Novels – and I *hope* that I write exciting, compelling stories which people will want to read.

WHAT ARE YOUR BOOKS ABOUT? I write mostly thrillers and horror novels.

BORN: 17 June 1949 in Solihull.

EDUCATION: St Alphage Church of England Primary School and Tudor Grange Grammar School for Girls – both in Solihull. BA in History and Politics at Warwick University; PGCE History at West Midlands Teacher Training College in Walsall; M.Ed. in English in Education at Birmingham University.

LIVES: Leamington Spa.

PREVIOUS OCCUPATIONS: I worked for the gas board for a year after leaving school and after university I taught English in various secondary schools. Later I went on to teach in Further Education. I currently run a Writing for Children module on the Open Studies Programme at Warwick University.

FAMILY/PETS: Terry, my husband, was a Head of School at Henley College of Further Education in Coventry and is now retired. We have a daughter, Catrin, who is seventeen and in the Lower Sixth at King's High School in Warwick. We have a ginger she-cat, Poppy, who has only half a tail!

HOBBIES: I read a lot. My writing permeates all of my life. To relax I go swimming and go to aerobics. I also watch films.

MOST TREASURED POSSESSIONS: My father's compass, my grandfather's watch-chain – which my mother wore as a necklace – and a fob from a watch that was once owned by my husband's grandfather.

LANGUAGES TRANSLATED INTO: Danish, Norwegian, Swedish, German and Serbo-Croat.

FAVOURITE PLACE: Llanstephan – a small village in Wales by the sea.

FAVOURITE BOOKS: I do not have a list of 'favourite books' as such, but certain books have stayed in my mind a long time. These include: *Wuthering Heights* by Emily Brontë, *The Weirdstone of Brisingamen* by Alan Garner, *The Heart is a Lonely Hunter* by Carson McCuller and *The House at Pooh Corner* by A.A. Milne.

FAVOURITE POEM: W.B. Yeats – 'He Wishes for the Cloths of Heaven'.

FAVOURITE MUSIC: I like early music – medieval to renaissance; English composers – Elgar's Cello Concerto, Vaughan Williams's *English Folk Song Suite*; folk-rock – Steeleye Span and early Fairport Convention (my favourite folk song is the Borders ballad, 'Tam Lin'). Two of my favourite albums are Bob Dylan's

Bringing it all Back Home and Van Morrison's *Astral Weeks*. My teenage daughter keeps me in touch with current trends in pop, and I do like some of the bands like Pulp, Blur and Catatonia.

FAVOURITE FILMS: *Thelma and Louise, Psycho, Alien, Don't Look Now*, Fritz Lang's *M*, Francis Ford Coppola's *Dracula*.

WHICH ONE OF YOUR CHARACTERS WOULD YOU MOST LIKE TO BE? Emma Tasker in *Colour Her Dead*. As a writer you can re-invent yourself. Emma is the type of person I would have liked to have been when I was seventeen.

WHAT WERE YOU LIKE AT THE AGE OF 11? A tomboy. I was out all the time playing and having endless adventures. My mother was very ill. I went out to escape that. I was also very shy, particularly around adults. I lived very much in the world of children.

ENJOYS VISITING SCHOOLS BECAUSE: I like keeping in touch with my readership, and as I don't teach any more it gives me a chance to see what young people are interested in.

WHY DO YOU WRITE? It's the most enjoyable thing I've ever done.

IF YOU WEREN'T A WRITER: I'd be a museum curator or an archaeologist.

AMBITIONS: To be famous, to live by the sea and to travel.

WHICH FOUR WORDS DESCRIBE YOU BEST? According to Terry, my husband – 'Intelligent, argumentative, funny, and passionate about her work.'

WHAT WOULD YOU LIKE TO HAPPEN IN THE TWENTY-FIRST CENTURY? I'd like people to finally take notice of the destruction that we're wreaking on the planet and to actually do something about it.

WHICH OF YOUR BOOKS WOULD YOU LIKE TO BE REMEMBERED FOR? I don't think in terms of immortality through fiction. I'm quite superstitious about all my books and I feel that if I preferred one novel over the others then they would be upset – I know it sounds ridiculous! Seriously, I care for all of them in different ways.

1 HOW THE READER BECAME A WRITER
(and the evolution of the novel *Every Step You Take*)

My mother read to me a lot and would take me to the library, where she'd choose her books and I'd choose mine. As a small child I was very fond of *Winnie the Pooh* and I was a fan of Beatrix Potter and Alison Uttley's *Sam Pig* books. Another book I loved was *When Jesus Came to Our House*. No one's ever heard of it. I was just fascinated by the idea that Jesus could be a real person who could come to your house and have tea with you! My father also read to me but his choice was different. He read things like *The Wind in the Willows*, and Kipling's *Just So Stories*, *The Jungle Book* and *Puck of Pook's Hill*. Books were almost a sort of organic part of my early childhood.

I progressed onto Enid Blyton and I particularly liked *The Secret Seven* series. The children in *The Famous Five* series were too snotty and snobbish and I was jealous because they could do whatever they liked and no one ever told them they couldn't camp out all night. They were always going off to mysterious islands in Scotland. Nobody does that! I wouldn't accept that, I wouldn't be the implied reader, I suppose. But the children in *The Secret Seven* were incredibly suburban, they only had a hut in someone's garden and the limit of their adventures would be the end of the street. I identified with that. I read comics – *Knockout*, *Swift* and *Girl* as well as my brother's *Eagle* and Marvel *Superman* magazines.

I also liked Malcolm Saville's books. His books have the same kind of structure as *The Famous Five* – with kids going off on adventures – but he has a stronger sense of place, and even then that was important to me. The stories were set in Shropshire, not like Blyton's in some vague Scottish island. It was much more real, and the children were too – they had real relationships with each other, and I liked that. I was also fond of historical novels, like Geoffrey Trease and Rosemary Sutcliffe. At about ten or eleven, I went through a phase in which I only read non-fiction and for hours I'd pore over Arthur Mee's *Children's Encyclopedia*.

I was a voracious reader. I read the whole time, but as a child I didn't feel any compulsion to write. I did not think I could do it. This was partly because my junior school at that time was more concerned with the look of your work – handwriting, punctuation, spelling, etc. – and getting people through the 11+. My grammar school was fairly academic. There was not much emphasis on creativity so I was not given a lot of encouragement. Perhaps this is why when I myself became a teacher, I tried to foster creativity as much as I could.

My father died when I was twelve and I used reading to escape. I read a lot of detective fiction – Arthur Conan Doyle, Agatha Christie – a taste I picked up from my mother. I used to dip into my brother's Pan Books of Horror, where I discovered American authors such as Edgar Allan Poe and H.P. Lovecraft. I also read *Dracula* and *Frankenstein*. In my early teens I liked long books, like *Gone with the Wind* and sagas. *Jane Eyre* was the only school set book that I read right through at one sitting. I went on to *Wuthering Heights*, then Hardy and D.H. Lawrence. In my late teens I went through a very pretentious phase of reading Dostoevsky, Tolstoy, Kafka, Camus and Sartre and books we weren't supposed to read like James Joyce's *Ulysses*. I also read J.D. Salinger's *The Catcher in the Rye*, which I loved!

I did my 'A' levels and then I took a year off before I went to Warwick University to do a History and Politics degree, after which I did a History PGCE. And after a short spell of supply teaching and part-time lecturing in a college, I got a job at Binley Park Comprehensive School in Coventry. I was there for nine years. I began teaching History there, but I rapidly became disillusioned with the subject – having to teach these huge chronological chunks – and I switched over to teaching English as soon as I could. The 1970s was an exciting time to teach English, with the revolution in the ways that English was taught and approached, and I was discovering so many exciting new authors I hadn't come across before such as Alan Garner, Helen Cresswell, Philippa Pearce, Robert Westall, Peter Dickinson and Penelope Lively. I enjoyed the freedom of teaching English. You could plan your work according to themes or authors, and you could incorporate different media. I really enjoyed the creativity of it. I felt a slight handicap in not having an English degree as I had to go straight into teaching English 'A' level, more or less.

From there I went on to become a temporary Head of Department in another comprehensive school in Coventry. Then in 1983 I took a sabbatical and went to Birmingham University to do an M.Ed. in English in Education. It was a seminal time for me. I got to read and study a lot more children's fiction and it proved to be a watershed in my feelings about writing. It got me thinking that I could write, which I hadn't even thought about previously. On the course we did a session on creative writing. And I thought, I like this, I can do this, and also the course tutor liked the piece that I wrote very much. So, I slowly started writing while I was still in full-time teaching.

I moved on to another school in Coventry – Whitley Abbey School, where I stayed until I left teaching full-time. Partly as a result of the teaching methods I came across on the M.Ed., I started writing alongside my pupils. I wrote one piece based on something that happened to me, and then I turned it into a fictional piece. My class responded so well to it and also their own writing was fantastic. We did lots of very interesting work together, because I'd opened up to them and shared my experiences with them.

Then, two important things happened at once. First, I was with a friend, a colleague, and we were in a pub one night and she told me about the school trip from hell – and she relayed all the events that happened to the party. Fascinated by this, I wrote all the details down. This is the very list:

> June 1987 – Brenda – school trip – near Barmouth – Cader Idris – involved in murder hunt – minibus stopped by police – murder in Staffordshire – 16 year old girl found in vestry – Saturday morning – weddings – school party – house – isolated on Cader Idris – get back – note on chair from police – go into room – order all windows and doors locked and barred – forget the one in the room – kids – rumours – alarm – night – sleepwalking around – banging doors – kid falls out of bed – thump – car passes – and dowses lights – it's a courting couple – waiting – they know who did it – he's on his way back to the house – caught two to three miles away walking up the road to the house.

At about the same time, I'd been talking to my Year 10 pupils about what books they ideally wanted to read, and they said something like Judy Blume or Robert Cormier, something exciting, contemporary and realistic and with a dash of romance, but set in England. So, I thought, why not write about my colleague's school trip as a novel? And the very day after I left that school I wrote the first two chapters of what was to become *Every Step You Take*. And more or less, those chapters have hardly changed from then to the published book.

But it wasn't easy. That sequence of events that I had been told made a good story, but it wasn't a novel, so I had to turn it into one. I realised I had to have a lot of other elements to it other than just the events. I wanted a parallel plot and to have all the various relationships going on. The holiday romance in the novel was in fact something that happened to a person I know – so I was actually bringing together two completely different events.

Often I'll get an idea, but it won't be complete. I may have a story or a plot, but it will need more. Then I have to wait until there is something else to add to it to make it whole. With this, the holiday romance was that extra ingredient I needed. That was the perfect parallel to the plot of the murderer coming towards the teenagers in the house. It took me about a year to write and another year or two to get it published. First I sent it around to various publishers and got rejections. Then I tried the children's literary agents. The second agent I contacted was Rosemary Sandberg and she liked my manuscript and wanted to represent me. I could hardly breathe I was so excited!

Rosemary had been an editor at HarperCollins and she made me rewrite a lot of it. She told me what to emphasise, what to lose, and to get rid of certain characters and to change the ending. Then, I was prepared to do anything to get in print! Rosemary knew the right editors to send it to. Macmillan had a good list of teenage thriller writers and she took it to them. Macmillan were interested, but thought the manuscript needed further work, and the issue was whether they were prepared to put in the time. And it's a big risk taking on a new writer. So I had a meeting with them. Also, they have to find out if they can work with you. But the editor, Susan Houlden, and I got on very well, and we found we had a good rapport; she agreed to publish *Every Step You Take*. Eventually I rewrote the novel three more times. Publishers are very careful with what they print and get many people to read the manuscript for feedback. Finally it came out, but it was a big hurdle to get over.

I was forty in 1989, and felt I had to make a choice – see Robert Frost's poem 'The Road Not Taken'. I thought that if I want to write and make a career of writing, I'm going to have to commit myself to it. I realised that it takes a long time to establish yourself as a writer and even longer to make a living out of it, so I wrote whilst I worked part-time in various jobs – EFL teaching, assisting overseas students and teaching Media Studies. As my writing took off, I found it really hard to do both. Now I teach just one course, Writing for Children on the Open Studies Programme at Warwick University.

2 WRITING: ROUTINES AND REFLECTIONS

I have a study where I do my writing, and it's the biggest room in the house. If I'm working on a specific piece, I'll get my daughter off to school and then I'll start for the day. Writing is very absorbing and time just disappears. I write solidly for hours with just occasional breaks. And if I overdo it I get really spaced out! I don't know if it's the word processor or that your head can't cope with ordinary things for a while. I usually write all morning, and in the afternoon I might read or make notes or do research. At any one time I'll be writing one novel and developing ideas for another, but I can't write two together.

It took me a long time to realise that writing is not just about sitting at a word processor or a pad of paper and getting things down. Writing is everything:

reading, going to the library, visiting places, researching, taking photos and even thinking – thinking is an inherent and *very* important part of the writing process.

Word processors have changed the whole concept of drafting in that it's not quite the same process as when people wrote by hand or typed their work. Then you would have to do numerous individual redrafts to get the final draft. Now, I draft as I go along, as I'm writing. The first draft is not the finished novel. Usually, there's a first draft which the editor will read through and comment on. In the meantime, I've had time to think about it and I'll have my own changes to make. So then I'll work on it again making both sets of alterations. All together, there'll be two or three different versions until I get to the final one. Originally I wrote by hand more or less and then typed it. The only time I write by hand now is when I get an idea and I'm on a train or away from the computer. And then I won't write it properly, I'll write it in note form. But if I think of a phrase I like I'll write that out in full.

I have many different notebooks and ideas books – too many. I lose track of them and I can't find them, and sometimes I can't find where I've written ideas down. I collect ideas and research material a long time before I get to writing a novel. I don't always write ideas down, but I do think that if it's a good idea I'll remember it anyway. Sometimes I get just fragments of an idea or of a book. One of my two Point Horror books – *The Vanished* – came to me in pieces, in various stages. And some ideas come from dreams. That happened with *Colour Her Dead*, the beginning of the novel came from a dream about a Yorkshire detective's murder investigation.

I have used the Internet. It can be very useful for research and I managed to get hold of masses of material for a new book that I've written which is about UFOs and alien abduction. The working title is *Missing Time*. I spent a lot of time browsing around various websites looking at information on UFOs, but I also came across a lot of stuff on ghosts and the supernatural, and some of that was useful. Researching this way, though, is very time consuming. The Internet is a bit like a library where all the books have been thrown on the floor and mixed in with good books you might want to look at are all kinds of trashy magazines. It takes ages to find what you want and you can come across so much rubbish.

I do different kinds of research. When I'm writing a thriller like *Colour Her Dead* I read books and magazines on real-life crimes and even newspaper reports on murders. You have to know when you're writing a thriller that the details of the murder are possible, so research is essential. I research usually two or three books in advance. And as I'm working towards a book I collect a lot of material. I pin photographs, press cuttings, leaflets, photocopies, illustrations, all kinds of things on to my cork notice-boards. As a result, by the time I get to writing the book, the raw material is practically all there.

When I'm writing I don't have a certain ideal reader in mind. Partly because I want to be read by either gender with the same amount of enjoyment. Though I have to be conscious of age, because that will determine the language I use, my sentence structures and the complexity of my narrative. There's no point writing in an elliptical manner for 8–9 year olds, because they won't be able to read it or won't want to read it. With my new six part *H.A.U.N.T.S.* series – aimed at 8–12 year olds – I've had to be disciplined and to simplify the way that I write.

While I'm writing, there are a number of voices talking to me. One is the voice of a young reader, saying 'No one would do that! That's stupid', – or 'No one talks like that!', or even 'No one wears those clothes!' So I've got to create characters, dialogue and situations that young readers will accept, relate to and believe in. Another voice says 'This is boring! Get on with it!' And another one is a more general reader – and I think many children's writers think this – of any age, child, teenage or adult that you're trying to please. On top of those there's an editorial voice saying 'You've said that before! That's a repetition – can't you think of another word? Not again!' Finally, there's your own critical voice saying 'This doesn't make sense. It's not gelling and coming together.' You have to satisfy this cacophony of voices while you're actually writing, and you have to still each one by writing well. They're definitely loudest in the first draft – if you get it right then, then they've got nothing to complain about.

Place is fundamental to my work. For me, it's one of the most important elements. I need to have a strong sense of place in my books – it's one of the areas that lends novels realism. When, like me, you're working within genres that are inherently unreal, say horror or the supernatural and even a thriller, you need to tack into a reality. A strong sense of place will give it just that, and makes it possible, believable, which is vital. I always have an actual place in mind when I'm writing – even down to small locations like bus stops or shops. Everywhere is a real place. But it will get changed as I fictionalise it. I hope I give my reader a sense of a real place but also something they can relate to. With each new place that my characters go to, I put a brief description in, but I choose places common to anywhere, so they can fill in the rest of the details themselves. I put in a few pointers, and they'll know what a MacDonald's or a school hall is like. I think long descriptions put young readers off, so I keep them short.

With regards to characterisation and narrative point of view, I tend to have one central character and the other ones grow around him or her, and they all have particular roles to play. The significance of each character does change as my novels progress, so someone who is key at the outset may become less so as the story moves forward. One of the advantages of writing in the third person as I do is that you can change the viewpoint to any number of people. As a result, you can have the story told briefly from the perspective of someone on the other side of the street who may be able to see something that one of your main characters can't see. By shifting the focus like that you're allowing the reader multiple viewpoints. As a writer I'm interested in incidental characters. They may not be important overall, but they can be catalytic or important for just a minute or two. And I like the idea of the story in a novel being picked up and carried on by different people, as in a relay race. It gives the reader a chance to meet and know lots of different characters – but they all interlink and they're all related to each other in different ways.

Sometimes your characters jump out at you fully fledged – they're there, they're that person, with that name and you'll know them well immediately. With *The Vanishing*, for example, I discovered Fraser very quickly. I knew his whole history, everything – it all just poured out as I was writing. Other characters prove harder to get to know. I may begin by thinking this person is female, aged sixteen, has blonde hair and blue eyes, wears these clothes – but that character is still anodyne, not fully fledged. Usually I'll have to find one thing about that character that's different and then they'll become real. I'm a terrible hypocrite – I tell my creative writing students to do character developing exercises – but I never really do that myself. With my earlier novels I used to write pages of notes about all the characters. Now I do them in my head. I give a lot of thought to them, just waiting for that one quality or detail that will make them come alive. There's a science fiction film called *The Invasion of the Bodysnatchers* in which these zombie-type people grew out of pods. If you're not careful, your own characters will be like that, a pod character that's not whole or fully formed, and will just sleepwalk through the novel not doing very much.

I sometimes map out the structure of the plot on paper, making huge messy diagrams. This can be before I begin or at some point during the writing. I do it to clarify the plot in my mind, to see if it will work. I don't do it all the time or stick to it rigidly. If a story is too 'worked out' it can lose spontaneity and die on you.

I'm as concerned with plot as I am with character. When you write for young people, you have to have a strong plot. Equally, you've got to have believable characters that your readers can care about – particularly if you're writing in the genres that I do. Otherwise, you wouldn't care if the characters were killed or whatever. You've got to care about them and you can only do that by developing credible characters within a strong plot. And plot, for me, has got to work and have an internal logic. There can't be any boggy areas where nothing much is happening, or any loose ends that don't make sense. There's got to be a coherent sequence of events that work by cause and effect – a knock-on from one to the other. You have to be able to see that *this* happened because of *that*. You have to be able to look forwards and backwards at any point.

You may have different plot strands working in different directions, or one plot working forwards and another underneath it moving backwards – but still they have to work together. An example of these contra-plots would be in *Colour Her Dead*. One plot involves two girls in the present conducting an ongoing investigation into something that happened in the past, and there's also another character, Alison, going back into her own past to solve the same mystery. Therefore, there's two connected plots occurring at once that will eventually come together. And as a general theme, I'm very interested in the past and how it affects the present.

I had a more defined and a feminist agenda in my first few novels – with date rape, relationships and male aggression – but I've lost that as I've gone on. I'm not an issues writer, but there are issues within all my novels. In *Ghost Chamber*, the book is about a family break-up as well as being a ghost story. Likewise, *The Vanished* is a ghost story but it's also about one character coming to terms with his brother's death. You can interweave quite serious issues into a book of any genre but I think without any issues at all it will just become an empty story. There has to more to think about than shock horror and scaring the reader.

I would not describe myself as a genre writer. I see myself more as a writer who chooses to write within particular genres. I only write what interests me. I wouldn't, for example, write romance. I get particularly annoyed when people suggest that I might be writing to a formula. I do not, and find the suggestion insulting. For me, some 'issue' books are more formulaic. My two horror books are written for Scholastic as part of their *Point Horror Unleashed* series. The *Unleashed* are certainly not written to a formula. They are all very different from each other – written by British authors – and are aimed at 12+ readers who might want to move on from the American *Point Horror* series to something a bit different and a bit more challenging.

I do like writing within genres, but there are some I wouldn't write in, such as romance or science fiction. And although I write within genres I have never been encouraged by a publisher to use formulas in my books. Yet editors do often tell me to develop romances between my characters more! Every editor I've ever had has said, 'Let's have a bit more romance in it'! With the *Point Horrors* – to be fair to Scholastic, they've never suggested what I should include. They'll give me good advice once I've written the book, such as where to build up tension or what to add or remove. They're excellent at that. Although I often leave an editorial meeting feeling that I won't be able to come up with new ideas for a book, often those new sections I've eventually written become the best bits, as I've been forced up a gear with my writing and the whole thing has improved.

When I give advice to people who want to write for children, I suggest they read a lot, see what other people are writing and how they write – and to do this before they even begin writing themselves. Next, you have to have a strong idea, and as original as possible – something fresh with a different way of approaching things, a fresh vision, a new point of view. If you produce a weaker version of what's already available, you don't stand a chance of getting published because it's a very competitive field. And you must be excited about what you do, and know about children and their tastes and interests now, not what was current when you were young. Being a parent and reading and sharing and discussing children's books with my daughter certainly helped me as a writer.

What I admire most in other writers is originality of vision – books that work on different levels and hold something for any reader, child or adult. A book like John Masefield's *Box of Delights*, for example, published in the 1930s but startlingly innovative and subtly influential. I admire Ursula le Guin's *Earthsea* trilogy for the meticulous way fantasy is underpinned by erudite research. I also like Catherine Storr's *Marianne Dreams*. I've never read another book quite like it. Another favourite is Maurice Sendak's *Where the Wild Things Are*. Deeply inventive, both in illustration and text, full of subtlety and humour. I love the way the world of the Wild Things literally grow around Max, and the way they are from his own world, in his own head. In my 'field', I like the work of the American thriller writer Lois Duncan. The most original books I have read recently are Philip Pullman's *Northern Lights* and *The Subtle Knife*. He has created a major new fantasy. I can't wait for the last part of the trilogy!

I'll always write for children. I think they're a good audience to have. Also, you do get a great rapport with children and teenagers when you go out to schools. Adult writers do go on book tours, but unless you're very successful you won't get to meet a lot of people. If I had an excellent idea – I'm impelled by ideas – for an adult book, then I'd write it. The only thing is that every time I've had an idea for an adult novel, I've found a way of writing it as a book for younger readers!

3 GROWING A BOOK

A *Point Horror* novel: *Blood Sinister*

Before I wrote *Blood Sinister*, my first *Point Horror* novel, I had never written a horror story or a fantasy or anything that involved the supernatural. I'll read a quote from Mary Shelley in her introduction to *Frankenstein*:

> I busied myself to think of a story . . . One which would speak to the mysterious fears of our nature and awaken thrilling horror – one to make the reader dread to look round, to curdle the blood, and quicken the beatings of the heart. If I did not accomplish these things, my ghost story would be unworthy of its name.

Now that's always the starting and finishing point for all the books I write in this genre, because that's what I set out to do too. *Blood Sinister* really began when I got my second 'bite' of Bram Stoker's *Dracula* and I went to see Ford Coppola's remake of the film. I went back and re-read the book and loved the way that the narrative was made up of letters and diary entries from different characters. It's so clever. Initially, I was going to use the same format – and write the whole novel as letters and diaries.

As I started to mull over various ideas, I got to thinking about the fact that Bram Stoker had published his novel in 1897. And I thought – what if somebody met a vampire before 1897? – that is, before people had read *Dracula* and knew about vampires. There had been various vampire stories before this time – as vampires had been an element of the gothic tradition for a long while – but few people would have known about them. So, developing the 'what if?', I thought – what if a girl from the Victorian era, a girl of about fourteen, encountered a vampire and didn't realise it?

So I had the situation, but I needed a way for her to meet the vampire. There is a doctor in *Dracula*, Dr Seward, and at the time I was thinking about this, *Middlemarch* was being shown on television. I studied *Middlemarch* for 'A' level so I knew the novel well. I went back to it to look at the character of Dr Lydgate – young, idealistic but ambitious, with pioneering ideas, misunderstood and mistreated in the provincial world of Middlemarch. The late nineteenth century was a time of medical research and discovery, so this kind of doctor fitted the period. The girl's father could be a doctor, like Lydgate, who had set up a hospital in the East End. He would work with the poor and needy, because he was a philanthropist, supported by a paying clientele of upper-class psychiatric cases – as was Dr Seward. This doctor was working before medicine was rigidly divided up into disciplines, so he would also be an expert in blood. Another reason that I set it in the East End was that I was interested in Jack the Ripper and the mysterious Ripper murders.

Now the whole story started to fall into place. There would be a young, cosmopolitan East European count with a blood disorder who would come to see the doctor for treatment – and then this would connect the girl with the vampire. Next I thought – what if this vampire comes to the East End and once he's been treated by the doctor, he goes out and starts killing women? I thought that all these details could be written about by the girl in her diary. And all these murders, I decided, would not be the focus of the story at first, but would gradually become the central element of the novel.

I gathered all these fragments together and started to develop a synopsis for the story. Originally it was only going to have this Victorian element. Though I didn't get too far with that, and the publishers were not very interested in the Victorian diary idea. I made notes as I went back on the train from London, framing the whole thing with the story of a modern girl – also called Ellen, and who would be the great, great granddaughter of the Victorian Ellen – finding the diary, which I admit is an old convention, but it works well. Then I got interested in the idea of the blood. I was reading about this theory that vampirism is a blood disorder, and that vampires lack something in their blood. It's like an anaemic condition, and the only way a vampire can overcome this is to feed off the blood of other people. So I was considering the idea of it being a real condition rather than just a supernatural condition.

When I started *Blood Sinister* as just a Victorian diary, Ellen's voice came straight away. I'd just been teaching Charlotte Brontë's *Jane Eyre*, which is also a first-person Victorian narrative. So I had a voice of that period in my head. And the two characters – Brontë's Jane and my Ellen – are of a similar age, and do have fairly similar personalities.

After a while it became clear to me that the framing device – the present-tense story with the modern-day Ellen – would not just serve as an excuse to open a diary and to read the Victorian story. I decided that as the book progressed, the modern-day Ellen would become more and more involved in her own story.

Ideas from notebook for *Blood Sinister*

I liked the idea of her reading the diary in which her ancestor meets a vampire without realising it. The present day Ellen would – with hindsight – very quickly know that the Count was a vampire. I also liked the idea of her reading a document that may seem or read like a fiction about a supernatural being, but really it's her great, great grandmother's diary. Again, it's my interest coming through of the past informing the present. By the time all these different ideas had gelled into a narrative, I'd completed a second synopsis and I had a contract with Scholastic to write it as a *Point Horror Unleashed* novel.

What I wanted to ensure with *Blood Sinister* was that there were lots of different elements to the book, and it wouldn't just be about shock horror. And so one theme I explored was the feminist issue of how difficult it was for a girl to become a doctor at the end of the nineteenth century. It's what her father is, and it's what she aspires to. And I decided that Ellen would finally become an eminent doctor whose speciality of course is blood – and that's where the 'Blood Sinister' comes from, because she's interested in Blue Baby Syndrome and rhesus positive and negative.

When I was researching this book I took photographs and made field notes in various graveyards. I studied these photos and I incorporated some of the details from them in the book – such as broken crosses, obelisks and rotting flowers. Although the book is set in Highgate cemetery, I didn't actually go there, I went to one in Coventry. There's one photograph that I used for the Count's tomb. I incorporated details such as the wrought iron gate and the way that the paint is flaking off it. I changed other details – for example, I put a coat of arms at the top of the gate. I had this actual photo on my desk the whole time as I was writing.

Photograph from cemetery for *Blood Sinister*

Blood Sinister would have taken a year in all to produce – from the very first idea to developing it and completing the last draft. And I did three drafts altogether. A lot of the alterations I made involved making sections more scary, and generally making more of situations and events. The story itself changed considerably over the three drafts. There are many elements in the novel that didn't appear in the first draft, and I changed the ending radically. It was the editor's idea that we divide the book into three sections – as she felt that it naturally and logically fell into three different parts. I came up with the quotations for each introductory page. The first of the three is taken from Bram Stoker's novel of *Dracula*:

'Take care,' he said, 'take care how you cut yourself. It is more dangerous than you think . . . '

I chose this as for me it was the most frightening part of the book. But also, I liked the sense in this passage that things are more dangerous than you're aware of, as there are things going on you don't know about. And that's what it's like at the start of my novel – as both girls, both Ellens, are innocents and are in danger but they don't know where the danger will come from. So I thought that was a fairly apt reference. It's lots of fun finding quotations.

I'm going to read a short passage from Chapter 4. It's from the Victorian Ellen's diary and it's a description of the Count's accommodation in the hospital:

> Whatever its original purpose, the room had been transformed from the last time I'd seen it. The Countess has taken a house in Highgate for the duration of her cousin's treatment and she must have scoured every shop in London to provide him with the most comfortable and sumptuous of furnishings. Oil lamps and candles compensate for the lack of natural light and cast a suffused glow over everything. Richly patterned carpets adorn the floors and walls, a heavy brocaded curtain, encrusted with gold and silver thread, cordons off the sleeping quarters. The more public area contains comfortable chairs and sofas. A beautifully carved table holds an exquisite chess set. The Count smiled as we entered and invited me to sit opposite him.

The Count's appartment is situated in a particularly grim part of the hospital – in an underground crypt that was believed to have been used by the Knights Templar for their occult rituals. The hospital is a very old foundation, as many London hospitals are. What I was trying to get across here was the continental flavour and almost decadent feel to the Count and Countess – and that this is not an English room; that it's been transformed into something almost oriental with its rich furnishings. I chose words like 'sumptuous' to create that sort of atmosphere. And with the line 'Oil lamps and candles compensate for the lack of natural light' there's a deep, hidden clue. There's no light as vampires don't like the light. So this may appear to be just a description of the room, but it's also an account of just how sinister he is if you like. 'Cast a suffused glow over everything' – that makes the room warm and inviting as well as sensual – as this is the place where the Count will entertain Ellen and where she will start to fall in love with him.

> Richly patterned carpets adorn the floors and walls . . .

– it's exotic, alien, different, it's like a cocoon, a private place.

> a heavy brocaded curtain, encrusted with gold and silver thread, . . .

– again, there's a feeling of richness and great wealth.

> cordons off the sleeping quarters.

– and it's important that she can't see the sleeping quarters as it's where the Count (being a vampire) keeps his sarcophagus, so that he can sleep in his own earth. So this gives you the feeling of the separation of a private and a public area.

> A beautifully carved table holds an exquisite chess set . . .

– now the reason Ellen is going to see the Count is to play chess and to teach him English, as I had to have a device for this girl to be entertained by him for long periods of time, and more or less on their own.

> The pieces are red and white gold . . .

– opulence. Made to the Count's order in Constantinople – he is a cosmopolitan traveller to exotic places. Based on a set he learnt about in the *Mabinogion* – he is erudite and widely read.

Overall in this passage I was trying to create this incredibly rich feeling – perhaps over-rich – and my choice of words is there to build that up. I think the words flow together to create that soft, dream-like quality to the writing. So I chose words that are not going to be dissonant and there's no harsh or short, sharp, clipped words – they're going to flow. The words describe the room, but in a way the words are the room as well.

I'm quite proud of the description of the Count's teeth a few pages later. It's where the reader – but not the Victorian Ellen – discovers that he's a vampire:

> He takes my fingers and kisses them again. Again, I feel a slight sting on my palm. He turns my hand and kisses it just above the wrist. It is still a queer sensation, but I no longer find it unpleasant.

He's actually cutting her wrist with his thumb nail and taking some blood from her, without her realising it.

> I have noticed that when he smiles, he rarely shows his teeth. I find myself glad of it. They are by far his worst feature. If they were otherwise, his looks would be almost perfect. They are not irregular, but they are unusual. The front ones are small, slightly backward sloping, sharp-edged, with tiny serrations. The canines, either side, are large and an odd shape, pointed, almost conical. They are pearly, semi-translucent, more the colour of bone than teeth. No, that analogy is not correct. I have to think about this. The thing they most resemble is the quill of a feather. I glimpsed them tonight, before his full lips shut them off from view. They are like those of another type of creature, something which belongs to a different species altogether. I try not to look at them, but feel compelled to do so. They give me an odd feeling inside as if something were not quite right.

It took me a long time to work this description out. I did it partly from a picture of Tom Cruise from the film *Interview with a Vampire* that I had on the cover of a film magazine. I liked the idea of the canine teeth being pointed. I wanted them to be different from human teeth – 'conical', as I put it, and an odd colour. I thought of a quill and then put it in. And I managed to convey something of my own struggle to portray the teeth in my narrator's own description by having the phrase, 'No, that analogy is not correct. I have to think about this.' Through this whole description I feel you get the sense of otherness. This passage was hard to do, but very satisfying.

4 VISITS TO SCHOOLS

As an ex-teacher it's very interesting to visit various schools and see what they're like, as each school has its own personality, ethos and feel to it. And as a writer now I can't just sit down writing the whole time. One of the important aspects of the job for me is to go out and visit people in schools and libraries and meet readers, teachers and librarians. At the moment, I only visit secondary schools, but with my *H.A.U.N.T.S.* series coming out I'll probably start visiting primary schools too.

Many of my visits involve performances, and schools do like me to go around as many classes as I can. Sometimes I'll do a year group or a couple of classes together. In libraries I have different classes coming in, and even different schools. I find that children can be quite subdued in libraries as they're out of their own environment.

Usually I begin my talk with discussing how I started writing and how I wrote my first novel, *Every Step You Take*. Then, depending on who's organising it, I'll talk about writing thrillers, and specifically *Colour Her Dead*. I'll go on to talk about *Dracula* and vampires and writing horror novels. I find it very important to get a rapport going with the children. As a teacher I've always tried not to talk for too long. So I'll ask them what they know about vampires and there'll be a forest of hands going up, and we'll talk for a bit, and that will break the ice. If I've mentioned *The Vanished*, I'll talk about local ghost stories and the oral tradition of storytelling, and ask them to tell me some scary stories. It's so important to get this kind of rapport going.

Sometimes I'll read something from one of my books, but I don't really like doing that. Though if I do read it's often from *Blood Sinister* – and I'll read the passage I discussed earlier with the description of the vampire's teeth. I'll ask the children what clues there are in the passage to indicate that the Count is a vampire.

If I'm at a school for a whole day, I'll talk to groups in the morning and I'll set up a workshop in the afternoon. Often I'm invited in specifically to conduct a workshop on writing horror stories. However, horror stories are particularly difficult for children as they go straight for the gore and the formulaic big scary house with a mad axeman! I see it as my mission in life to show them the difference between what is frightening and what is disgusting, and to get them thinking of something more original!

I'll talk about sense of place – and not setting a story in a stereotypical spooky house, but somewhere that they know. So they'll talk about this and then describe it. We'll then switch to thinking about what has previously occurred in the place they have chosen and what might happen now – and we'll get ideas flowing from that. Next we'll consider the characters, and how they get involved. So, we'll be brainstorming three areas – character, place and plot. The children will be working on each of these separately and then put them together into a story. Obviously time is limited, so at the end of the workshop they'll have outlined their ideas which they can then write up later in class. Classes quite often send me their finished stories and I'm more than happy to respond.

Another story-writing exercise I do is to take a local paper and cut out loads of stories or news items. I'll get the children in groups to discuss the other possible details behind these stories. I'll tell them that the newspaper clipping only gives brief details, but behind it is a whole human story of what has actually happened. So, working from the short piece they'll make their own story around that event. That always works well. Children like the fact that these events really happened, and they enjoy creating background stories to them – wondering why this or that happened, inventing names for other people involved and thinking of the various events that led up to this particular story.

Some children find it easier physically to draw something to generate either a place or a person. Because of this, another thing I do is to get them to draw around their shoes – it sounds very silly, but it works well! Then they swap their shoe outline with a partner, and then within the shape they describe their character from the shoe upwards. They start by describing the person's shoe, socks, trousers, skirt, jumper, up to a more general description of the character. So they build the person, from the feet upwards.

General advice I give children about writing is that they must make the place they are writing about real and believable and they must trust their own world. Children will sometimes say that their own lives and their own worlds are boring and not worth writing about, and that in a story everything is different from real life. I respond by saying that I believe that a story *is* real life, but it's the *detail* of your everyday life that makes your story real – realism, detail, observation – things that you see and hear. I tell them to consider this before they even think of writing about how they can write these details into a story. Sometimes I'll give them the photographs of cemeteries that I took when I was researching *Blood Sinister*, and I'll ask them to consider and write about everything they can see in the photographs: the grass, the tombstone – is it marble or granite?, is it dirty, green or brown? From this they find lots of material to write about. It's a case of accessing what they already know about that's important.

I also discuss the basic story structure of beginning, middle and end and the fundamental nature of plot; that is, cause and effect – if this happens what will happen next, and what will happen as a result of that? I say that an ending must bring the plot strands or events together, and must satisfy the reader – it must be a logical conclusion of what has gone before. To achieve this, they must plan their stories out beforehand. I'll also mention avoiding clichés and falling back on stock answers and structures they've learnt from other stories.

When I was in Devon last year, one girl, a very able reader, said, 'I just love your books. What I love about them is that I can sit down and read one in an afternoon from beginning to end.' She also said that she wanted to read them from start to finish. I do deliberately try to inject that sort of compulsiveness into my work. I also like it when children clearly understand how a book works and when they say that they enjoyed an ending to a book or ask me how I've worked out a plot at the end of a book, like in *Colour Her Dead*. So they're reading *you* – the writer – as well as the book. I like that. And I certainly aim to write my novels in such a way that anybody can read them and that they're accessible and that people can get different things out of them.

Teachers are usually very good. They'll give out class copies of my books or they'll do readings in the library beforehand. As long as the children know who I am and why I'm there, that's all I ask for. I can't insist that everyone has read my work.

5 ON WRITING HORROR/THE HORROR PHENOMENON

My interest in horror began when I read Bram Stoker's *Dracula* at the age of eighteen. It was such an epiphany for me. I just loved it. What a fantastic story! I was reading it one night all alone in the house as my mother and brother were away. I couldn't put it down. But then I got quite frightened. The thing that really freaked me out was the passage in which the Count couldn't be seen in the mirror. And the more I read the more scared I became! Eventually I had to ring up a friend and go and stay at her house for the night!

And that led me on to reading *Frankenstein*. I became totally engrossed in that world, though I didn't find the idea of the monster as interesting as the concept of the vampire in *Dracula*. But I loved the way Mary Shelley creates this dream-like horror – and horror on many levels, as well as the sympathy she generates for the monster. And all those philosophical levels – with the Promethean myth of humans creating life, the anti-Enlightenment concept that science is not the answer to everything, and that through science we create something that is beyond our control. I found parts of it very chilling indeed – such as when Dr Frankenstein is going through the charnel houses to collect the human limbs. I think it's one of the most quietly frightening passages in fiction that I know. It's masterly. And it's amazing how, at the age of nineteen, Mary Shelley could write a novel such as this and understand the ruthlessness of men, and also how she manages to balance the reader's sympathy for the doctor. I read the other day that the *Frankenstein* story fits in with an Innuit myth that there is a malevolent spirit wandering the Arctic – just as the monster does in Shelley's novel. I'm fascinated by the sources of novels, and perhaps it was a wisp of a story such as this that might have reached Mary Shelley's ears and she remembered it, consciously or otherwise.

I don't enjoy 'gore fests', but there are certain contemporary adult horror novelists whom I admire – these include Shirley Jackson, Jonathon Aycliffe, Tom Holland, Anne Rice and Stephen King. There's something Stephen King once said that I bear in mind when writing in this genre. He said that he will try and terrify his reader, and if he can't terrify the reader he will try and horrify the reader – and if he can't horrify, he'll go for gross-out. So, terror is the highest level, the hardest to attain, and gross-out, the gore element, is the easiest. This suits me as I don't believe teenage horror should be very gory. I tend to go for creepiness – like the Count's teeth I was describing earlier in *Blood Sinister*. If you describe intestines spilling out it's just a gross-out, but if you're comparing teeth to a quill it's more effective, I think. At times I might describe rotting or ghost-like corpses, but that's different. It's the small details – the off the wall details – that really horrify, not the blood spurting from every artery! It's the small subtle details I try for. Oddly, my thrillers have more gore than my horror novels!

Until quite recently I think the horror genre was taken quite seriously. It's a recent phenomenon that it has been downgraded or derided. Maybe it's because of film and comics, I don't know. There was a horror comic scare in the 1950s – which was related to horror films too – which gave it a bad name, especially in relation to children's reading. But it has a pedigree, if you take the gothic as horror, with everyone from Shakespeare onwards busily mining it for what it's worth – with Robert Louis Stevenson, Charles Dickens, Arthur Conan Doyle, the Brontë sisters, Nathaniel Hawthorne, Edgar Allan Poe, the list just goes on. I have no problems with the genre.

Contemporary writers I admire include Stephen King, not just because he's a master of the medium but because I think he's a good writer, and also because he writes very interestingly on the horror genre itself. Although he's seen as a horror genre writer, he fits well into mainstream American writing. He's excellent on representing small town American community life. And just because he translates the paranoia, isolation, fear and prejudice that occur in small, isolated communities into supernatural phenomena it doesn't detract from the way he examines those lives. He's very good on character as well.

How would I define horror? I gave a lot of thought to this when I started writing it. I read a lot about the literary and filmic horror genres when I began – writings by Stephen King and Carol Clover. I still find it difficult to say exactly what it is. It contains elements that are not in the thriller. For me, thrillers are totally realistic, set in this world – and whatever happens in a thriller it occurs in this world. A thriller will centre around a violent act like a murder. And it will be a 'Whodunnit' or a 'Whydunnit'. Yet horror will have other aspects to it. It has an otherness, the uncanny, the supernatural in it, something that doesn't belong to this world. With horror there are forces that erupt into the normal world that are dangerous because they are not governed by the rules of the world. The forces do not have to be supernaturally powerful, they can be superhumanly powerful. And horror can also include science fiction, as with the *Alien* films.

Horror has developed a lot through the medium of film. Film has made it into one of the great popular genres and this is perhaps one of the reasons why people have derided it. Some people, such as critics, have a disliking for popular films and genres – the things that people actually like to see and read.

Altogether I'm not happy with 'horror' as a definition for what I do. And 'gothic' has literary overtones. One of my next books is partly about UFOs and alien abduction. I researched the area a lot as I was writing the book, and there's a term in UFOlogy – the study of UFOs – which is 'high strangeness'. It denotes events when people are abducted and experimented upon. For me, 'high strangeness' is a more appropriate definition for my work – as in my novels strange things happen, but lots of ordinary things happen too. I'm quite happy to be categorised or marketed as 'horror', but really, with my writing there's a lot more to it than simply horror.

In a way, the teacher in me never dies. I inject all these issues in a book such as female emancipation, education and women becoming doctors at the end of the nineteenth century. Teenagers will happily read all this because it's also a book about a vampire. But if you wrote a worthy book about a girl becoming a doctor at the end of the 1800s they wouldn't be so keen to read it.

I mainly visit secondary schools – Years 7 and 8. And a lot of boys of that age, 11–13 year olds, still read *Goosebumps* quite happily. They don't feel embarrassed about it, even though the books are aimed at the junior age range. These boys are probably still into *Goosebumps* because their reading ability age is below their chronological age. I look at this situation through my teacher's eyes and I know the tussle that exists with boys in Years 7 and 8 who don't read or aren't reading, or have low reading ability levels. So, anything that they'll read avidly at that age has to be good.

I'm sure that part of the popularity of *Goosebumps* and *Point Horrors* is due to the fact that you get more rewards as a reader. You get thrills and spills. It can be incredibly subtly written, but you get emotional rewards for reading it. It's exciting, scary, it pushes your buttons. Whereas you can get another book that's, say, of a different style, which will still push those buttons it's harder to see what the author is doing and you don't get the same kind of reaction. As a result, a naïve or inexperienced reader may find it harder to get the emotional rewards from the more complex, sophisticated narrative. I think also that children like to be scared, but within a safe environment. You can put the book down – you can shut it, and it's gone. It's safe, and you the reader are in control of it. And with a book you have more control than you do with a film. As a reader, you generate the images yourself, in a film they're generated for you. It's almost like a rites of passage thing that boys watch horror films and try not to be scared, but it's clear that they are.

Because I write the kinds of novels I do, I occasionally have to defend myself against the view that horror published for children is formulaic rubbish, a low grade form of literature, an easy way of getting children to read. Obviously, I disagree. The genre contains some very fine and powerfully original writing. Some of it is formulaic, but so is the writing in other genres. Some children, maybe all children at different stages of their reading, feel safe within the familiar. As for 'an easy way to get children to read' – what's wrong with that? If children are reading – shouldn't we all be glad? Adults are not required to subsist on a fiction diet consisting only of the Booker Prize list. Like adults, children will read what they find stimulating, entertaining, interesting. You can't stop them reading what they like. I believe that reading the kinds of books they enjoy can give them the confidence to try other types of fiction.

So, regarding *Point Horrors* and *Goosebumps*, I feel that anything that children read avidly has got to be a good thing. And I don't think that children are going to live entirely on a diet made up of *Goosebumps*. If they want to read them, then why not? People in my generation read the whole of Enid Blyton. There were hundreds of her books. R.L. Stine has now become the Enid Blyton of the late twentieth century! It says something about the change in society. I think children read him, as well as other *Goosebumps* and *Point Horror* writers, in the same spirit, for the same reasons, for the same sort of enjoyment. I don't think the genre is harmful at all.

Just as children used to enjoy reading *The Famous Five* because of the heroic nature of the child protagonists, with horror books too it's the children that over-come the monster or villain in the end through their own resources. And I think that's something that people often ignore when they talk about horror. It's mythic almost – you have this supernatural, superhuman enemy and children have to band together, they have to be independent, resourceful, loyal to each other, intelligent, courageous, wily and possess lots of other positive character traits to overcome the evil. Those that don't, they fall by the wayside – they're victims. The vain, the stupid and selfish don't stand a chance, so you have to learn fast. There are many positive qualities to be found within horror which children can see, and with which they can identify. Some adult readers don't seem to realise this – they kind of miss the point!

SELECTED CURRENT TITLES

Blood Sinister (Scholastic – *Point Horror Unleashed*)
The Vanished (Scholastic – *Point Horror Unleashed*)
Blood Tide (Scholastic – *Point Horror Unleashed*) (September 1999)

Every Step You Take (Macmillan)
Colour Her Dead (Macmillan)
Midnight Hour (Macmillan)
Truth or Dare (Macmillan) (mid-1999)

Soul Taker (Hodder & Stoughton)
Ghost Chamber (Hodder & Stoughton)
H.A.U.N.T.S. series (Hodder & Stoughton)

An introduction to . . . Norman Silver

WHAT TYPE OF BOOKS DO YOU WRITE ? Novels, such as *No Tigers in Africa* and *The Blue Horse*, short stories such as *An Eye for Colour*, picture books such as *Cloud Nine* and poetry collections such as *The Walkmen Have Landed* and *Choose Your Superhero*.

WHAT ARE YOUR BOOKS ABOUT? Young people journeying to find themselves.

BORN: Cape Town, South Africa, 1946.

EDUCATION: B.A. (Hons.) in Philosophy and English Literature at Witwatersrand University in Johannesburg, South Africa. M.Sc. in computer programming at Essex University, England.

LIVES: Suffolk.

PREVIOUS OCCUPATIONS: I've worked in remand homes for young adults and taught computer programming. I took up writing full-time in 1987.

FAMILY: I live with my wife, a clinical psychologist. We have two children in their early twenties.

AWARDS: *No Tigers in Africa* was decorated with the German Blue Cobra Award (1992) – an annual award that is given to literature for young people that 'reports on the Third World without prejudices or opinions, in an entertaining rather than in an instructive manner'. *No Tigers in Africa* was also shortlisted for *The Guardian* Children's Fiction award.

LANGUAGES TRANSLATED INTO: Spanish, Swedish, French, German, Greek, Italian, Dutch.

WHAT WERE YOU LIKE AT THE AGE OF 11? Shy and perplexed.

ENJOYS VISITING SCHOOLS BECAUSE: I enjoy the creativity of young people.

WHY DO YOU WRITE? Because I love splashing around with words.

IF YOU WEREN'T A WRITER: I'd be a computer games programmer.

AMBITIONS: To experience life joyously.

WHAT WOULD YOU LIKE TO HAPPEN IN THE TWENTY-FIRST CENTURY? Outbreak of peace.

WEBSITE: http://www.storybook.demon.co.uk

I HOW THE READER BECAME A WRITER

I was born in Cape Town, South Africa. And the first book that I remember reading was an illustrated children's encyclopedia. I absolutely loved that book. I immersed myself in it totally for a number of years. Apart from that, I didn't read very much at all. My dad told me a few bedtime stories when I was very young, but not that many.

When I was fourteen or fifteen I had a teacher who was very keen on us reading. She would bring in books for sale and she often asked us what books we were reading. I always used to tell her I was reading *Tarzan* and *William* books – and it used to infuriate her! The truth is, I did read *Tarzan* and *William* at that age! But also at night I would be reading poetry – some American poets like Lawrence Ferlinghetti, and of course I never used to tell my teacher during class I was reading all that stuff. It was just rebelliousness. And I was tremendously shy as a teenager. I didn't like to read out loud in class. I spent most of my days in class with my head tucked down behind the person in front of me – so the teacher wouldn't see me!

My dad wasn't conventional, and he fancied himself as a little bit knowledgeable about things literary. He was quite well read, but he wasn't an academic person or anything. And he was moderately encouraging with my writing. He'd written a few poems himself and had read them to me, and I thought that perhaps I could write poems as well. But I never told him I was writing them either. All my writing then was done behind my locked bedroom door, very, very late at night, around midnight – from the age of fifteen to the age of twenty-three. One of my poems at that time – 'The Ripening Fruit' – was read out on an afternoon radio programme of the South African Broadcasting Corporation. And later, I had a little Oscar Wilde-type story read out as well. I don't remember the name of it, but I'm sure it had a fisherman in the title. Apart from those, I let very few people read my work then, except for my girlfriend.

Later on, when I was studying at Witwatersrand University in Johannesburg, I joined a writing group run by Lionel Abrams, and I enjoyed that very much. It was a really powerful experience of enjoying the act of writing. I wrote a lot when I was with that group. Week after week, I was producing poems, stories and plays. They were all pieces I felt inspired to write by being in that group, and by being with other people who were writing. Lionel would encourage me to be bold in my work, because I was not very confident then. And just being with other writers like that was exciting for me.

In 1969, my wife and I got married and came to England to pursue our academic studies. My wife was to study psychology, and I was to study philosophy. I didn't write another word from that moment – the moment we got on the boat to come to England, the night of our wedding day – until 1986. So that was a gap of seventeeen years. It was because I was going through change, very intense personal change. It was the openness of everything in England – being able to go to uncensored films, or read books that were banned in South Africa, meeting people that were different from myself, who had different views about everything. I felt I was going through a metamorphosis. Had I stayed in South Africa I would have carried on writing – there wouldn't have been that gap, but coming over here, my desire to write was put to the back of my mind.

When we arrived here, I started my Ph.D., but I didn't finish it. And I had a number of jobs before I started writing full-time. I was house father in remand homes in London and Bristol. I sold antiques and antique paintings for a while. And then I took an M.Sc. in computer programming at Essex University and later taught computing at a technology centre. It was when I was working at the technology centre that I started writing in my spare time. After a year of doing that, I made the conscious decision to write again and decided to take a year off work.

During that year I worked on a science fiction-type story, which didn't get anywhere. And around that time I went on a weekend writing course with Geraldine Kaye. It was an important weekend for me because Geraldine said that in her work she wrote about displaced people – people who had been born in one country, yet now lived in another. I came away from that course with the whole of *No Tigers in Africa* in my head. But also at that time it suddenly occurred to me that everybody's experience was unique and worth writing about. Until then I'd had this South African inferiority complex that the world was happening outside of South Africa. And then I connected to my South African past, to when I saw a play in Johannesburg called *The Blood Knot*. It was written and directed by Athol Fugard – and he acted in it as well. Seeing that had been a tremendously powerful experience for me. It dealt with racial issues and the bond between blacks and whites. So those two things came together – meeting Geraldine Kaye and connecting with my South African past. However, none of the events in *No Tigers in Africa* are autobiographical – except for Selwyn's love of rugby and poetry – but the emotional journey Selwyn undertakes is pretty much what I went through.

Having written *No Tigers in Africa*, I specifically sought out a creative writing course run by a writer who I thought might be sympathetic or helpful in some way. I found one with Hanif Kureishi in Cambridge. He was kind enough to read the manuscript over the weekend and suggested I send it to a friend of his at Faber & Faber for a critical reading. Janice Thompson, the children's editor at Faber, gave me a call and said that she wanted to publish it. At the same time I got my agent Laura Cecil. And after that, *No Tigers* was published. When I was writing *No Tigers* I was writing poetry alongside, and I've continued that pattern ever since.

2 WRITING: ROUTINES AND REFLECTIONS

I write in my little room – a room with a desk and a computer. I usually spend from 9 to 5 in that room, either writing or editing or researching something. I work on a word processor – I've worked on one since 1986. I *never* write by hand.

At any one time I have a number of projects on the go. Now, I'm just completing a book of magical tales – which I've been working on for the last year and a half – several picture books, a novel set in the new South Africa and also a new collection of poetry.

I store all my ideas in my head! I work on the basis that what is significant will remain in my memory and what isn't will fall away. I do let things grow or gestate in my head for quite a long time before I ever start writing. Occasionally with a poem I'll write the idea down as it occurs. But whether they're ideas for stories or poems they'll take a while to get to the stage where I'm working with them on the word processor. I've never used a notebook for ideas – that would be too much of a distraction to my life.

Usually, ideas for poems come tagged as ideas for poems. I just know that certain ideas should go into a poem. But occasionally one has crossed over. My picture book *Cloud Nine* started life as a poem. Poetry allows me to explore a variety of themes in one book, which I can't do in a novel or even in a book of short stories. You can only explore thirteen or fourteen ideas in a book of thirteen or fourteen short stories. I think that part of the pleasure I get from writing a collection of poetry is being able to switch from one topic to another. And disguised within the serious material in my collections is a kind of spectrum of stuff which ranges from humorous to lightweight and everything between. My collections are like an assortment of chocolates, and hidden amongst the poems are some that have a deeper subject matter than they appear to have. Somebody might just pluck one of those out, thinking it's lightweight or it's going to be humorous or whatever, only to find they've picked out a poem of a different kind, but hopefully it's still interesting to read!

And I love writing for young people. Unlike adult literature, there's no room for artifice and there has to be a fairly direct communication. There's no need to be unduly complicated. I feel that that matches perfectly with the material that wells up from within me – it comes up in that sort of uncomplicated way. Somebody who was reading one of my short stories recently said that it was very simply written, and I thought, great!

When I'm writing I don't think about readers or particular groups of readers. All I'm aware of is the younger age limit – I never think of the upper age limit, I always try to keep that as open as possible. What I'm in touch with is the corresponding age of myself. I think that's who I'm writing for.

I test out my work within me as I'm writing it. When I finish something, I might show it to my kids – although they're twenty-one and twenty-three – to give me some feedback, and my wife as well if she has the time. My children have been very helpful in the past, and I have made changes on their recommendations. As I sit at the word processor, I read and re-read my work until it's right. But this process of checking whether something's working is happening within me as well. So by the time it reaches my children or my wife it's already gone through that process, and then I'm asking them to look for the small details.

With all of my novels so far, from *No Tigers in Africa* to *The Blue Horse*, the first person has seemed the most appropriate voice. I started out with that form of narration for my South African books – and looking back, I think it's because I needed literally to hear that South African accent and I heard it clearest when I was writing in the first person. Then apart from that, there's the usual business that the first person helps you to get into the character's head in a particular way and to see events through their eyes. That suited my first three books. Likewise, in *The Blue Horse* I really wanted the reader to meet this person Alex, and I thought the best way was with the first person voice.

People often ask me how I achieve the teenage voice or teenage point of view. It's not so difficult for me because I have a rebellious view of society – which I've never grown out of and I don't intend to. When I'm writing I just have to make contact with that part of myself which is out of sync with what society expects. I really begin to hear that teenage voice the more I work with a teenage character. I just have to find it within myself, that teenage voice – it's in there, very clearly, still. I don't feel that because I'm in my fifties that voice has gone away, it's still active – as is the voice of myself as a child.

It has been said that my novels are 'issue books', but I personally don't like labelling them in that way. For example, with *The Blue Horse*, although it deals with the issue of facial disfigurement, I feel it is not exclusively about such disfigurement but more about an individual human being who finds himself suddenly in a difficult situation, challenged by circumstance to find resources within himself to cope with life. And I guess I may write other books in this vein, but I won't be thinking of them as issue books.

3 GROWING A BOOK

The Blue Horse

The Blue Horse began when the children's programme *Jackanory* got in touch with my agent and they requested a story from me. One of the producers there wanted me to write an issues-based story for the programme – for example, the war in Yugoslavia or something. I was quite intrigued with the idea of writing for *Jackanory* – I'd seen some of their more recent programmes and I'd enjoyed them a lot, so I was quite excited about doing this project.

When I started to figure out what topic I wanted I suddenly remembered that my wife, five years before that, had asked if I knew of any books for kids who were facially disfigured, which would give them some sort of positive experience. Most facially disfigured characters in fiction are rather nasty – in fact most disabled people in fiction often appear as villains or horror figures. And when I'd looked into it five years previously, I hadn't found anything suitable for a child to read. Another factor in writing the story was that when I lived in Cape Town as a child I sometimes came into contact with a relative who had suffered severe facial disfigurement in his teens after accidentally setting himself on fire.

As soon as the *Jackanory* offer came about, I knew then that facial disfigurement was exactly what I wanted to write about. I had the feeling that I wanted to tackle it head on. But at the same time, it had to be for younger viewers. On top of this was the matter of how we would present a facially disfigured person on *Jackanory* – either in illustrations, or the person reading the story would be facially disfigured – which I thought presented some really interesting possibilities.

So then the story started to grow in my head and I began to realise that Alex, the main character, was actually going to be heroic – as are all people who confront their own fears or disabilities. I thought the best way of showing this in the novel would be to have a parallel story of a fantasy hero which would be told by Alex's grandfather. Part of my intention was to allow a young reader to feel by the end of the story that Alex was truly heroic. I also wanted to consider what a hero actually is – for often heroes are larger-than-life mythic figures. I've always felt that people who confront their own fears are more heroic than most archetypal heroes. So in the book I wanted people to meet an everyday heroic figure. Once I'd

Rough artwork by Jilly Wilkinson for *The Blue Horse*

discovered the form, that of two stories in parallel, what I'd also found was that the piece was as much a reflection on fantasy reading as it was on the heroism of real life. But everyday heroes can also be seen to be mythical figures. These two types of hero play on each other.

I really enjoyed developing those two parallel stories. And what I tried to do was not to have the two plots corresponding too closely. They don't map directly onto each other in terms of events. I wanted an element of arbitrariness. I trusted totally on the storytelling part of myself to let that happen. In fact, for the writing of the whole thing, there was no time when I altered one plot to parallel the other in any way.

One thing I knew in advance of writing *The Blue Horse* – before I even knew its title or even the plot, but when I'd decided it was going to be about a person with facial disfigurement – I just knew that there was going to be something blue in the story. But why, I have no idea! Then, I wasn't quite sure what was going to be blue in the story. I had many other such hunches, but only some of them were realised in the book. First of all I had the idea of the accident with the horse, but I didn't know that the horse would be blue at that point. It was at a later stage that the blueness attached itself to the horse! Now, if the horse had only been blue in the fantasy story, it would have had no real significance. But the blue horse in the everyday story becomes a mythic creature in this boy's life.

These metaphors in my novels – like the blue horse, the tigers in *No Tigers in Africa*, the snakes in *Python Dance* and the chameleon or the ladybug in *An Eye for Colour* – for me, they act as little doorways into the psyche of a character, those subterranean parts of a character. Using metaphors is instinctual for me, and it's also my own way of entering into the inner world of dreams and myths. These metaphors introduce some sort of dreamscape – another form of reality – into the everyday lives of my characters. I do like this idea of the mapping together of myths and dreamscapes with a waking reality.

I wrote *The Blue Horse* in its original form for *Jackanory*. And obviously, they didn't need a novel, they just needed some form of manuscript which they could work from to produce a programme. The original text must have been about sixty pages long. When it was finished, I gave it to them and they loved it. But then the programme was axed. At that point my editor, Janice Thompson at Faber & Faber, said she would really like to see it done as a novel. I went back to it and did a second draft. I extended it to its present form of a hundred pages. I didn't add anything new to the two storylines, I just expanded upon a few individual scenes and sections that were already there. And because I had more time I was able to elaborate parts of the fantasy sequence as well as the real-life step-family. However, the overall style was very similar in both versions.

The illustrations for *The Blue Horse* were done by Jilly Wilkinson. *Jackanory* were going to use her for their programme. Jilly was very sympathetic to the story because members of her own family had also been involved in a car accident. And when *Jackanory* fell through, my editor at Faber readily agreed that Jilly should do the illustrations for the book. It was the first illustration job Jilly had done since the accident, and it seemed so right for her to do it. Jilly showed me her illustrations at all the various stages of production, and I was extremely pleased with how she interpreted the story.

Storyboard for artwork by Jilly Wilkinson for *The Blue Horse*

I'm not a first drafter! I did do two main drafts for *The Blue Horse*, though it doesn't mean that I don't go over each draft a large number of times. I work them, and re-work them, page by page, paragraph by paragraph, sentence by sentence. I look at it all. I call it polishing. I just go on and on polishing a draft until I feel it's ready. I spend as long on that process as I do writing it. I never keep the original versions, I just work on the one document on the computer. And it's impossible to tell on the computer what the original was like compared to the final draft. So any book that I've done, if it's taken a year, then probably it's been six months to get it into a first draft, and then another six months to go through it. With a novel I'll work on it until I feel that anything I do from that point on is not going to do it any good. For a while, all the changes I'm making will be improving it and polishing it, and then it reaches a point where it's beginning to be unnecessary or to clutter the story, so I stop.

More time is spent on the beginning of a story than anything else. I just keep working on those first couple of pages. Until I get the tone of my work, it doesn't move any further. So the usual order of production is, first, to gestate the idea; then, second, to go for those opening couple of pages to see what it's going to sound like. Then once I've wrestled with it and got it nearly right – the train leaves the station! I'll begin the story proper. And now I'll work on it non-stop until I get to the end. This writing phase is pretty intense. Once I've finished, I might leave it for a bit, work on other things and then return to the polishing stage later.

The only book I've used paper for is *No Tigers in Africa*. When I came back from the creative writing weekend I'd been on with Geraldine Kaye, I wrote down about twenty points – a sequence of plot details or stages. And when I looked back at it later, those stages were what I actually used in the book. I've never done that again! Usually, those developments – those plot stages – are in my head before I begin a novel, and I know I will go through each of these with my main character. I'll always know the rough feel of the ending, but in the writing there can be a lot of surprises. And I always allow room for that. There could be tremendous variation in how the story actually comes out, even though I have the rough idea at the beginning of how things will turn out.

Generally speaking, plot and character work together for me – when an idea comes I have the feeling of a character in a situation or in a crisis. From there, my plotting starts with my main character's need to get out of his situation. And that will start to generate the plot. I then start to expand the character to make him go for one choice rather than another. I never think of a character in isolation – that wouldn't work for me. I'm always thinking of a character in a social or personal situation, or whatever, but in some kind of turmoil, usually. That scenario drives the plotting forward. But I'll also have various other plot ideas – I'll know that other events will happen down the line – so that will affect how my character starts to be formed, and then the character takes a step forward, and I'll see that affecting the plot.

4 VISITS TO SCHOOLS

I really enjoy working with young people. Even before I began writing, I was working with young people – when I was teaching computer programming, and before that, when I worked in remand homes. And I enjoyed it when my own children were young.

Before any visit I usually do quite a lot of preparation. I have ways that I've been doing prose and poetry exercises with various groups over the last eight years. And I like to find out exactly where the class is at that I'm going to be working with. If it's necessary, I'll modify the activities I already have.

Most schools ask for either a workshop or a reading, and state whether they want me to do prose or poetry. I'll either go in for a day, a number of days or for a whole week. Generally, the prose sessions need more time, especially with the older groups. With secondary school children I usually do work based on their own experiences and on people they've known well in their lives. We'll start with characters and events, and then we'll work towards the idea of creating a short story out of these experiences. Often I'll read one of my own stories and point out its structural elements and offer the students a sort of skeleton structure on which to hang their own story.

With younger groups we work from our imaginations – perhaps to produce a picture book. I often use my own picture book *Cloud Nine* as a model. With the class I go through the plot stages of the book and then discuss ways that this structure can be varied so that it becomes the story of another kid in a different situation, going off on a different adventure.

The way I help children to overcome the blank page is to generate enthusiasm. When someone is enthusiastic about something, it becomes easier to draw it or write it or sing it or whatever! If you're bored with it, *that's* the problem – not the blank page. If there can be some excitement about putting something down, it makes the task much easier. For example, during a five-day workshop in a special school, I came in one morning and asked the class, 'Shall we write poetry today?' The entire group of kids yelled out, 'Yeah!!' When it's like that, there's no problem of a blank page any more. They can't wait to write down their ideas.

Occasionally a student will come up to me after a reading and say, 'That poem you just read, that's the first poem I've ever enjoyed.' Any writer visiting a school loves hearing that sort of response. And when participants in a workshop say, 'Can we write more poetry?' – I find that inspiring. Sometimes when I go into a class I'll start off by asking 'Who hates poetry?' And if at the end of the session one of those students softens their attitude, that can be very rewarding.

Teachers can prepare for my visits in many different ways. Some read my work to their classes or else they pin up extracts of my work on the walls of the corridors or classrooms. Others share their own excitement about the upcoming visit and transmit this feeling to their students. Sometimes it's disheartening if you sense the teacher feels you've just come in to take the class off his or her hands, so that they can catch up on marking or some other task. Whereas you go into other schools and you feel this tingle of excitement. You just know the teacher has helped to make it a special day and told the class that it's their chance to ask questions about your books. Teachers' responses vary from being absent, to sitting in a corner doing their own work, or, in most cases, actively participating. I don't mind if they don't participate, if they don't join in with the writing, especially if they feel they're better occupied helping less able individuals to enjoy the writing exercise I've set the class. But most teachers are quite wonderful once they've taken the trouble to invite you in!

5 METHODS OF RESEARCH

I do all kinds of research, usually during the planning or the gestation period of a book. The nature of the research very much depends on the book that I'm working on at the time. For instance, after I'd written the first draft of *The Blue Horse* – a book about facial disfigurement – I decided it would be a good idea to get in contact with Veronica Kish and James Partridge of Changing Faces, the facial disfigurement charity. Veronica is the children's specialist and James is the founder-director of the charity. I asked both Veronica and James if they could read the manuscript, and they were very keen. When they'd read it, they called me for a meeting. I was very encouraged by their enthusiasm. James made one or two suggestions which I incorporated into the book. One of these was that it would be good if the family in the story saw an advert of people with really beautiful faces – so that kind of suggestion I welcomed and included.

When Jilly Wilkinson (the illustrator) and I were thinking about the pictures for *The Blue Horse*, and what the boy Alex should look like, we asked James for advice. When we came to the last picture of the story, I always wanted a frontal shot of Alex's face. James gave us various diagrams which were very useful. James and I also discussed the type of operation that my character Alex would have had, and also the damage that Alex would have incurred to his face. And although I never made the details very explicit in the book, I had all those details in mind as I wanted it to be factually accurate. So, one of the functions of the research I do is to ensure I'm getting my facts right. And before I started writing that book I also read case histories of people with disfigurement as well as looking into the psychological and physical therapy that people have after accidents. I read James Partridge's autobiography too.

Research for my novel *Python Dance* involved reading a lot of newspapers. The book is set in South Africa in 1966, and I spent a lot of time in the newspaper library at Colindale, examining their microfiches of newspapers from Johannesburg of that year – *Johannesburg Star*, *Daily Mail*, *Sunday Times* and *Drum*. I was looking for all different things: the advertisements from that time, names of the hit records, the current films, which horses were winning the races, etc. I also discovered that it was a year with a bad drought – and I actually followed the progression of the drought in my book. Researching *Python Dance* was the only time I've used notebooks to collect information in. I had loads of notebooks with loads of stuff – I had much more than I could use – but it was fun choosing what information I needed for the novel.

I've also used interviewing for purposes of research during one visit to South Africa; I used a tape recorder and spoke to a huge number of people. I started off with about three or four interviews with friends of people I know – and they then suggested other people that I should see. This was a very enjoyable and most valuable way of gathering information.

I don't use external or real events to generate the events of a novel. I have an idea of the character inside the plot, in a situation, as I've described before. I use the research to fill that out. I once went on a creative writing weekend where the tutor asked us to do two exercises: the first was to take a newspaper article and turn it into a short story, and the other was for each member of the group to contribute plot and character details to a group story – then we each had to go off and finish the

Final artwork by Jilly Wilkinson for *The Blue Horse*

story on our own. Both of those I see as external methods, whereas I tend to work from an internal point of view in that my main character will have some connection with my own experience. I then open out from that point and research where I need to in order to fill out details. I do sometimes allow research to influence plot, but the impulse for the plot will never come from another source. The drought in *Python Dance* is just about the only time I've allowed an external source to influence the way that a story is told.

SELECTED CURRENT TITLES

South African trilogy (Faber & Faber)

No Tigers in Africa
An Eye for Colour
Python Dance

The Blue Horse – illustrated by Jilly Wilkinson (Faber & Faber)

Poetry collections

Choose Your Superhero (Hodder & Stoughton)
Words on a Faded T-shirt (Faber & Faber)
The Comic Shop (Faber & Faber)
The Walkmen Have Landed (Faber & Faber)

Picture book

Cloud Nine – illustrated by Jan Ormerod (Bodley Head)

An introduction to . . .
Jacqueline Wilson

WHAT TYPE OF BOOKS DO YOU WRITE? I mostly write novels for seven- to twelve-year-olds – including *Double Act*, *The Suitcase Kid*, *The Lottie Project* and *The Story of Tracy Beaker* – but I've also written very short stories for beginner readers and a trilogy for teenagers.

WHAT ARE YOUR BOOKS ABOUT? They're realistic modern books about children with problems. They sometimes deal with very sad subjects like divorce and bullying but the children always find a way of dealing with these issues. I know my books sometimes make my readers cry – but I put in lots of funny bits so that they can have a good laugh too.

BORN/LIVES: Bath, 17 December 1945. My parents were billeted there during World War Two, but most of my life I have lived in and around Kingston, Surrey, which is where I live now.

EDUCATION: I went to two primary schools, one in Lewisham and one in Kingston. I attended Coombe Girls' Comprehensive School, and then I did a one-year secretarial course at Carshalton Technical College. In my late thirties, early forties – just to prove to myself I could have gone to university – I did an 'A' level in English Literature and got an 'A' grade!

PREVIOUS OCCUPATIONS: I worked as a journalist for D.C. Thompson in Dundee for a couple of years in my late teens and later I was a freelance writer.

FAMILY/PETS: My daughter, Emma, is 32, and an academic at Cambridge. I'm separated from my husband. I don't have any pets, but I'd like a dog or cat in the future, though only when I've stopped travelling around so much.

HOBBIES: Reading. Going to art galleries and films. I swim three-quarters of a mile every morning. My totally naff hobby is line dancing – I adore it! And my serious vice is collecting books – I've got over 10,000.

MOST TREASURED POSSESSIONS: The stories that my daughter wrote for me when she was little. She made them into little books with lots of beautiful illustrations.

AWARDS INCLUDE: *The Story of Tracy Beaker* – Oak Tree Award 1991; Sheffield Children's Book Award 1991; shortlisted for the Carnegie Medal 1991. *The Suitcase Kid* – Children's Book Award 1993; shortlisted for the Carnegie Medal 1993. *The Bed and Breakfast Star* – Young Telegraph / Fully Booked Award 1995. *Double Act* – Smarties Prize 1995; Children's Book Award 1996; Sheffield Children's Book Award 1996; Highly Commended for the Carnegie Medal 1996.

LANGUAGES TRANSLATED INTO: Most European languages and Japanese.

TELEVISION PROGRAMMES: *Cliffhanger* was produced by Channel 4. *Double Act* and *The Suitcase Kid* have had recent interest from two production companies. I've been asked by the BBC to write an original drama series for young teenagers – though whether it will happen I don't know. Television can be a wonderful shop window if your work is being shown, and you reach a great many more people. It's not my top priority – I'm more interested in writing books.

THEATRE: *The Suitcase Kid* was adapted for the stage by Sam Snape, and I'm currently writing a play – *The Dare Game*. It's a new story about Tracy Beaker – for the Contact Theatre in Manchester. I'm also going to do it as a book.

FAVOURITE PLACE: New England – though I love *old* England too.

FAVOURITE BOOKS: Children's – *Nancy and Plum* by Betty Macdonald (now out of print) and *The Greengage Summer* by Rumer Godden. Adults' – *The Bell Jar* by Sylvia Plath and *The Accidental Tourist* by Anne Tyler.

FAVOURITE POEM: 'The Fat White Woman' by Frances Cornford.

FAVOURITE MUSIC: Anonymous Four – a quartet of female medieval choral singers. I play them when I'm writing. Also anything by Queen and very corny country music!

FAVOURITE FILMS: *Thelma and Louise* and a 1950s film, *Mandy*, about a deaf girl.

WHICH ONE OF YOUR CHARACTERS WOULD YOU MOST LIKE TO BE? Charlie in *The Lottie Project* because she's bright, intelligent and full of beans.

WHAT WERE YOU LIKE AT THE AGE OF 11? I loved reading. I kept a diary. I knew I wanted to be a writer, but mostly I kept quiet about it because I didn't want people to tease me.

ENJOYS VISITING SCHOOLS BECAUSE: It keeps me in touch with what is going on in schools. I like meeting lots of children and it's fun hearing what they think of my books.

WHY DO YOU WRITE? I can't imagine what my life would be like if I didn't write. I don't know *why* I write. I can't seem to help it.

IF YOU WEREN'T A WRITER: If I had the talent, I'd be an illustrator.

AMBITIONS: I'd like to make it on a line dancing team!

WHICH FOUR WORDS DESCRIBE YOU BEST? Imaginative, friendly, anxious, determined.

WHAT WOULD YOU LIKE TO HAPPEN IN THE TWENTY-FIRST CENTURY? For people to value creativity a little more and technology a little bit less.

WHICH OF YOUR BOOKS WOULD YOU LIKE TO BE REMEMBERED FOR? *The Illustrated Mum.*

I HOW THE READER BECAME A WRITER

I wish I could say that my first book was a wonderful literary text, but it was *Pookie* by Ivy M. Wallace. I loved it. It was all about a rabbit called Pookie who was the odd one out in his family because he was white and all the others were brown. As he wasn't wanted he left the burrow and had a terrible time and he ended up in a wood. Kind Belinda, the woodcutter's daughter, came along and nursed him. And Pookie lived happily ever after with Belinda! The book had a little bit of text and large, brightly coloured illustrations, which I pored over.

I imagine that my mother would have read *Pookie* to me just once or twice, as my parents weren't particularly into reading aloud to me. But even before I could read the words myself I would spend hours just looking at this book, and I'd make up my own stories about all the characters. So I was a totally committed book person even before I could actually read. Though when I did, I learned to read quite quickly. By six, I had read a great deal of Enid Blyton. I really liked the *Faraway Tree* books and the *St Claire's* series. I didn't like *The Famous Five* books. I would enjoy the first chapter when they went off to the seaside to have a picnic, but I was irritated by the adventures. I wanted the stories I read to be really true to life, with strong convincing characters and lots of detailed description of clothes and Christmas, books and birthday parties. I loved Noel Streatfeild. Her characters were ultra-realistic and could be bad-tempered or jealous. And I also loved *Nancy and Plum* by Betty Macdonald. It's a totally girlie book. I read it again and again and I adored it.

By eight, I was reading some adult books with child characters because I found them more truthful. I read Catherine Cookson's books about a girl named Mary Ann who had a drunk for a father. Mary Ann was forever getting into fights. I also read Rumer Godden's books with child characters. For a while there was a down-market women's magazine called *Woman's Companion*. It had a serial story called 'The Latchkey Child' which I totally adored. I read any kind of thing. The joy of growing up in my sort of household was that I had no concept of what was considered literature. I just went for subject matter.

I would spend all my pocket money on notebooks and maybe a new biro. I would sit and write a new story on the Saturday. I'd write some more of it on Sunday, and by Monday I'd think it was rubbish and I'd tear it out and start another one. By Saturday, I'd be ready for another notebook. I used to copy illustrations and pictures from books as well. The only story I've kept from my childhood – which I wrote when I was nine – is 'The Maggots'. It was reasonably influenced by a book I loved called *The Children From One End Street* by Eve Garnett. Like that book, 'The Maggots' is about working-class children.

Most of the stories that I wrote then were like juvenile versions of what I do now – stories about families with problems. I wrote the whole time. By the age of eleven I knew very much I wanted to be a writer, but mostly I kept quiet about it because I didn't want people to tease me. Being an only child was brilliant training for being

THE MAGGOTTS.

BY

JACQUELINE AITKEN.

Story written by Jacqueline Wilson at the age of 9

The Maggotts.

Chapter 1
Meet the Maggotts

When Alfred Maggott was married he stated he wetix children and children he got. You see Daisy Maggott wanted children too, and everything Daisy wanted she was sure to get. The Maggotts had seven children, four girls and three boys. The oldest, Marilyn is dead keen on boys. Boys are dead keen on her too. She is fifteen. She is very pretty with blonde hair hanging round her shoulders and bright blue eyes.

Then comes Marlene the brainy one. She is twelve and has passed the school up to the high school. Her interest is books. You can't drag her out of them. She has brown eyes and brown hair in a very short pony tail. She also wears National Health glasses.

Ten year old Mandy comes next. She has short dark plaits and hazel eyes. She is mad about films. She wants to be an actress when she grows up.

Then come the nine year old twins who have brown hair, blue eyes and they are always getting into trouble. The are called Marmaduke and Montague.

Now Mervyn. He is a curly golden haired tell-tale of seven.

The baby of the Maggott family is two x year old Marigold shortened t Goldie. She looks like Mervyne and a usally eating, breaking things and screaming. Now back to alf and a writer – having to amuse myself and to use my imagination in that way. I've always been very happy with my own company.

My mum and dad didn't get on, and my home life was a bit tempestuous, and I kept quiet about that too at school. I got used to having different sorts of lives. There was my life with my family. There was my school life. There was my writing life. And there was my own private imaginative play life. I gave up proper dolls at ten or eleven but played endless games with paper models from fashion magazines until I was well into my teens.

In 1959, when I was thirteen, I kept a diary and I had two books on the go. One was Catherine Cookson's *The Devil and Mary Ann* and the other was Nabokov's *Lolita*. *Lolita* had just come out in hardback. My father bought it but didn't read it. It was the first book of Literature – with a capital 'L' – that I ever read. I had no idea that you could do this sort of thing with language. I found it incredible – absolutely riveting. I savoured every sentence. I was very interested in the Lolita character. Knowing my parents would be horrified at the idea of me reading it, I took the cover of *Lolita* off and put the cover from *The Devil and Mary Ann* on instead! Now, I'm such a literary snob, I'd do the opposite! Right throughout my teens I read a great deal – including *Jane Eyre, Wuthering Heights*, all of Jane Austen, some Dickens and a little Virginia Woolf, but I managed to miss out on so many standard classics because I didn't know they existed.

I quite liked moving up to the comprehensive school as they had a special stage with curtains, and I rather fancied acting. I joined the drama club, but I only got small parts. I worked very hard at English and Art and I cared passionately about my English essays. And at fifteen I wrote my first full-length novel about two sisters who set off in a car for Europe. My school was heavily into sport, and I was useless at all games, so I didn't particularly appreciate my school life. Having said that, I've had the delight of being asked back to the school as an 'old girl' and to present the prizes. And there is a year group which they've named after me – 7 Wilson – which I think is wonderful. The atmosphere of the school has changed out of all recognition. It's a lovely school now, and I'm really proud that I went there.

It sounds stupid, but I had absolutely no idea you could leave school and actually do 'A' levels at a college of further education. So I went to Carshalton Technical College and learnt shorthand and typing and office skills. But this probably enabled me to start my career as a writer earlier than if I'd done 'A' levels – because, a year or so later, having had a couple of jokey articles accepted by D.C. Thompson in one of their magazines, I went to work for them as a junior journalist in Dundee. I was recruited to work on their new teenage girls' magazine. The magazine was eventually called *Jackie* because I was the youngest journalist there and I think they wanted a catchy name and they'd gone through the *Bunty*'s and *Judy*'s. And Jackie was a very 1960s name – with Jackie Kennedy very much in the news.

However, when I began at D.C. Thompson I was put to work on a woman's magazine called *Red Letter*, which was for – as they put it in those days – 'house-wives'! I had the wonderful job of writing short stories and seeing them in print every week. I also wrote readers' letters – when no one had written in! – and also the horoscope column and articles about pregnancy and babies. I was eighteen and had never been pregnant. It's amazing what you can do with a bit of research and imagination! All this was invaluable training, because it taught me not to be precious about writing, to be adaptable, to turn my hand to anything and to write whenever it was needed.

At nineteen, I got married, returned to Kingston, and I thought I would try to earn my living in a freelance capacity. I sold some articles and short stories. I'd already written a couple of adult novels and a children's novel which I didn't manage to sell. I eventually had another go at writing a book for children and it was published. This was for a series of early readers for Leila Berg called *Nippers*, about inner city children. My book was called *Ricky's Birthday*. I was thrilled to bits when it came out.

Next came my five crime novels for adults. The books are quite explicit sexually, which does worry me in that I have various young fans who have these quests to find everything I've ever written. I would be very perturbed if they read these. They're not still in print, but they do surface in libraries. All of these books have child characters in them, and a couple of them had early teenage girl characters, and even as I was writing these I knew that what I really wanted to do was to write *for* children. But, I don't know why, I just got caught up in writing for adults instead. Sometimes because you write in a particular way that comes naturally to you it's almost as if it's too easy – so you try some other field that seems 'harder'.

After that I wrote my first hardback book for children called *Nobody's Perfect*. That was published in 1982 by Oxford University Press, for 12–16 year olds. I did another seven or eight books of this type for OUP – including *Falling Apart* and *The Dream Palace*. Compared with my current work, these books had a far more literary style, they had denser text, and were much longer books, dealing with complex issues for older girls. I loved writing them, but they were of their time. Then in 1990 I moved over to Transworld, and started to do work illustrated by Nick Sharratt. I concentrated on books for 8–12 year olds, and it made a real difference, for everything just started to take off.

2 WRITING: ROUTINES AND REFLECTIONS

I can write anywhere and at any time, and I don't have to have certain music playing or be in a specific place before I can write. I have a little study upstairs which is really my spare bedroom with a desk, a chair and a lot of books. I write in there, or at the kitchen table or curled up in the living room. I often write on trains because I visit so many schools and libraries. I feel worried if I haven't written at least two pages a day of whatever book I'm currently writing. I don't write in the evenings or weekends, but I will use that time to respond to post – I get about three hundred letters a week from children, which includes batches from whole classes. I keep every letter and try to reply to all of them.

I write with any kind of black felt tip pen, in my little squiggly writing. I feel very comfortable writing in longhand in these Claire Fontaine A4 notebooks that I buy. What I like about these books is that they're firm, so I can even write if I'm standing up waiting at a station. I only write on the right-hand side of the page, so when I'm re-writing I can put additional changes onto the left-hand side. I'll do one draft by hand – with some occasional amendments – and then I'll type out a second draft on my ancient, manual Olivetti typewriter. I change bits and pieces as I type. Then I'll send it off. I have to use a typewriter as I can't use a computer. I'm hopeless with technology and I'm frightened of machinery!

I've learnt that you can't remember all the ideas you have, they leak straight out of your head. I'll jot down a few lines in my ideas book – though having said that, it's often the ideas that I remember without having to refer to the book that will eventually get used. But more than anything else, my ideas book gives me a feeling of security. All writers get asked where we get our ideas from. No writer can ever come up with a reasonable, convincing answer. You just don't know – an idea bobs into your head, just like that. The notebook gives you the feeling that there's always something to work on. As a fiction writer, it's frightening – you do literally have to conjure things up out of nothing. Even half a page of jottings in the book can be a big help.

Originally, I would write my books on spec, and the publisher would respond with a 'yes' or 'no'. Now I've got to the pleasant position where I get my work commissioned. It used to be that the publisher would ask for a synopsis, for if they're putting down hard cash and they're wanting to put you on their publishing list for next year, they need to know more or less what this next book will be about. I found doing a synopsis the most difficult thing of all, for although I would know vaguely what I was going to do, I didn't really want to detail all the ins and outs of the story because I wanted to keep it alive, and also I might have wanted to do it quite differently when I got down to writing it. Nowadays, my contracts will simply say 'An untitled book for 8–12 year olds', and I may or may not discuss some of the details with the editor. This system works well for me as I prefer to let an idea simmer in my head and not discuss it with anybody at all, and then develop it myself. If I talk about something before I've written it I have this superstition that I might lose confidence in it completely or I'll be concerned that it sounds awful or banal.

I still get very worried each time I send a new manuscript off that people will think, 'Oh dear, she's really lost it this time, this is useless.' Half-way through a book I'm practically weeping and saying, 'This just isn't working, what am I going to do?' Yet I don't generally go back and re-read stuff from the beginning at that point because it would make me too depressed. I think, never mind, go on to the end, and when it's all done I can go back and change the bits I don't like. Every book I've written I've agonised over at certain points in the writing stages. Usually, I'll send the manuscript first to my agent, Caroline Walsh, who'll read it immediately and send it on to Annie Eaton, my editor at Transworld. If I need a bit more confidence, I'll get my daughter Emma to read it, as I did with *The Illustrated Mum* recently. Emma is always ultra complimentary!

Do I get emotionally involved when I'm writing? Well, I've never cried or laughed out loud at anything I was writing, but I do feel as if I'm living whatever my character is doing. It sounds fey, but it's as if I'm taken over. If anybody ever comes into the room when I'm writing, I jump, because it's as if I'm in a different world. I do get heavily involved with what I'm doing, though as far as I can tell it doesn't physically show itself outside. My new book, *The Illustrated Mum*, is a very sad book. I certainly felt for my characters, and I became them as I wrote the book, but I didn't write it in floods of tears.

In my books I tend to focus on the child that's the odd-one out, the child that doesn't fit in for whatever reason, the outsider. As a writer I'm interested in the relationships between children and their friends, enemies, siblings, parents. And I'm also very interested in the way things are *right now* – and trying to reflect the different things going on in children's lives. My books tend to get mentioned when social issues crop up, and people often think that I consciously look for new issues to write about. But I don't work that way at all. I think of the child first, and its particular circumstance, and then I get drawn into thinking about it. It isn't until the book's written that I realise that it's actually about divorce or bullying or whatever. And I'd like to think that there's more to my books than simply the issues. However, when children write and say that one of my books helped them through a certain situation – as they often do – I feel very touched and pleased.

I'll use *Bad Girls* as an example. That book started because I met an interesting little girl at a school, who was wearing glasses with these rainbow frames that I admired. These glasses stuck in my mind. From there I became interested in writing about a child who wasn't a fierce, sparky, bossy, determined, powerful girl as many of my other characters are. I wanted to write about a shy, quiet, babyish girl because I feel that nowadays this kind of girl isn't represented in books. I thought, why would she be like this – possibly because she had older parents who'd waited ages before they had a child, and they would baby her and she'd be special to them. Then I thought, how is this kid going to get on at school? She'd probably be very bright, and wear very childish clothes, and be horribly teased. Then it became a book about bullying as a result of simply thinking about *her* – the character – not the issue.

I write in the first person mainly because it's what I've enjoyed most as a reader, and it's the way I write most naturally. I find that mostly children seem to respond more readily to something written in the first person, because automatically you're on the same wavelength, and you become that child. I find it the easiest way for me to identify with my main character. With *Girls in Love*, I didn't have to try and remember what it was like to be thirteen and to compare it with thirteen-year-old life now, all I simply did was start 'I'm Ellie' and immediately I've become her. I instinctively do this, without really thinking about it too much. I don't consciously use children's slang or anything. It just comes out. Though I do think about my characters quite hard before I write about them – particularly when I'm swimming in the mornings! I always know what my characters like best to eat, their favourite television programmes and things like that. I get to know them very well.

Nowadays, even kids from arty, literary homes want more immediacy in a text. They want to get sucked in straight away, they don't want to have to work too hard at things. If it's not immediately grabbing their attention, children will dismiss it, say 'This is boring' and put it down. When I moved to Transworld I consciously changed my style. I began writing in the first person, broke up the text more and made my writing more jokey. I generally try very hard indeed to write about what I consider to be quite complex things but in an easy and accessible way. I don't think I need to compromise my stories in any way whatsoever by putting it in colloquial language. Having said that, I do use a lot of wordplay and odd descriptive phrases and wacky imagery that is different for children – but still it's accessible because it's coming from a child narrator.

I'm a very firm believer in accessibility. Because there are so many other things that children are also interested in, you've got to go with what modern children are now about. They want liveliness, humour and adult situations. Most kids watch all the soaps. And in their books they want to meet themselves in their own domestic situations. As a child, I loved reading problem pages in magazines, and I think modern children do too. Some children have told me that they enjoy my books because I deal with the situations that they're facing in their lives. Many have said 'How do you know what it's like?' – as if I've opened up their heads and peered inside!

Some writers believe that doing journalistic work affects your writing style. I feel that you can learn to be versatile but your own, true style is always there. I feel there is a direct line – wholly unaffected by my journalism – stretching from 'The Maggots' through to my work now. If you've been a young journalist and you've seen all your favourite bits subbed straight out, you learn to accept the editing process. I don't always comply, but I'm always willing to listen. I've learnt not to react initially, and to go away and mull things over. It means that I'm not one of those writers that won't allow anyone to change a single word.

Perhaps surprisingly, boys do respond very positively to my books. They don't seem to mind that I usually have girls as the central characters. Even the toughest boys seem happy to read something like *Double Act* with two girls on the cover. I think it's because my characters are funny and tell jokes and muck around – they're not girlie-girls. Also, Nick Sharratt's illustrations look unisex, and with their bright covers they look quite cool to buy – they're not the glossy, Barbie type. The response from boys in schools can be just as positive as girls, but 80 per cent of my post is from girls.

I always like to have different devices for telling stories – and not just boring old chapters! For *Cliffhanger*, I had the idea of Tim writing the postcards to act as a trailer before each chapter. In *Buried Alive*, I wanted a similar device but something different, so I had Tim and Biscuits write their holiday diaries. *The Suitcase Kid* has an alphabet structure. And in *The Lottie Project*, there are sections of Charlie's school project throughout. I really like playing with the form of a story and it livens things up for my child readers. Children say to me, 'I like the way you tell your stories.' What they're referring to is not my prose style, but the devices I use. Each of my Transworld titles has its own special form. And it's fun for me, trying to think up different narrative devices.

The one children's book of the last ten years that has most impressed me is an American book called *Catherine Called Birdy* by Karen Cushman. It's a medieval girl's diary – yet it's funny, accessible and totally original. Karen Cushman's second book, *The Midwife's Apprentice*, is almost as good. Another American book I really like is Virginia Euwar Wolff's *Make Lemonade*. I like Morris Gleitzman's writing style too – I especially like his book *Water Wings*.

3 GROWING A BOOK

Double Act

I'd just given my editor, Annie Eaton, the manuscript of *The Bed and Breakfast Star* and I told her that next I wanted to write a book about identical twins. Annie said that their twinness should be integral to the story, but I'd need to have a good plot too. So I went away thinking that it was not enough just to have a thoughtful, introspective book about what it's like to be twins. I realised that I needed some action, something to get the plot moving so that a reader could get caught up in the story. This was helpful for me – to prove to Annie that there was a story, that some action would be happening. I knew that I could write about all the things I wanted to – such as these two odd little girls with their rituals and games – but they had to be in a conventional story with a plot.

Here's a list of the rough notes and ideas I made before I even began writing:

Garnet and Ruby
Told in tandem
Ruby writing most –
Garnet adding and embellishing, doing the pictures
Mum died – live with Gran and Dad
Gran too old
Dad meets teacher at her OU summer school
Children's bookshop
Make more of a story if start with Dad and Gran and meeting the bottle blonde
Make clearer who is who
Dad opens bookshop
Garnet and Ruby hate it
Start more simply

This is simply a list I made of random bits and pieces and would have been made while I was still writing *Bed and Breakfast Star*. I keep all my early drafts and notes in folders, as well as the research I do for a book. For *Double Act*, I collected clippings from magazines and newspapers on twins. Really, it's security, as I don't do that much research, but because I'm interested in the subject matter I'll collect things. In the end, I'll probably use about 5 per cent of the material from the research. I would have read it all, and have been unconsciously absorbing it. Generally, most of the research I do is as I'm about to start writing the first draft.

With this book, first I wrote the synopsis, with a working title of 'Ruby and Garnet':

Ruby and Garnet

Ruby and Garnet have lived with their Dad and Gran ever since their mother died. But now Gran is finding it hard to cope and Dad meets Rose, who sells bric-à-brac at boot fairs. Dad is made redundant. Gran is ready to move into a labour-saving sheltered flat and Dad wants to join forces with Rose and buy a run-down shop in the country, to have as a book/junk shop. All this will be dealt with briskly by the twins so that the reader isn't bogged down with detail.

So, everything is changing for the worst, from the twins' point of view. They can't stand Rose. They miss their Gran. They hate the country village. They're teased by the local children. They do their best to retreat into their own world of twinness, inventing their own maddening method of speaking half a sentence each and doing their best to walk in step. They're doing it deliberately, but Dad is very worried that they've gone a little crazy. And they're certainly driving everyone crazy. Ruby and Garnet want to escape, but don't know how. Then Ruby sees an advert for a television version of Enid Blyton's 'The Twins at St. Clare's' to be filmed during the summer holiday at a big girls' public school. She thinks this is their great chance. They pool their savings, sneak off to London to attend the audition, a big adventure in itself and get a shock when they arrive to find hundreds of twins, all desperate for the part. Ruby realises they're not such an amazing novelty after all, but she still hopes they might win out against all the enormous competition. When it's their turn to do their two minutes' worth, poor Garnet fluffs and gets flustered and is useless. Ruby is furious with her. Dad and Rose are furious with both twins when they eventually trail home because they've obviously been worried silly.

I've lost a couple of pages of this, but I've got the final piece, which matches the final plot fairly accurately. This is once Garnet has gone to the boarding school:

So both twins grow and benefit from being away from each other. But they're still best friends as well as sisters, thrilled to be together again at half-term. Then they're both bridesmaids in dark red velvet dresses at Gran's wedding.

Gran's wedding: that's something that didn't happen in the book – perhaps I could put that into a sequel! Overall, I did stick fairly closely to my original intentions, as you can see. This synopsis would have taken about a week in all to plan, organise and type up, but I would have been deliberating about it for a while before that.

This is my first manual draft [see manuscript page illustrated]. I wrote it out like this, and then I typed it out and sent it off to Transworld. At that stage, although they were commissioning me, they wanted to see exactly what I was doing. This is not a synopsis, this is the introduction to the book, sample pages that I did for the publisher. My working title, as you can see, was still 'Ruby and Garnet'.

Because I'd already done the introduction in longhand, I didn't allow myself the luxury of completing it in that way. I actually wrote the rest of it on the typewriter. And, as always, as I went along I did a carbon copy – one for myself, and one for the editor. The majority of that first draft would not have been altered at all, though a few pages would have been rewritten. The writing of the entire book would have taken some four or five months in total.

Throughout the manuscript, I made notes for the illustrator, Nick Sharratt. For example:

And then we grew up a bit and we could toddle around. [*Picture of toddler twins playing with two large toy giraffes.*] [*Photograph of mum holding both girls. They're around four or five.*]

We're twins . I'm Ruby . This is Garnet.

I'm Garnet .

We're identical . There's very few people who can tell us apart . Well, that is of them uncle ... we star telling . I tend to go on & on . Dad ... knows ... Garnet is much quieter .

That's because I can't get a word in edgeways

We are exactly the same height and weight . I ... to eat a bit more ... than Garnet . If we have chips I tend to slove mine down quickly & then maybe half of Garnet's . She doesn't mind .

Yes I do

But I don't get fatter because I charge around more . I eat sitting still . Garnet will hunch up over a book for hours but I get the fidgets . We're both quite good at running, Garnet and me . At our last sports day at school we beat everyone, even the boys . We came first . Well, I did, actually . Garnet came second .

Manuscript page from *Double Act*

The first idea – with the giraffes – didn't get used though. Here's another bit:

This is Rose. [*Picture of plump blonde, actually rather charming and around 30. Has a rose motif on one item of clothing. She dresses in a jumble-arty sort of way.*]

No. THIS is Rose. [*This time Ruby has supposedly drawn Rose. She is much, much fatter and looks very stupid and her worse points are exaggerated.*]

As I go along I do these notes to suggest to Nick different ways of doing the illustrations. How annoying it must be for him, to have a writer taking over and doing all this! Generally, he's been so sweet and kind and done what I've asked.

In the first full draft I had a lot more of the twins' imaginary games, and bits about the books they read. I wanted it originally to be a 'bookish' book – with Dad having the bookshop – and I wanted all sorts of references to other books. I do like the idea that children might pick up on these books I've referred to and go and read them. But the manuscript was getting too long, and Annie Eaton, my editor, did suggest that I needed to cut these bits out. I can see that possibly these are the parts that non-literary kids would skip. Transworld have a brilliant ploy to get me to cut material. They say, 'We won't be able to use as many of Nick's illustrations.' And I think, oh no, we can't have that! So, I will cut. With *Double Act* we got rid of about fifty or sixty pages altogether.

I'm going to read a section from the book. It's at the start of Chapter 3, and Garnet is speaking:

I hate changes. I want every day to be the same. I've always been like it, even before Mum died.

I couldn't stand our first day at school.

Everybody stared at us because we were different. And the whole day *was different. We couldn't play our games and talk in our own private language. It felt like we couldn't even be twins, because the teacher sat me on one side of the classroom and Ruby on the other. She said it was so she could tell us apart.*

I felt as if she'd somehow torn us apart. I didn't feel like a whole person at all. I felt like a half, as if an arm and a leg and most of my head were the other side of the room stuck to Ruby. I didn't know how to think without her.

Well, naturally. I'm the oldest. I'm the DOMINANT twin. That's what they call the one that's born first. That's me. I'm the Big Cheese. You're just the Little Crumb.

They're arguing backwards and forwards and Garnet is stressing how they do everything together – they even go to the loo together. There's a picture of both twins on the lavatory! I like slightly rude bits in children's books, and I know children enjoy them too.

I picked this passage because it shows that I'm on the side of children who are slightly different or worried or anxious. Although I choose to write in the most simplistic way I can, and in the way a child would write, I still select my language carefully and put a spin on the different words. I have Garnet saying 'Everybody stared at us because we were different. And the whole *day* was different.' At this new school, suddenly, and for the first time ever they're put on different sides of the

ONE

We're twins. I'm Ruby. She's Garnet.

We're identical. There's very few people who can tell us apart. Well, until we start talking. I tend to go on and on. Garnet is much quieter.

Illustrations by Nick Sharratt and Sue Heap for Page 1 of *Double Act*

classroom. And Garnet says, 'I felt as if she'd somehow torn us apart.' I had this bizarre image of Garnet literally being torn apart. I like to play around with words and try and find both a literal and then a more bizarre and imaginative meaning. Each time I use a particular word I like to put a little twist on it to try and bring out any extra meaning. It's like savouring sweets. You suck them a bit to see what different flavours you can get out of them. Sometimes it's a pun and it will make you totally groan:

> Dad reads great fat books too but they're not modern, they're all classics – Charles Dickens and Thomas Hardy. If we have a look at Dad's book we wonder what the Dickens they're on about and they seem *very* Hardy, but Dad likes them.

The title became *Double Act* for a number of reasons. Although Transworld agreed that Ruby and Garnet were right as character names – with Ruby being the precious stone and Garnet being the semi-precious stone – they felt that 'Ruby and Garnet' as a title had an old-fashioned ring to it. We couldn't use 'twin' in the title as I'd already done a book called *Twin Trouble* for another publisher. My husband actually suggested *Double Act* (though he hadn't read the manuscript) and we went for that as it captured the fact that they do literally act, and it's also an act they put on – and from every angle, it's a perfect title.

In *Double Act* there are two illustrators. Nick Sharratt had the brilliant concept that he would illustrate all the Ruby parts and Sue Heap would illustrate all the Garnet parts – which creates another doubleness to the book, which I'm very pleased with. I think it works brilliantly. And they've collaborated again with *Buried Alive!* – Nick did Tim's holiday diary and Sue Heap has done Biscuit's diary. Again, that works beautifully too.

The Suitcase Kid

I knew I wanted to write about a child whose parents had divorced and was being shuttled backwards and forwards between two homes. This seemed to me to be something that was happening more and more, and was very difficult to deal with. I'd got most irritated by reading accounts in newspapers and seeing documentaries in which the adult divorcees would say, 'It was traumatic for us, but fine for the kids. You know what kids are like, they bounce back.' I felt that although some kids might, I know many kids who are traumatised by the whole thing, and it takes them years to get over it.

I wanted to write something from a child's point of view to show how difficult it was, and to highlight the problem of getting used to new step-siblings and different living circumstances. I didn't want it to be *too* heavy a book. I wanted to show that a child could get through this and out the other side and to feel that they were coping. So, with this one, I did very much start with an issue, because I felt cross thinking about this and from knowing that people are not considering this from the children's point of view and just how much it can hurt them.

I also wanted to write about a child who was quite babyish, but who was tall; the sort of child that people would be irritated by because he or she appeared young for their age. I had already had the idea for this type of girl a while before. And I thought, yes, she is the right character for this book, and she will have some little toy creature that she loves and needs to have with her. But she's not a cute little girl and because she's tall people expect her to behave in a mature way. So I put this character into this situation – the context of divorce.

I was looking for a name for the Sylvanian Family Rabbit. I got thinking about what rabbits like to eat, and 'Lettuce' cropped up. And I thought, no, it was too wet and limp! I was after something that was sturdy but little and then I came up with 'Radish' the rabbit. It sounded alliterative, and I went with it. I chose this particular toy as I had my own Sylvanian Family Rabbit as a mascot that had originally been my daughter's. And I have to say that Radish is definitely my most popular character to date.

The alphabet framing device did not come straight away. I began by doing a chapter and a half – telling it completely straight, with Andy narrating and telling the story right from when her parents had had their final row and had decided to divorce. Yet I felt uncomfortable with this for two reasons. One was that I had hit on a new device for me, a different way of telling the story with *Tracy Beaker* – and I

is for Radish

Illustration by Nick Sharratt from *The Suitcase Kid*

wanted some kind of unusual way to tell Andy's story too. Also, I realised that if I told it consecutively, and exactly how things happened, it was going to run into really serious problems, because there would inevitably be material that wasn't suitable for the target readership of 8–12 year olds – such as when parents argue and shout at each other and the children overhear. It would be too depressing and too awful for this age group to read. Yet I didn't want to fudge things – I needed to show that things could be awful, but I wanted to hint at these worst moments rather than feature them.

I needed a 'camera'-type narrative device that would allow me to home in on a situation but then stop just before it gets totally ugly. As a result, I would be jumping in and out of the story at various points. I needed a device to allow me to do this – to feature specific parts of the story – and therefore avoid a child having to read all the distressing moments. I knew that children that have been through divorces would be able to fill in the gaps – all the terrible things that parents yell at each other.

I decided early on to have a family counselling scene and I knew that in those rooms they have different toys to enable children to act things out. I knew that they have building blocks and I thought about these blocks having the letters of the alphabet printed on them, and I suddenly thought, hey, how about telling the story in the form of an alphabet! At the beginning, it was easy – 'A is for Andy', as was the first half of the alphabet – but I hadn't thought about the Y or Q or Z! But I found that it actually gave me ideas for the narrative itself – such as 'U for unconscious' – which Andy is when she returns to Mulberry Cottage, and it enabled me to have the dream sequence which I couldn't have had otherwise. I don't know if I would have thought of that in the story without that deliberate device prompting me to come up with something. And the same happened with other letters too. So, the alphabet structure provided me with plot details that wouldn't have otherwise occurred to me. For the most part, I was lucky in that my plot and the alphabet synchronised naturally together. But quite how my translators get on with this book, I don't know!

Originally the book was to be called 'Time to Go Home'. When I wrote it, the most popular children's video at that time was the BBC *Watch with Mother* compilation, including an episode of *Andy Pandy*. All the children in the schools I visited knew the video and *Andy Pandy*. It's where I got Andy, my main character's name, from. At the end of the *Andy Pandy* programme there was a song called 'Time to Go Home'. I thought this was a good title for the book, as the whole point was that Andy hasn't got a home any more. Transworld didn't think it was a snappy enough title, and we eventually decided on *The Suitcase Kid*. I don't know where I got it from, but I know that kids in America that have two homes are called 'suitcase kids' as they are forever packing their suitcases.

4   VISITS TO SCHOOLS

I visit hundreds of schools and libraries and bookshops. I always take Radish – the little rabbit in *The Suitcase Kid* – when I'm talking to primary school children. I tell the children that Radish stands on my desk and keeps me company when I write. When I'm stuck for an idea I play all sorts of silly games with her. I even tie elastic round her ankle and encourage her to try her paw at bungee jumping. The children generally have a bit of a giggle at this and realise I'm not just going to drone on about description and paragraphs and capital letters.

I've been on visits when teachers have said to me, 'The children are having difficulties with punctuation. Will you stress to them how important punctuation is?' I feel that if you're telling somebody that's just set out to write a story that they've got to have speech marks here and a comma there, you'll kill their story stone dead. Surely it's best to write the story and to imagine it as hard as you can first, and then you can go back and do an exercise on how to punctuate it. I also think that teachers demand a great deal from children, when they ask something like 'I want you to write about your summer holiday, right now.' And children are expected, just like that, to start off. Most professional authors would not be willing to sit down in a room full of people and be given a title and told to get cracking, and then, forty minutes later, to have produced a coherent story!

When I go in to schools I take in my black folder. In it I keep things like 'The Maggots' – the story that I wrote when I was nine. It's good for showing children how we used to write in those days – very neatly and in brown ink – and also it's useful for explaining how schools in the 1950s were compared with now.

In my talks I tend to concentrate on *The Story of Tracy Beaker*, which is about a girl who lives in a children's home. I'll often read the dare scene from the book because it's rude and funny! It's the part of the story where Tracy dares Justine to say the rudest word she can think of when the vicar comes round the home, and then Justine dares Tracy to run all the way round the garden stark naked. This passage always goes down very well!

During my talk to the children I'll show this booklet I have called *My Book About Me* which I was given by a woman from the Foster Care Association. It's a booklet that all children in care are encouraged to fill in. I show the children this partly to let them see how I got the idea for the format of *Tracy Beaker*. There's a 'Things I Like' page in the booklet and I go through each of the individual sections asking the children to give their own responses – to tell me their own lucky number, favourite colour, best friend, favourite food, and so on. These are easy things that all children – no matter what their abilities – can join in and have fun.

In the book, Tracy is advertised in the paper. And as research for this book I collected some cuttings of real child advertisements from newspapers. I read these out to the children and get them to think about what it must be like for adopted children in this situation. If a school asks me to do a workshop, I find it a very useful device to use *Tracy Beaker*. In the book, there are two advertisements – Tracy's own idealised version in which she stresses all her good points, and then there's the social worker's realistic and downmarket version. I get the children to do two such versions for themselves – one stressing their good points, the other concentrating on their worst side. This gets the children to think in different ways. And I'll do my pair of adverts too. At the end, we read them all out to each other.

For the next exercise, I'll get them to invent a character. I'll say that it will be a child that is going to live at the children's home and will get to know Tracy Beaker. I'll tell them it can be a child or teenager, a girl or boy. Next we'll run through the list of favourite things in the *My Book About Me* – and they have to fill in all the details, actually thinking in character. The more imaginative children will think up all kinds of things for their character, and those children who do not have so much imagination can think of a person similar to themselves. Then I'll give them a five-stage structure to use with their character so that everyone can write a story about settling into the children's home – with a little adventure to liven things up. To finish, I'll get a few volunteers to read their pieces out. I do this writing exercise – modified according to the age group – with children from Year 3 all the way up to Year 9.

I have a whole variety of activities I can do across the age ranges. If a class has read a particular book and the teacher wants me to do work that will fit in with that, then I'll try to go along with what they want to do. I'm reasonably happy to do whatever a school requires. But *The Story of Tracy Beaker* tends to work best as it offers a whole range of possibilities and related activities.

5 WORKING WITH NICK SHARRATT

It was David Fickling that brought Nick and me together. David is now Editorial Director at Scholastic, but he was my editor at Transworld at the time. *The Story of Tracy Beaker* was going to be my first title for Transworld, and I wanted lots of illustrations that were supposedly done by Tracy herself. I asked David if it would be possible to have lots of black and white illustrations throughout, and he was very enthusiastic.

David knew Nick from when he was previously at Oxford University Press, and he sent me a book that Nick had illustrated – an anthology of poems called *A Gerbil in My Hoover*. I liked Nick's illustrations immediately – they were very

fresh and modern and funny. And that was that, Nick has done every book of mine for Transworld ever since, from *The Story of Tracy Beaker* onwards. Nick has an amazingly expressive style, in that he can, with just that stark, simple line, have something that's very funny or indeed very sad. Yet there's a complexity about his illustrations and it's not until you look very carefully at them that you see the very clever way he has of conveying all sorts of emotions with just the raise of an eyebrow or the little quirk of a mouth. He likes putting in extra details that are not in my text – as he did with *The Lottie Project*, which I think are the best illustrations that he's done for me.

So *Tracy Beaker* was the first book we worked on together, and I didn't know as I was writing the book who the artist was going to be, so I wrote all these bossy little instructions throughout the manuscript. I was delighted when Nick did them so wonderfully. Initially, I had Tracy wearing different clothes. I made reference to her wearing jeans at one point, though Nick had drawn her in a little skirt and jumper. I pointed this out to someone at Transworld who said they would ask Nick if he could draw her in jeans instead. Then I thought, how boring, for him to have to go through and change all his illustrations! And all I would have had to do was to write 'skirt' instead of 'jeans'. So I did. It wasn't that important to me whether she wore jeans or she didn't. I prefer her in a skirt because it makes her more distinctive, and it's a classic shape that won't date, so I'm grateful to Nick for that. It's important to make characters look modern and up to the minute and yet not actually put in the very latest clothing.

Nick and I come from different backgrounds and we're very different people but we seem to totally understand each other. Occasionally, Nick will have his own ideas for illustrations and that's great. Sometimes I'll just put the word 'Picture?' in the text and Nick will follow it up with something.

When a book is ready to be illustrated, the publishers pass on my manuscript to Nick. There will be notes throughout the text wherever I feel a picture will be appropriate. Sometimes I'll be very specific in my notes about what I think would look good. But I always say to Nick that he should override my notes if he wants to or to go for a different idea that he may have. Nick will send the roughs to the editor who will then pass them on to me. I nearly always find that the illustrations are perfect, because Nick reads every word of my text and knows – often even better than me – exactly what is going on in the story. When I've sent the roughs back he'll complete the illustrations. But I don't usually suggest ideas for the covers. Nick designs these himself.

I do feel that Nick's illustrations make my books more accessible to the sort of child that might have problems without the pictures to help them into the text. I've been illustrated by many other people, all of whom I admire, but there's none who can get inside my head and respond in the way that Nick can. And they're the sort of illustrations children love. I've never met a child that doesn't like his work. And children like to copy his illustrations themselves.

Nick has served me so well. No writer could be luckier than me. Sometimes I worry terribly about him working for other writers – I do feel he commits adultery – and many times over! Recently, both *The Lottie Project* and *My Granny's Great Escape* by Jeremy Strong were shortlisted for the Children's Book Award. Both books were illustrated by Nick. And it was wonderful because the Federation of Children's Book Groups decided to give Nick a special artist's award. I was really thrilled for him. I've been lucky enough to win awards myself and remained composed – but when Nick went up to get his award I cried!

SELECTED CURRENT TITLES

Transworld titles

Bad Girls
The Bed and Breakfast Star
Buried Alive!
Cliffhanger
Double Act
Glubbslyme
The Lottie Project
The Monster Story-Teller
The Mum-Minder
The Story of Tracy Beaker
The Suitcase Kid
The Illustrated Mum (forthcoming)

Trilogy for teenage readers

Girls in Love
Girls Under Pressure
Girls Out Late (November 1999)

Puffin titles for younger readers

The Deep Blue
The Left Outs
Mark Spark in the Dark
The Werepuppy
The Werepuppy on Holiday

Titles by Nick Sharratt

Scholastic:

A Cheese and Tomato Spider
Don't Put Your Finger in the Jelly, Nelly!
I Went to the Zoopermarket
Ketchup on Your Cornflakes?
Stamp Mania
The Time it Took Tom (with Stephen Tucker)
Very Sticky Christmas Book

Walker Books:

My Mum and Dad Make Me Laugh
Rocket Countdown!
Animal Orchestra
Dinosaurs' Day Out

A miscellany of information on children's books

ADVICE ON AUTHOR VISITS

Looking for an author? This booklet is 'a directory of authors, illustrators and poets who participate in book events' and is published annually by Young Book Trust and the Reading and Language Information Centre. See 'Information Centres' (pp. 260–3) for the addresses of these organisations.

Blueprint – a handbook of writers in education projects: written by Liz Fincham, this handbook is published by West Sussex Advisory Service, North East Area Professional Centre, Furnace Drive, Furnace Green, Crawley, West Sussex RH10 6JB. Tel: 01293 553297, Fax: 01293 533359

A Novel Experience: Fiction Writers in Education – available from London Arts Board. Tel: 0171-240-1313.

Other publications that can provide information on publishers and agencies are *The Writers' and Artists' Year Book* (A&C Black) and *The Writers' Handbook* (Macmillan) – both of which are updated annually.

The following organisations give advice to schools on booking authors for school visits:

The Arts Council (see 'Information Centres')

National Association of Writers in Education (NAWE)
PO Box 1
Sheriff Hutton
York YO6 7YU
Tel/fax: 01653-618429
Website: http://www.nawe.co.uk

The Poetry Society (see 'Information Centres')

'Speaking of Books' – 'At last! Here's an easy way to arrange just the right visitor for a school or reading-group – also to guarantee back-up information together with a book supply on a sale-or-return basis. Since January 1998, 'Speaking of Books' has been backed by Puffin, Orchard, Random House, HarperCollins, Walker and other leading publishers. Jan Powling – "Hopefully, I'm not just solving the problems teachers or book group organisers have in finding an author, illustrator, poet or storyteller to meet their particular needs . . . I'm also helping the speakers themselves by making sure visits are less of a hit-or-miss affair. Basically what we offer is the equivalent of one-stop shopping – a call to us and we'll organise the rest."'

Jan Powling
Speaking of Books
9 Guildford Grove
Greenwich SE10 8JY
Tel/fax: 0181-692-4704

Young Book Trust and Young Book Trust Scotland
(see 'Information Centres')

ADVICE FOR ADULTS ON WRITING FOR CHILDREN

The City Literary Institute: an adult education college that runs a variety of writing courses, including writing for children.
16 Stukeley Street
London
WC2B
Tel: 0171-242-9872

Arvon Foundation: residential writing courses, including writing for children. Centres also in Yorkshire and Scotland.
Totleigh Barton, Sheepwash, Beaworthy, Devon EX21 5NS. Tel: 0140-923338
or
Lumb Bank, Heptonstall, Hebden Bridge, West Yorkshire. Tel: 01422-843714

MA in Writing for Children – King Alfred's College, Winchester
'A new and unique creative writing course to help you develop your abilities and talents as a writer for a child audience. The MA in Writing for Children can be studied on a one year (full time) or two year (part time) basis.'
Postgraduate & Advanced Studies Office
King Alfred's College
Winchester
SO22 4NR
Tel: 01962-827375
Fax: 01962-842280

The Writers' Advice Centre for Children's Books
Editorial and marketing advice by editors currently involved in children's publishing.
Day courses and conferences. Send SAE for details.

Palace Wharf
Rainville Road
London W6 9HN
Tel/fax: 0181-874-7347

ANNUAL BOOK EVENTS AND FESTIVALS

World Book Day: Shakespeare's birthday, 23 April.
Children's Book Week: one week in early October.
National Poetry Day: usually falls on the first Thursday in October.
International Children's Book Day – 2 April – Hans Andersen's birthday.
Anne Frank Day – 12 June.
Northern Children's Book Festival (see p. 264).
Edinburgh Book Festival – part of the Edinburgh Festival in August.

COMPETITIONS – CHILDREN'S OWN WRITING

Apple Tree Award. Closing date by end of Spring term. 'A writing competition for children who have difficulties with reading, writing and communication. There are three sections: 5–7, 8–11 and 12–16 years. Entries can be submitted in the following formats: handwritten, typed, computer generated, sound tape, signed video, braille, rubus, Blissymbols. Any non-print format must be accompanied by a written script.'
National Library for the Handicapped Child
Reach Resource Centre
Wellington House
Wellington Road
Wokingham
Berks RG40 2AG

BBC Radio 4 Young Poetry Competition (8–21 years)
BBC Broadcasting House
Whiteladies Road
Bristol BS8 2LR

Roald Dahl Foundation Poetry Competition (7–17 years)
PO Box 1375
20 Vauxhall Bridge Road
London SW1V 2SA
Tel: 0171-824-5463

W.H. Smith Young Writers Competition (up to 16 years)
Strand House
7 Holbein Place
Sloane Square
London SW1W 8NR

Welsh Academy Young Writers Competition (up to 18 years – closing date July)
PO Box 328
Cardiff CF2 4XL

Write Away – 'a competition for pupils aged seven to 11. It is a chance for juniors to find an audience for their writing, to explore new styles and voices – and to win cash prizes . . . A competition organised by *The Times Educational Supplement*, the National Association for the Teaching of English and McDonald's Restaurants Ltd to give young writers the opportunity to reflect on their lives.'
National Association for the Teaching of English
50 Broadfield Road
Sheffield S8 0XJ

Contact the publicity departments of the following publishers for details:

A&C Black competition: 0171-242-0946
Puffin Wondercrump competition: 0181-899-4000

COMPETITIONS – ADULTS WRITING FOR CHILDREN

Scholastic / Independent competition. Annual competition for original short stories for 6–9 year olds. Details in *The Independent* (March/April) or from:
The Publicity Department
Scholastic Children's Books
Commonwealth House
1–19 New Oxford Street
London WC1A 1NU
Tel: 0171-421-9000

Write a Story for Children Competition
The Academy of Children's Writers
PO Box 95
Huntingdon
Cambs PE17 5RL
Tel: 01487-832752

INFORMATION CENTRES AND CHILDREN'S BOOK ORGANISATIONS

The Arts Council (publishes a magazine entitled *Writers on Tour*)
Alison Combes
Literature Officer
The Arts Council of England
14 Great Peter Street
London SW1P 3NQ
Tel: 0171-333-0100/Fax: 0171-973-6520

The Arvon Foundation (Writing courses – some for children)
Lumb Bank
Heptonstall
Hebden Bridge
West Yorkshire
Tel: 01422-843714

Bethnal Green Museum of Childhood
Cambridge Heath Road
London E2
Tel: 0181-983-5200

The Centre for the Children's Book
(Mary Briggs / Elizabeth Hammill)
Pendower Hall Education Development Centre
West Road
Newcastle upon Tyne NE2 4RU
Tel: 0191-2743620 or 0191-2813702
Fax: 0191-2747595

The Children's Book Circle.
Membership – contact Gaby Morgan – Tel: 0171-881-8000. 'A discussion forum for anyone interested in children's books. Monthly meetings addressed by a panel of invited speakers.'

CIRCL . . .
The Centre for International Research in Childhood: Literature, Culture and Media.
'CIRCL . . . is a centre fostering international collaborative research on children's literature and media. One current project is "National Cultural Identity in Children's Literature and Media".'
Department of English
University of Reading
PO Box 218
Reading RG6 6AA
Website: http://www.rdg.ac.uk./~lnslesko/circl

Roald Dahl Museum (part of Buckinghamshire County Museum)
Church Street
Aylesbury HP20 2QP
Tel: 01296-331441

The Federation of Children's Book Groups.
An organisation for all those interested in children's book groups.
7 Carrs Lane, Birmingham B4 7TQ

IBBY (International Board on Books for Young People). 'IBBY is an international network; a forum for people working in all areas connected with children's books

and reading. IBBY organises a biennial International Congress; a forum for members. IBBY has a strong commitment to supporting the growth of children's literature and literacy in developing countries.'
British Section of IBBY
Roehampton Institute
Downshire House
Roehampton Institute
Roehampton Lane
London SW15 4HT
Tel: 0181-392-3008
Fax: 0181-392-3031
E-mail address: kreynold@roehampton.ac.uk

National Association of Writers in Education (NAWE)
This national organisation actively promotes writing in education and co-ordinates activities between teachers and writers. NAWE publishes a magazine entitled *Writing in Education*.
PO Box 1
Sheriff Hutton
York
YO6 7YU
Tel/fax: 01653-618429

Poetry Library
'The Poetry Library has a large collection of poetry for children and young people and the people who work with them. Our collection ranges from nursery rhymes to rap, includes poetry by children and readings and performances on video and audio cassettes by modern poets.' Many free services to schools and teachers.
Level 5, Royal Festival Hall
London SE1 8XX
Tel: 0171-921-0943/0664

The Scottish Poetry Society
Tweeddale Court
14 High Street
Edinburgh EH1 1TE
Tel: 0131-557-2876

The Poetry Society
The Poetry Society is an organisation whose aim is to promote poets and poetry. Information packs for primary and secondary schools are available from the Education Officer. Their journals include *Poetry News* and *Poetry Review*. The Society runs a Young Poetry Competition, which is free to entrants aged between 11 and 18. Twelve winners go on a poetry writing course at an Arvon Foundation centre. 'Young Poetry Unplugged', on the third Thursday of every month, is open to young people from 11 to 18; they can read their own poetry or their favourite poets' work. Held at The Poetry Café – next door to The Poetry Society. Booking via The Poetry Society (0171-420-9880) is recommended.

22 Betterton Street
London WC2H 9BU
Tel: 0171-420-9880
Fax: 0171-240-4818
E-mail: poetrysoc@dial.pipex.com
Website: www.poetrysoc.com
Education Officer direct line: 0171-420-9894

Reading and Language Information Centre – 'The Centre offers an extensive programme of courses and conferences for teachers on all aspects of language, literacy and the English curriculum.'
University of Reading
Woodlands Avenue
Reading RG6 1HY
Tel: 0118-9318820
Fax: 0118-9316801
Website: http://www.rdg.ac.uk/AcaDepts/eh/ReadLang/home.html

Reading is Fundamental – 'a non-profit organisation that inspires children to become strong, motivated readers . . . RIF provides books for children to choose and own at no cost to them or their families . . . RIF helps families become involved with their children's reading, enjoying stories and books together . . . RIF brings together readers and writers, creating new generations of readers.'
Swire House
59 Buckingham Gate
London
SW1E 6AJ
Tel: 0171-828-2435
Fax: 0171-931-9986
Website: www.literacytrust.org.uk

Ty Newydd Writing Courses – run with support from the Welsh Arts Council
Taliesin Trust
Ty Newydd
Llanystumdwy
Criccieth
Gwynedd LL52 0LW

Young Book Trust
'Book Trust is the national, independent educational charity concerned with books and reading. Young Book Trust (YBT) is the arm of the organisation which works with and for all those interested in children's reading. Our London-based library contains the vast majority of current children's books published in the UK. Books are displayed in the collection for two years and then sent on to the National Museum of Childhood in Bethnal Green. All books received by the library are added to our extensive database, which forms a unique resource in children's literature. The database, to date, holds in excess of 26,000 titles. Services are

available for Teachers, Librarians, Parents, Students, Researchers, Writers and Illustrators. You can visit our library – and our Beatrix Potter Study Room – between 9 a.m.–5 p.m. Monday to Friday. Please telephone first for an appointment. Please note that books cannot be borrowed from the library.'

Book House
45 East Hill
London SW18 2QZ
Tel : 0181-516-2977

Young Book Trust Scotland
137 Dundee Street
Edinburgh EH11 1BG
Tel: 0131-229-3663

MA COURSES IN CHILDREN'S LITERATURE

Postgraduate Master of Arts courses in Children's Literature are now run at the University of Reading, the University of Warwick, the University of Wales and at the Roehampton Institute. Prospectuses for these courses can be obtained by contacting these numbers:

University of Reading, Tel: 0118-9875123
Roehampton Institute, Tel: 0181-392-3000
Trinity College, Carmarthen (University of Wales), Tel: 01267-237971
University of Warwick, Tel: 01203-523523

MAGAZINES AND JOURNALS

Books for Keeps – 6 Brightfield Road, Lee, London SE12 8QF. Tel: 0181-852-4953

Carousel – 7 Carrs Lane, Birmingham B4 7TG

Children's Literature Association Quarterly (USA) – Children's Literature Association, PO Box 138, Battle Creek, MI 49016

Children's Literature in Education – Geoff Fox, University of Exeter, School of Education, St Luke's, Exeter, Devon EX1 2UU

Horn Book (USA) 11 Beacon Street, Suite 1000, Boston MA 02018. Website: http://www.hbook.com

In Brief – contact Centre for the Children's Book or Waterstone's bookshops

The Lion and the Unicorn (USA) – Johns Hopkins University Press, Journals Division, 2715 North Charles Street, Baltimore MD 21218 – 4319

Orana (Australia) – Australian Library and Information Association, PO Box E441, Queen Victoria Terrace, Kingston ACT 2604

School Librarian – School Library Association, Liden Library, Barrington Close, Liden, Swindon SN3 6HF

Signal: Approaches to Children's Books – Thimble Press, Lockwood, Station Road, South Woodchester, Stroud, Glos GL15 5EQ

Writing in Education – published by NAWE – National Association of Writers in Education. NAWE, PO Box 1, Sherriff Hutton, York YO6 7YU. Tel/fax: 01653 618429

Young Writer 'It's fun and instructive. Designed to build any child's confidence. *Young Writer* is a forum for young people's writing – fiction and non-fiction, prose and poetry.' – Kate Jones, Glebe House, Weobley, Herefordshire HR4 8SD. Tel: 01544-318901. Website: www.mystworld.com/young_writer

NORTHERN CHILDREN'S BOOK FESTIVAL

'What is NCBF?
–   the biggest annual children's book festival in the UK
–   free to all children and families
–   a regional event across the whole North East of England
–   held over 2 weeks in November'
Jan Clements
Northern Tyneside Children & Young People's Library Service
St Edmund's Building
Station Road
Beckworth
Tyne & Wear NE27 0RU
Tel: 0191-2008223
Fax: 0191-2008231
Website: http://www.chilias.sunderland.ac.uk/ncbf/ncbf.htm

'READATHON®'

'The Readathon concept is simple. Children undertake to read books, or do other literacy-based activities, in return for pledges of money from family and friends. All money raised is donated to two charities who care for sick children. The event is staged mainly in schools, and is supported by the Arts Council, children's publishers and booksellers nationwide.'

'Please join Readathon. Not only will your pupils be encouraged to read good books, they will help sick children at the same time.'
Roald Dahl, Readathon Chairman, 1988–1990.

Readathon
Swerford
Chipping Norton
Oxon OX7 4BG

Tel/fax: 01608-730335
Website: www.readathon.org
E-mail: readathon.org

REFERENCE TEXTS AND FURTHER READING

The following publications provide useful introductions and insights into various aspects of children's literature.

Aidan Chambers – *Booktalk* (Bodley Head)
Margaret Clark -- *Writing for Children* (A&C Black)
Liz Fincham – *Blueprint: A handbook of writers in education projects* (available from West Sussex County Council)
Peter Hunt – *Introduction to Children's Literature* (Oxford)
Peter Hunt (ed.) – *Children's Literature – An Illustrated History* (Oxford)
Stephanie Nettell – *Meet the Authors and Illustrators* (Scholastic)
Chris Powling and Morag Styles – *A Guide to Children's Poetry 0–13* (Reading and Language Information Centre, University of Reading)
Kimberley Reynolds – *Children's Literature in the 1890s and 1990s* (Northcote House)
Michael Rosen and Jill Burridge – *Treasure Islands 2* (BBC)
John Rowe Townsend – *Written for Children* (Bodley Head)
Anthony Wilson with Siân Hughes – *The Poetry Book for Primary Schools* (The Poetry Society)
Writers' and Artists' Year Book (A&C Black) – updated annually
The Writers' Handbook (Macmillan) – updated annually
The Children's Book Handbook (Young Book Trust)

WEBSITES

Publishers

A&C Black – e-mail enquiries@acblack.co.uk
Bloomsbury – http://www.bloomsbury.com
Dorling Kindersley – www.dk.com
OK UK Books – www.okukbooks.com
Puffin – www.puffin.co.uk
Routledge – www.routledge.com
Scholastic – www.scholastic.co.uk
Transworld – e-mail info @ transworld publishers_co.uk

The Routledge website above offers a menu of further website addresses to visit.

Further publishers' website addresses can be found in *Writers' and Artists' Year Book* (A&C Black) and *The Writers' Handbook* (Macmillan).

Others

Argosphere – language and cross-curricular activities for 3–13 year olds:
www.argosphere.co.uk

The Children's Literature Web Guide (USA) – set up and maintained by David K.
Brown at the University of Calgary:
http://www.ucalgary.ca/~dkbrown/index.html

CIRCL . . .
The Centre for International Research in Childhood: Literature, Culture and Media.
University of Reading: http://www.rdg.ac.uk./~lnslesko/circl

The Poetry Society – www.poetrysoc.com

Poetryzone – a poetry website for children. Roger Stevens writes: 'Hi. As I've
travelled around the UK visiting schools to perform my poems and give poetry and
writing workshops, I've often wished that there was some way that children could
publish their poems. I do read and hear some wonderful and beautiful poetry and
verse. The internet, of course, makes this possible – which is why I've started the
POETRY ZONE. Please encourage your children to send me their poems. I will
publish as many as space permits and make all the poems sent available as
downloadable files to our visitors. If you would like to know more about this site or
have any constructive comments to make about it, I'd love to hear about them.'
www.poetryzone@ndirect.co.uk

The UK virtual library, set up by Gateshead MBC, Libraries & Art Service in
conjunction with the University of Sunderland:
http://www.chilias.sunderland.ac.uk

Waterstone's bookshop – http://www.waterstones.co.uk

Printed in the United Kingdom
by Lightning Source UK Ltd.
122286UK00005B/137/A